PERSONAL TAX

Qualifications and Credit Framework

Level 4 Diploma in Accounting

British Library Cataloguing-in-Publication Data

A catalogue record for this book is available from the British Library.

Published by
Kaplan Publishing UK
Unit 2, The Business Centre
Molly Millars Lane
Wokingham
Berkshire
RG41 2QZ

ISBN 978-0-85732-886-1

We are grateful to the Association of Accounting Technicians for permission to reproduce past assessment materials and example tasks based on the new syllabus. The solutions to past answers and similar activities in the style of the new syllabus have been prepared by Kaplan Publishing.

We are grateful to HM Revenue and Customs for the provision of tax forms, which are Crown Copyright and are reproduced here with kind permission from the Office of Public Sector Information.

CONTENTS

KAPLAN PUBLISHING

INTRODUCTION

HOW TO USE THESE MATERIALS

These Kaplan Publishing learning materials have been carefully designed to make your learning experience as easy as possible and to give you the best chance of success in your AAT assessments.

They contain a number of features to help you in the study process.

The sections on the Unit Guide, the Assessment and Study Skills should be read before you commence your studies.

They are designed to familiarise you with the nature and content of the assessment and to give you tips on how best to approach your studies.

STUDY TEXT

This study text has been specially prepared for the AAT AQ2013 qualification but is also suitable for the AQ2010 syllabus.

It is written in a practical and interactive style:

- key terms and concepts are clearly defined

- all topics are illustrated with practical examples with clearly worked solutions based on sample tasks provided by the AAT in the new examining style

- frequent activities throughout the chapters ensure that what you have learnt is regularly reinforced

- 'pitfalls' and 'examination tips' help you avoid commonly made mistakes and help you focus on what is required to perform well in your examination.

- practice workbook activities can be completed at the end of each chapter

WORKBOOK

The workbook comprises:

Practice activities at the end of each chapter with solutions at the end of this text, to reinforce the work covered in each chapter.

Students may either attempt these questions as they work through the textbook, or leave some or all of these until they have completed the textbook as a final revision of what they have studied.

ICONS

The study chapters include the following icons throughout.

They are designed to assist you in your studies by identifying key definitions and the points at which you can test yourself on the knowledge gained.

 Definition

These sections explain important areas of Knowledge which must be understood and reproduced in an assessment.

 Example

The illustrative examples can be used to help develop an understanding of topics before attempting the activity exercises.

 Activity

These are exercises which give the opportunity to assess your understanding of all the assessment areas.

UNIT GUIDE

Personal tax is divided into two units but for the purposes of assessment these units will be combined.

Principles of Personal Tax (Knowledge)

2 credits

Calculating Personal Tax (Skills)

3 credits

Purpose of the units

The AAT has stated that this unit is to enable students to understand the impact and significance of taxation on individuals. All sources of income for individuals, such as employment income, capital gains, income from land and property and investment income are covered. By studying these taxes, students can appreciate the tax implications for their own personal situation, and that of clients.

Learning objectives

This unit will enable the students to:

- demonstrate an understanding of legislation and procedures relating to personal tax

- understand the current taxation principles of income from employment, investment income, property income and capital gains tax

- calculate income from all sources and apply relevant allowances, deductions and reliefs to prepare accurate income tax computations

- calculate the income tax liability of an individual

- calculate the capital gains tax liability of an individual

- prepare accurate computations and complete sections of relevant tax returns

Learning Outcomes and Assessment criteria

The unit consists of five learning outcomes testing Knowledge and Skills, which are further broken down into Assessment criteria. These are set out in the following table with Learning Outcomes in bold type and Assessment criteria listed underneath each Learning Outcome. Reference is also made to the relevant chapter within the text.

Knowledge (K) and Skills (S)

To perform this unit effectively you will need to know and understand the following:

		Chapter
1	**Understand legislation and procedures relating to personal tax**	
1.1 K	Explain the main current legislation relating to personal taxation	Throughout
1.2 K	Explain the main legislative features relating to income from employment and savings, including exempt savings income	3, 4, 8
1.3 K	Explain the responsibilities that individuals have for disclosure of income and payment of tax to the relevant tax authorities	11
1.4 K	Explain the main features of the self-assessment system of taxation	11
1.5 K	Describe the duties and responsibilities of a tax practitioner	11, 16
1.6 K	Identify sources of taxation information for individuals	11
1.7 K	Explain the tax authority's filing and payment process in relation to all personal income	11
1.8 K	Identify the main legislative features relating to dividend income from UK registered companies	8
1.9 K	Identify the main legislative features relating to property income from furnished and unfurnished rented property, rent a room scheme, holiday lets and buy to let investments	6

		Chapter
2	**Calculate income from all sources and identify taxable and non-taxable items**	
2.1 S	Prepare computations of emoluments including assessable benefits	3, 4
2.2 S	List non-savings, savings and dividend income checking for completeness	8, 9
2.3 S	Prepare schedules of income from land and property determining profits and losses	6
2.4 K	Describe taxable and non-taxable sources of income from employment, including assessable benefits	3, 4
2.5 K	Describe taxable and non-taxable savings income	8
3	**Apply current legislation to calculate the tax payable on income**	
3.1 S	Apply allowances that can be set against non – savings income	9
3.2 S	Apply deductions and reliefs and claim loss set-offs	9, 10
3.3 S	Account for personal allowances	9
3.4 S	Calculate income tax payable	2, 9, 10
3.5 S	Describe taxation relief which can be given on income from employment including deductible (allowable) expenses, pension's relief and charitable donations	3, 10
3.6 S	Describe types of relief which are available on property income including allowable expenses, wear and tear allowance, renewals allowance, loss relief – and the circumstances in which each apply	6
4	**Account for capital gains tax according to current legislation**	
4.1 K	Identify the main features of the capital gains tax system	12, 15
4.2 K	Describe chargeable and exempt assets	12,13
4.3 K	Describe the process for relief of current year allowable losses and for losses unrelieved in the current year	12

Delivery Guidance

The AAT have provided delivery guidance giving further details of the way in which the unit will be assessed.

Employment income

Employment income is a key area of this unit and will feature in multiple tasks within the assessment.

Students can expect questions on:

- the differences between, and indicators of, employment and self-employment.

- the basis of assessment for employment income.

- income assessable from employment income

- computation of various benefits in kind, including:

  - provision of cars, including fuel for private motoring

  - beneficial loans

  - living accommodation, including job related accommodation

  - use of assets

  - pool cars

  - vans, including fuel for private motoring

  - other taxable and non-taxable benefits (as this list is quite extensive, there is a separate list provided at the end of the guidance notes).

- recognition of allowable expenses and deductions, including:

  - mileage allowances

  - expenses payments and reimbursed expenses

  - charitable giving through a payroll deduction scheme.

It is also expected that students will be able to explain employment income in terms of providing basic advice to tax payers. For instance, being able to explain how job related accommodation operates is as relevant as being able to compute the taxable benefit in kind of accommodation. Also, students may be expected to explain how a potential benefit in kind can be adjusted to make it tax free.

Students will mainly be required to complete computational style questions for this topic area, but some written tasks can also be expected.

Excluded topics

Calculation of car benefit where the emission figures are not given.

PAYE system.

Identification of P11D employees.

National insurance contributions

The list of other taxable and non-taxable benefits in kind

- Provision of meals and food vouchers
- Employers contribution to occupational pension schemes
- Parking facilities
- Sporting and recreational facilities
- Provision of childcare
- Mobile telephones
- Annual staff parties
- Long service and suggestion scheme awards
- Assets transferred to/bought by employees
- Goodwill gifts
- Private Medical and health screening
- Job related living accommodation
- Late night taxis
- Household costs for employees working from home
- Removals expenses and benefits
- Re-training and training expenses and benefits
- Employees working away or on international work
- Scholarships
- Entertaining expenses
- Gifts to employees
- Cycles and subsidised transport

Property income

Income from property is an important aspect of income tax, and students must be able to show knowledge of such income from a variety of sources.

Students can expect questions on:

- furnished and unfurnished property
- rent a room schemes
- furnished holiday lettings
- buy-to-let investments

Computation of rental income, associated expenses and profit or loss arising, are important. Students need to know about the wear and tear allowance and the renewals basis. In addition, students must be able to apply the rules for any losses arising from these sources of income.

Written and computational style questions can be expected that explore both the amounts taxable and allowable, and also the knowledge that underpins this source of income.

Excluded topics

Leases

Savings income

Both taxable and non-taxable savings income is expected to be covered.

In particular, students can expect questions on:

- bank interest
- building society interest
- dividends
- individual savings accounts.

The computations of gross interest received, tax deducted at source, net interest received and how the income is taxed within the tax computation of an individual can all be expected. Students need to demonstrate that they understand how tax credits on dividends operate within an individual's tax computation.

These questions will be mainly computational in nature, but understanding of the rules may also be assessed. This is particularly so for the topic of ISAs.

Excluded topics

Junior ISAs.

National savings and investments.

Child benefit.

Payment of tax

Students will need to be able to collate different types of income subject to income tax and apply the rules for different tax bands and rates. This includes all rates for all levels and types of income.

The impact of pension payments on taxation liabilities, both occupational and private, will need to be understood. Such knowledge could be assessed through both computational and written style questions. The impact on the basic rate band needs to be understood together with how taxpayers with income falling in all tax bands receive tax relief on their pension payments. Also, students should be able to explain the differences between occupational and private payments.

The impact of charity giving also needs to be understood. Giving through employment and direct gift aid needs to be understood, including the differences in how tax relief is obtained. Extension of the basic rate band applies also here.

Personal allowances must be understood, including age allowance.

An understanding of the payments on account system is crucial with students expected to answer questions that involve both the computational aspects of this payment system, and to provide explanations to clients on how they are worked out.

Excluded topics

Complexities of pension payments, such as annual allowances or lifetime allowances.

Taxpayers under the age of 16.

Married couple's allowances.

Blind person's allowance.

KAPLAN PUBLISHING

Written advice to clients

This area underpins all the other specific taxation areas assessed within this unit. Students can expect written questions on:

- what taxation documentation individuals need to maintain and for how long

- the responsibilities individuals have for disclosing full and accurate information to HMRC

- the duties and responsibilities tax practitioners have to clients and HMRC

- the sources of tax information for individuals

- how the various penalties and interest are applied by HMRC in relation to filing and payment processes for income tax and capital gains tax.

This topic area will be assessed via a free text written response from the student. The questions will usually be client focussed so students will be expected to address their answers in a manner appropriate to such an audience.

Excluded topics

Complex computations such as daily interest.

Tax returns

There are three tax returns which are assessable:

- employment income

- property income

- capital gains.

Capital gains tax

Students must appreciate who and what is taxable under this heading. The impact that relationships between connected persons have on disposal of chargeable assets needs to be understood.

Computations can be expected on:

- chargeable assets being disposed of

- enhancement expenditure

- part disposals

- chattels

- share disposals, including matching rules, bonus issues and rights issues
- exempt assets, including principal private residence.

Students also need to be able to appropriately apply the annual exempt amount and understand how the relief for losses work. Finally, students must be able to compute the actual capital gains tax payable, based on the individual's income tax situation.

This topic area will mainly be assessed via computational style questions, but students must also be able to show understanding of the rules that underpin this topic.

Excluded topics

Takeovers and reorganisations.

Business reliefs such as rollover, gift and entrepreneurial.

Small part disposals of land.

Small part disposals rules as applicable to rights issues.

THE ASSESSMENT

The format of the assessment

The assessment has 11 tasks.

Task	Learning outcome	Assessment criteria	Maximum Marks	Title for topics within task range
1	1, 2	1.2, 2.1, 2.4	9	Benefits in Kind – provision of cars
2	1, 2	1.2, 2.1, 2.4	10	Benefits in Kind – all excluding cars
3	1, 2, 3	1.9, 2.3, 3.2, 3.6	10	Income from property
4	1, 2	1.2, 1.8, 2.2, 2.5	6	Investment income
5	1, 2, 3	1.2, 2.1, 2.2, 3.1, 3.2, 3,3, 3.5	12	Computation of total and taxable income
6	1, 3, 5	1.4, 3.4, 5.3	10	Computation of tax payable and payment of tax
7	1, 5	1.1, 1.3, 1.5, 1.6, 1.7, 5.1	10	Theory underpinning topic and penalties
8	5	5.2	7	Tax returns
9	4	4.1, 4.2, 4.5, 4.6	12	Basics of capital gains tax
10	4	4.5, 4.6	8	Taxation of shares
11	4	4.3, 4.4, 4.7, 4.8	6	Capital gains tax exemptions, losses, reliefs and tax payable

Time allowed

The time allowed for this assessment is **2 hours**

Pass mark

The pass mark is 70%.

AQ2010 syllabus and assessment

This text/workbook has been primarily prepared using the AQ2013 syllabus.

However, it is also suitable for students studying the AQ2010 syllabus as the overall content is similar.

The key differences between the two are in the assessment method as follows:

- The AQ2010 syllabus assessment has twenty three tasks covering similar areas to the AQ2013 one, but the assessment is divided into two sections:

- Section 1 has fourteen tasks and covers:

  – General tax

  – Employment income

  – Investment, savings and dividend income

  – Payment of tax

  – Tax returns

- Section 2 has nine tasks and covers:

  – Property income

  – Capital gains tax

- A question requiring an extended written response from the learner will be included in Section 1.

- Both sections have to be passed to achieve competence.

- The AQ2010 assessment does not show the mark allocation for the different tasks.

KAPLAN PUBLISHING

STUDY SKILLS

Preparing to study

Devise a study plan

Determine which times of the week you will study.

Split these times into sessions of at least one hour for study of new material. Any shorter periods could be used for revision or practice.

Put the times you plan to study onto a study plan for the weeks from now until the assessment and set yourself targets for each period of study – in your sessions make sure you cover the whole course, activities and the associated questions in the workbook at the back of the manual.

If you are studying more than one unit at a time, try to vary your subjects as this can help to keep you interested and see subjects as part of wider knowledge.

When working through your course, compare your progress with your plan and, if necessary, re-plan your work (perhaps including extra sessions) or, if you are ahead, do some extra revision / practice questions.

Effective studying

Active reading

You are not expected to learn the text by rote, rather, you must understand what you are reading and be able to use it to pass the assessment and develop good practice.

A good technique is to use SQ3Rs – Survey, Question, Read, Recall, Review:

1   Survey the chapter

Look at the headings and read the introduction, knowledge, skills and content, so as to get an overview of what the chapter deals with.

2   Question

Whilst undertaking the survey ask yourself the questions you hope the chapter will answer for you.

3 Read

Read through the chapter thoroughly working through the activities and, at the end, making sure that you can meet the learning objectives highlighted on the first page.

4 Recall

At the end of each section and at the end of the chapter, try to recall the main ideas of the section / chapter without referring to the text. This is best done after a short break of a couple of minutes after the reading stage.

5 Review

Check that your recall notes are correct.

You may also find it helpful to re-read the chapter to try and see the topic(s) it deals with as a whole.

Note taking

Taking notes is a useful way of learning, but do not simply copy out the text.

The notes must:

- be in your own words
- be concise
- cover the key points
- well organised
- be modified as you study further chapters in this text or in related ones.

Trying to summarise a chapter without referring to the text can be a useful way of determining which areas you know and which you don't.

Three ways of taking notes

1 Summarise the key points of a chapter

2 Make linear notes

A list of headings, subdivided with sub-headings listing the key points.

If you use linear notes, you can use different colours to highlight key points and keep topic areas together.

Use plenty of space to make your notes easy to use.

3   Try a diagrammatic form

The most common of which is a mind map.

To make a mind map, put the main heading in the centre of the paper and put a circle around it.

Draw lines radiating from this to the main sub-headings which again have circles around them.

Continue the process from the sub-headings to sub-sub-headings.

Highlighting and underlining

You may find it useful to underline or highlight key points in your study text – but do be selective.

You may also wish to make notes in the margins.

Revision phase

Kaplan has produced material specifically designed for your final examination preparation for this unit.

These include pocket revision notes and a bank of revision questions specifically in the style of the new syllabus.

Further guidance on how to approach the final stage of your studies is given in these materials.

Further reading

In addition to this text, you should also read the "Student section" of the "Accounting Technician" magazine every month to keep abreast of any guidance from the examiners.

TAX RATES AND ALLOWANCES

Note: Tax rates and allowances that you need in the examination will be given to you.

These allowances are provided for use in this Study text.

Tax rates and bands

	%	£
Basic rate	20	first 32,010
Higher rate	40	32,011 to 150,000
Additional rate	45	over 150,000

Savings income is taxed at 10%, 20%, 40% and 45%.

(10% applies to a maximum of £2,790 of savings income only where non-savings income is below this limit)

Dividends are taxed at 10%, 32.5% and 37.5%

Personal allowance

Personal allowance	Born after 5.4.1948	£9,440
Age allowance	Born between 6.4.1938 and 5.4.1948	£10,500
Age allowance	Born before 6.4.1938	£10,660
Income limit for age allowance		£26,100

Car benefit percentage

Emission rating	%
Zero	0
75 g/km or less	5
76 g/km to 94 g/km	10
95 g/km	11 + 1 for every 5 g/km above 95 g/km

Diesel engines – additional 3%

The figure for fuel is £21,100.

Authorised mileage rates

First 10,000 miles	45p
Over 10,000 miles	25p

Van scale charge

Charge	£3,000
Private fuel provided	£564

Capital gains tax

Annual exempt amount	£10,900
Tax rate	18%
Higher rate	28%

HMRC official rate of interest 4.00%

Introduction to personal tax computations

1

Introduction

The Personal Tax assessment covers two taxes relating to individuals:

- Income tax
- Capital gains tax

This chapter outlines how this study text approaches the taxes.

CONTENTS

1 Tax years
2 Taxation of individuals

1 Tax years

Every individual taxpayer pays tax based on a tax year.

This study text bases computations around the tax year 2013/14.

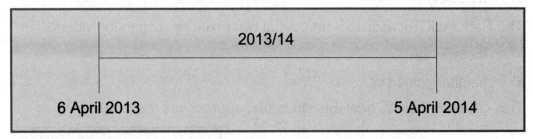

The tax year 2013/14 runs from 6 April 2013 to 5 April 2014.

Tax returns are completed for this period (see Chapter 11).

This study text will explain which items go into the tax returns and tax computations for the tax year.

2 Taxation of individuals

2.1 Two main taxes

The two main taxes applying to individuals are:

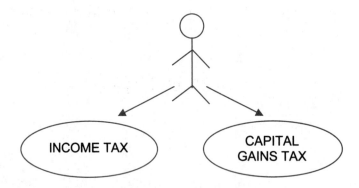

- Income tax (Chapters 2 – 11); and
- Capital gains tax (Chapters 12 – 15).

Chapter 16 then looks at:

- the duties and responsibilities of a tax adviser.

2.2 Income tax

Income tax applies mainly to:

- amounts earned in day to day work; and

- income generated from assets (for example dividend income on shares).

You will discover how to calculate an individual's income tax payable.

The ways in which the tax payable by an individual can be reduced are also considered.

2.3 Capital gains tax (CGT)

CGT applies mainly when we sell assets.

However, certain assets are exempt from CGT and there are other ways of reducing the gains.

You will discover how to calculate an individual's CGT payable.

3 Summary

Taxation of individuals is based around:

- Tax years.

The two main taxes applying are:

- Income tax; and

- Capital gains tax.

Principles of income tax

Introduction

In the assessment you will have to calculate what income is taxable for an individual and calculate an individual's income tax payable.

In this chapter we look at the basic proforma income tax computation with a view to building this up over the next few chapters.

KNOWLEDGE	CONTENTS
Explain the main current legislation relating to personal taxation (1.1 K)	1 Sources of income 2 Proforma income tax computation
SKILLS	
Calculate income tax payable (3.4 S)	

1 Sources of income

1.1 Main sources

Individuals essentially obtain income from two main sources.

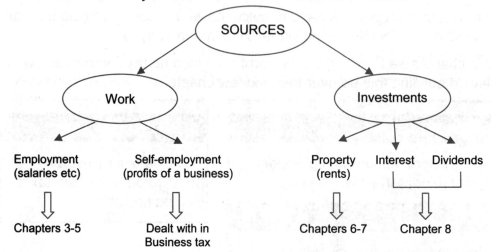

1.2 Classification of income

Income can either be classified as:

- **Taxable income** – which is shown on the income tax computation (section 2 below), or

- **Exempt income** – which it is not shown on the income tax computation (1.5 below).

1.3 Taxable income

Each type of taxable income has a slightly different tax treatment.

The types of taxable income, which are each considered in detail in the following chapters, are:

Taxable income	Includes
Employment income	Salaries, wages, bonuses, benefits
Property income	Rents receivable less expenses of renting
Interest	Interest received from, for example, building societies, banks, etc
Dividends	Dividends received from UK companies

The computation of income from self employment is not considered in this study text as it is outside the scope of Personal Tax (it is covered in Business Tax).

Income from self employment does, however, form part of an individual's taxable income. In an assessment question you will be told the amount of taxable self employment income to include if necessary.

1.4 Deduction of tax at source

Income is always shown 'gross' in the income tax computation.

However, sometimes individuals receive income 'net' of tax. This means that the person paying the income has deducted tax before paying the income, and has paid the tax to HM Revenue and Customs (HMRC) on the individual's behalf.

These sources of income need to be 'grossed up' and the gross amount included in the income tax computation.

 Example

Amy received bank interest of £800 in 2013/14. This was received net of 20% income tax.

Calculate the taxable income that will be shown in her income tax computation.

Solution

In Amy's income tax computation there will be taxable income of:

$$\text{Amount received} \times \frac{100}{100 - \text{Rate deducted}}$$

$$= 800 \times \frac{100}{100 - 20} = 800 \times \frac{100}{80} = £1,000$$

The assessment will usually state amounts **received**.

Where tax is deducted at source, the amount received will be the net amount. Take care to gross this up in the computation. ×

For these types of income:

    Amounts received = NET

    Taxable income = GROSS

Throughout the next few chapters, it will be indicated where income is received net and how it should be grossed up.

1.5 Exempt income

Exempt income, as stated earlier, does **not** go in the income tax computation.

Exempt income includes the following:

- Interest on NS&I Savings Certificates.

- Interest on Save As You Earn (SAYE) sharesave accounts.

- Interest on delayed income tax repayments.

- Interest, dividends and capital gains arising in respect of ISAs (individual savings accounts).

- Damages for personal injury or death.

- Scholarships and educational grants.

- Prizes, lottery winnings and gambling winnings.

- Statutory redundancy pay.

- Some social security benefits, including housing benefit, working tax credit and child tax credit. Child benefit is also exempt but it triggers a tax charge for high income individuals. Calculation of this charge is not in the syllabus.

This is not a complete listing of exempt income, but does cover the main examples that appear in exams.

2 Proforma income tax computation

2.1 The main tax rates

For 2013/14 an individual must pay income tax on total taxable income at the basic, higher and additional rates.

Total taxable income is found by adding up the amounts of taxable income from all the different sources and deducting any available reliefs and allowances.

The basic rate of 20% is charged on the first £32,010 of taxable income.

The higher rate of 40% is charged on taxable income between £32,011 and £150,000.

The additional rate of 45% is charged on taxable income in excess of £150,000.

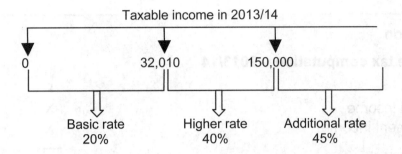

Special tax rates may apply to certain types of investment income as explained in Chapter 8, but other income is taxed at the above rates.

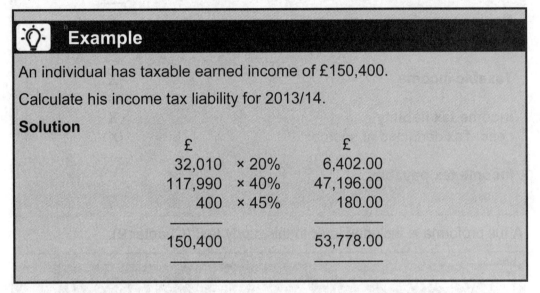

Example

An individual has taxable earned income of £150,400.

Calculate his income tax liability for 2013/14.

Solution

£		£
32,010	× 20%	6,402.00
117,990	× 40%	47,196.00
400	× 45%	180.00
———		———
150,400		53,778.00
———		———

2.2 Proforma income tax computation – overview

The following is an overview of the construction of a personal income tax computation.

It is essential to focus your attention on the key headings within the structure. They will be explained in more detail in the following chapters.

A Person

Income tax computation – 2013/14

	£
Earned income	X
Investment income	X
Total income	X
Less: Reliefs	(X)
Net income	X
Less: Personal allowance	(X)
Taxable income	X
Income tax liability	X
Less: Tax deducted at source	(X)
Income tax payable	X

A full proforma is included later in this study text (Chapter 9).

Activity 1

Mark the following statements as true or false.

		True	False
1	Interest from a building society account is exempt		
2	Income from an ISA account is taxable		
3	If Ben receives £120 of bank interest then £144 is included in his income tax computation		
4	The basic rate of income tax is 40%		

KAPLAN PUBLISHING

3 Summary

The chapter has prepared the foundations to gradually build up a full income tax computation by looking at:

- Taxable income.
- Exempt income.
- The proforma income tax computation.

4 Test your knowledge

 ## Workbook Activity 2

Ben has taxable income of £39,140.

What is his income tax liability for 2013/14? Give your answer in pounds and pence to the nearest pence.

Workbook Activity 3

Mark the following statements as true or false.

		True	False
1	Income tax is payable on lottery winnings.		
2	Bank interest received of £600 is grossed up to £720 in the personal income tax computation.		
3	Statutory redundancy pay is exempt from income tax.		
4	There are two rates of income tax – 20% and 45%		

KAPLAN PUBLISHING

Introduction to employment income

Introduction

The assessment will include testing of knowledge of the different elements of an individual's employment income.

This will include some or all of the following:

	£
Cash income	X
Benefits (Chapter 4)	X
Less: Allowable expenses	(X)
	___
Employment income	X
	___

We will first cover the taxation of cash income and the deduction of expenses. Benefits will be covered in Chapter 4 and the employment income supplementary pages of the tax return in Chapter 5.

KNOWLEDGE

Explain the main current legislation relating to personal taxation (1.1 K)

Explain the main legislative features relating to income from employment (1.2 K)

Describe taxable and non-taxable sources of income from employment (including assessable benefits) (2.4 K)

SKILLS

Describe taxation relief which can be given on income from employment including deductible (allowable) expenses, pension's relief and charitable donations (3.5 S)

CONTENTS

1 Employment status
2 Earnings
3 Allowable expenses and deductions
4 The PAYE system

1 Employment status

1.1 Introduction

An individual who works may be either an employee or self-employed (including business partners).

It is important to distinguish between the two because an employee is taxable on his employment income whilst a self-employed individual is taxable on his trading profits. The rules for the two types of income are different.

This text is concerned only with the calculation of employment income; the calculation of trading income is dealt with in the Business tax paper.

1.2 Contract of service

In many instances it will be a straightforward matter to decide whether an individual is an employee or is self-employed. If it is not clear, there are various matters to take into account.

HM Revenue and Customs (HMRC) may be asked to give a status ruling to ensure that there is no doubt. The HMRC online Employment Status Indicator can also be used to determine the status of an individual.

The basic distinction is that an employee has a **contract of service,** whereas a self-employed person will have a **contract for services.**

Some of the features of a contract of service are:

- The employer is under an obligation to offer work and the employee is under an obligation to carry it out.

- The employer will control how the work is carried out.

- The employee will be committed to work a specified number of hours at fixed times and places.

- The employee must do the work himself; he cannot arrange for someone else to do it.

- The employee does not take any financial risk.

- An employee does not usually have to provide their own equipment.

- Employees are entitled to paid holidays and sickness benefits.

Activity 1

For each statement, tick either employment or self employment:

	Employment	Self employment
Contract of service is for:		
Contract for services is for:		
A high level of control by another over the work performed would indicate what type of relationship?		

2 Earnings

2.1 Types of income

Employment income covers all earnings received from an employment. Such income includes salaries, wages, bonuses, commissions, directors' fees, tips, expense allowances and benefits.

Benefits are dealt with in Chapter 4.

Any pension income resulting from an employment is also taxable income.

2.2 Basis of assessment

The expression 'basis of assessment' means which income should we tax in which tax year.

The basis of assessment for employment income is the **receipts basis**.

This means that income is taxed in the year in which an employee receives it or becomes entitled to the payment, if earlier.

Example

Bertha receives her salary on the last day of the calendar month.

In the year to 31 December 2013 her salary is £1,000 per month. In the year to 31 December 2014 her salary is £1,100 per month.

(a) What is her taxable employment income for 2013/14?

(b) Would this be different if her salary was paid in advance on the first day of the month?

Solution

(a) **2013/14 – taxable employment income**

	£
In year ended 31 December 2013	
30 April 2013 to 31 December 2013 (9 months)	
(9 × £1,000)	9,000
In year ended 31 December 2014	
31 January 2014 to 31 March 2014 (3 months)	
(3 × £1,100)	3,300
	12,300

(b) **2013/14 – taxable employment income**

	£
In year ended 31 December 2013	
1 May 2013 to 1 December 2013 (8 months)	
(8 × £1,000)	8,000
In year ended 31 December 2014	
1 January 2014 to 1 April 2014 (4 months)	
(4 × £1,100)	4,400
	12,400

2.3 Bonuses

One of the main areas that can cause problems is bonuses.

Many individuals receive bonuses (for example sales representatives). The bonus may be based on the employer's accounting period (e.g. sales made in that period). However, the employee may not be entitled to payment until after the end of the period.

Remember that the employee will not be taxed on the bonus until he is entitled to receive it.

 Example

Gordon is a salesman working for Jones Ltd. He is entitled to a bonus each year based on the sales he has made in the company's accounting period ended 31 December.

His recent bonuses have been as follows:

For the year ended	Date of payment/entitlement	£
31 December 2011	10 April 2012	8,000
31 December 2012	8 April 2013	10,000
31 December 2013	4 April 2014	9,500
31 December 2014	8 April 2015	7,500

What is the amount taxable in 2013/14?

Solution

The taxable amount is that paid in 2013/14.

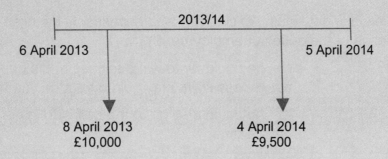

Hence the total taxable bonus in 2013/14 is £19,500.

Note there will be no taxable bonus in 2014/15.

3 Allowable expenses and deductions

3.1 Principle of allowable expenses

Allowable expenses are those that can be deducted from earnings to arrive at the taxable employment income.

3.2 Wholly, exclusively and necessarily

The general rule for an expense to be deducted from earnings is that it must be incurred 'wholly, exclusively and necessarily' in the performance of the duties of employment.

If in doubt about an expense in the exam, return to this rule to seek guidance.

The expense cannot be deducted **just** because it makes the job easier.

 Example

A bank manager joined a golf club with a view to taking potential clients there. In his opinion it would make his job easier because in the relaxed atmosphere the potential clients would be more likely to put business his way.

Can he claim the membership fees as an allowable expense?

Solution

No.

The expense is not wholly, exclusively and necessarily incurred in the performance of the duties of employment.

| NECESSARY | – | No, he could try to win business at his office. It is not necessary to play golf to be a bank manager! |
| EXCLUSIVELY | – | No, he could also go to the golf club in his own private time. |

3.3 Other specific allowable expenses

Set out below are specific expenses that are allowable.

- **Costs of business travel and subsistence.**

    Business travel includes journeys made in the performance of an employee's duties. It does not include travel between home and the permanent workplace (i.e. ordinary commuting).

    If an employer pays for business travel (e.g. via an expenses claim), then the amount paid is employment income. The employee can then deduct the allowable travel expenses that he incurred.

    However, special rules apply if an employee uses his own vehicle for business travel.

Under the 'Approved Mileage Allowance Payments' (AMAP) system, only amounts paid in excess of the approved rates are taxable.

If the amounts paid are lower, the employee can claim the shortfall as an allowable expense.

The approved rates are:

Cars

First 10,000 business miles per tax year	45p per mile
Additional mileage	25p per mile
Motor cycles	24p per mile
Bicycles	20p per mile

These are given in the exam if needed.

 Example

John has travelled 12,000 business miles in 2013/14 in his own car. His employer pays 42p per mile.

(a) How much of the mileage allowance is taxable?

(b) How would your answer differ if John's employer paid 38p per mile?

Solution

(a) Taxable mileage allowance

	£	£
Income (12,000 × 42p)		5,040
Less: Allowable expense		
10,000 × 45p	4,500	
2,000 × 25p	500	
	———	(5,000)
		———
Taxable amount		40
		———

(b) If John's employer paid 38p per mile, the total amount received by John would be 12,000 × 38p = £4,560.

John could deduct the shortfall of £440 (£5,000 – £4,560) as an allowable expense.

- **Professional subscriptions.**

  Professional subscriptions (e.g. annual subscriptions to AAT, subscriptions to trade associations, etc) are allowable expenses. Compare this to golf club subscriptions mentioned earlier.

- **Amounts donated under the payroll deduction scheme.**

  Under this scheme employees can have sums deducted from their salary on a weekly/monthly basis by their employer and paid directly to charity. This is also referred to as payroll giving or Give As You Earn.

- **Contributions to company pension schemes.**

  Where an individual contributes to the employer's own company pension scheme (also known as an 'occupational pension scheme'), the amount contributed is deducted directly from wages/salaries.

  The amount deducted is an allowable expense (see more on pensions in Chapter 10).

- **Entertaining.**

  Where an employee incurs entertaining costs, (e.g. for entertaining clients), he will usually reclaim the costs from the employer. Or he may have a regular specific 'entertaining allowance' which is always spent, e.g. £100 per month.

  In both of these situations there should be nothing chargeable.

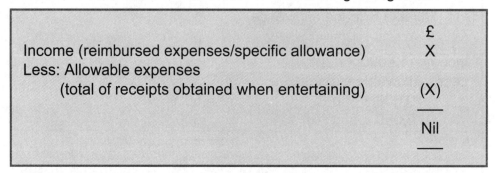

	£
Income (reimbursed expenses/specific allowance)	X
Less: Allowable expenses (total of receipts obtained when entertaining)	(X)
	Nil

However, if the employee pays for entertaining costs out of a general round sum allowance, no deduction for allowable entertaining expenses is available.

3.4 Dispensations

Where expenses are reimbursed by an employer, HMRC allows for dispensation treatment of those expenses, as long as they are incurred 'wholly, exclusively and necessarily' in the duties of employment.

As the expenses automatically cancel out the original expenditure, the details do not need to be entered on the tax return.

3.5 Proforma employment income computation – 2013/14

	£
Salary/fees/commission/bonus etc	X
Expense allowances and reimbursed expenses	X
Benefits (see Chapter 4)	X
	X
Less: Professional subscriptions	(X)
Donations under payroll giving schemes	(X)
Occupational pension scheme contributions	(X)
Entertaining expenses (where reimbursed or paid from a specific entertaining allowance)	(X)
Expenses incurred wholly, exclusively and necessarily in the performance of duties	(X)
Taxable employment income	X

Activity 2

Underwood

Underwood is employed as an insurance salesman at a monthly salary of £950.

In addition to his basic salary he receives a bonus which is paid in May each year and which is related to the sales achieved by Underwood in the year to the previous 31 October.

His bonuses are as follows:

Bonus for year to	Paid during	£
31 October 2011	May 2012	1,920
31 October 2012	May 2013	1,260
31 October 2013	May 2014	2,700

Underwood made the following payments in respect of his employment in 2013/14.

	£
Contribution to occupational pension scheme	342
Subscription to Chartered Insurance Institute	100
Payroll giving scheme (in favour of Oxfam)	200
Gym membership – often meets clients at the gym	150

Using the following proforma calculate Underwood's taxable employment income for 2013/14.

£

Salary

Bonus

_____

Less Allowable expenses

_____

Taxable employment income

_____

4 The PAYE system

4.1 Principle of the PAYE system

The PAYE system is a method of collecting income tax at source from the earnings of employees.

The aim of the PAYE system is to remove the requirement to submit a tax return from as many people as possible (i.e. all of their tax is deducted at source by their employer and paid to HMRC on their behalf).

The PAYE system will not be examined in the Personal Tax assessment.

Activity 3

Mark each of the following statements as true or false

		True	False
1	Sally is paid her bonus for the year ended 31 December 2012 in May 2013. Her bonus will be taxed partly in 2012/13 and partly in 2013/14.		
2	If Chen Li is paid 50p a mile by his employer for business mileage, there will be no tax consequences.		
3	Gail is employed as an electrician. Her subscription for the Financial Times is an allowable employment expense.		

5 Summary

The important aspects of this chapter are:

- **Basis of assessment** – when employment income is taxed.

  Bonuses are often tested here. Remember that a bonus is taxable in the tax year in which the employee is entitled to receive it.

- **Allowable expenses** – these are often included in an exam.

  Remember that for the expense to be allowable it must be incurred 'wholly, exclusively and necessarily' in the performance of the duties of the employment.

6 Test your knowledge

 Workbook Activity 4

Egbert is the sales director of Pinafores Limited.

The company paid the following expenses on behalf of Egbert in the year ended 5 April 2014:

	£
Business entertainment	
Sums reimbursed	46
Sums paid to third parties	62
General expenses allowance	500
Travelling and subsistence (all business related)	
Fares, hotels, meals etc	938

Egbert advises you that 35% of the general expenses allowance was used in entertaining customers and the balance was spent on business travelling.

Required:

What is the total of the allowable expenses in Egbert's employment income computation for the year 2013/14?

A   £1,546

B   £1,371

C   £1,046

D   £1,309

 Workbook Activity 5

Alan is the finance director of a large company and incurred the following costs during 2013/14.

Which one is deductible from his employment income?

A   Subscription to the local health club where he often meets clients

B   Travel between the two offices of his employer

C   Tips to taxi drivers if he chooses to take taxis home from work

D   Cost of two new suits bought to impress clients

Workbook Activity 6

Charles Thackery has the following income for 2013/14:

			£
(a)	Salary as a sales representative paid on the last day of the month:		
	year ending 31 December 2013		16,000
	year ending 31 December 2014		18,000
(b)	Bonus based on the company profits for the accounting year to:		
	30 September 2013 (paid 1.12.13)		600
	30 September 2014 (paid 1.12.14)		900
(c)	Mileage allowance paid (8,000 miles @ 50p)		4,000
	The allowance was only paid for business mileage.		

Based in the information above, answer the following questions:

1   What is the taxable salary for 2013/14?

2   What is the taxable bonus for 2013/14?

3   What is the taxable/allowable mileage allowance for 2013/14?

Workbook Activity 7

Bartholomew, age 45 years, has been employed by Telnet TV Ltd in central London for several years as a television producer.

The following information is available for the year 2013/14:

(1)   His annual salary is £52,000.

(2)   On 31 May 2013 he received a bonus of £7,644 in respect of the company's year ended 31 March 2013.

The bonus for the company's year ended 31 March 2014 paid on 31 May 2014 was £10,400.

(3) Telnet TV Ltd has a registered occupational pension scheme to which it contributes 10% of employees' basic salary. Bartholomew is required to contribute 5% of his basic salary.

Required:

Calculate the amount of employment income chargeable on Bartholomew for 2013/14 using the following proforma.

	£
Salary	
Bonus	
	____
Less Pension contributions	
	____
Assessable employment income	
	____

 Workbook Activity 8

Mel earns £45,000 per year as a copywriter for Columbus Ltd. Columbus Ltd prepares accounts to 31 March each year.

For the last two years, Mel has earned bonuses from her employer as follows:

	Paid	£
Year ended 31 March 2013	1 June 2013	8,000
Year ended 31 March 2014	1 June 2014	11,000

In addition, Mel incurs expenses in travelling to client's offices of £2,000 in 2013/14.

What is Mel's assessable employment income for 2013/14?

A   £51,000

B   £53,000

C   £54,000

D   £56,000

Employment income – benefits

Introduction

In this chapter we look at the different types of benefit an employee could receive and how they are taxed.

This is an important area of the syllabus. The first two tasks in the assessment will test the rules for benefits.

KNOWLEDGE

Explain the main current legislation relating to personal taxation (1.1 K)

Explain the main legislative features relating to income from employment (1.2 K)

Describe taxable and non-taxable sources of income from employment including assessable benefits (2.4 K)

SKILLS

Prepare computations of emoluments including assessable benefits (2.1 S)

Make computations and submissions in accordance with current tax law (5.1 S)

CONTENTS

1   Classification of benefits
2   Exempt benefits
3   Benefits assessable on all employees and directors
4   Benefits assessable on P11D employees

1 Classification of benefits

1.1 The three categories

Benefits are split into three categories:

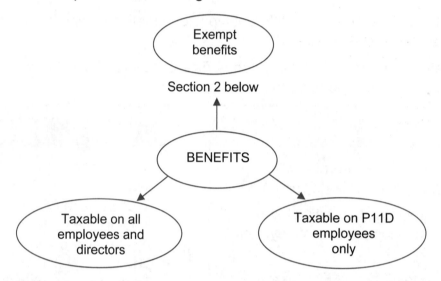

In an exam you can expect benefits from each category. The tasks concerning benefits will be a major part of the assessment.

The P11D is the name of the HMRC form used by employers to report details of benefits and expenses for directors and employees earning at the rate of £8,500 per year.

1.2 General points

Before we consider the specific benefits, here are some general points which are *frequently* examined.

- If an employee pays his employer for a benefit, the taxable amount is reduced.

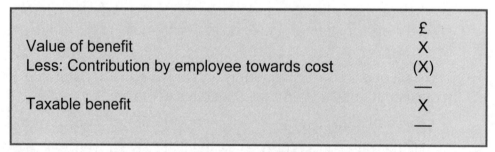

	£
Value of benefit	X
Less: Contribution by employee towards cost	(X)
Taxable benefit	X

The only exception to this rule is that partial payments for private petrol cannot be deducted (covered later).

- An employee may be able to claim that a benefit (or part of it) was provided wholly, exclusively and necessarily for the purposes of the employment.

- In such situations you should first calculate the benefit, and then claim an expense deduction to reduce it.

- For most benefits **time apportion** the taxable amount if the benefit was only available for part of the tax year.

- This adjustment should be calculated in **months** and is a very popular adjustment in exam questions.

2 Exempt benefits

2.1 Types of exempt benefit

The exempt benefits which are specified as examinable are:

- Job related accommodation (see 3.2 below).

- Subsidised canteen provided it is available to all staff and is not part of a salary sacrifice scheme.

- Removal expenses up to £8,000 for a new employment or if an employee's job is relocated. This can include hotel costs whilst looking for somewhere to live, legal and estate agents' fees and any other costs related to the removal. There is a time limit such that if an employee needs to move in 2013/14 then expenses must be incurred or benefits provided by end 2014/15.

- Personal expenses (e.g. telephone calls home, newspapers, laundry) paid by the employer whilst the employee is required to stay away on company business. The payment limits are up to £5 per night in the UK and £10 per night for overseas. If the payments exceed these limits then the **whole** amount is taxable.

- Workplace nurseries (crèches) (provided by employer). These can be at workplace or in other premises that the employer manages and finances.

- The cost of childcare provided by an **approved** child carer subject to a maximum depending on the tax status of the employee:

  - Basic rate taxpayers –   the first £55 per week

  - Higher rate taxpayers –   the first £28 per week

  - Additional rate taxpayers –   the first £25 per week

- Contributions by an employer to a registered pension scheme.

- Sport and recreational facilities available for all staff but not to the public generally. Facilities can also be used by former employees and employees' families.

- The provision of one mobile telephone per employee (including smartphones). Tablets and computers used to make telephone calls are not exempt because they use the internet to make the calls.

- The expenses of work related training borne by the employer including associated costs such as books.

- Retraining courses for employees made redundant to provide them with skills to get a new job or become self employed.

- Contributions by an employer towards the additional household costs incurred by an employee working from home instead of at the employer's premises. Only payments above £4 per week require supporting evidence.

- The funding of an annual party or similar event (e.g. Christmas office party or staff summer outing) up to £150 per attendee per year. If the event costs more than £150 per head none of the amount is exempt. If employees attend two events with total costs more than £150 then only one of the events (with a cost below £150) can be exempt. The more expensive of the two events should be chosen for the exemption.

- A long service award of £50 for each year of service provided service is at least 20 years. The award must not be in cash and the recipient must not have had an award within the previous 10 years.

- Awards in accordance with a staff suggestion scheme. These reward employees for suggestions that improve the employer's business and which are not made as part of the employee's normal job. Awards up to a maximum of £5,000 can be exempt.

- Non-cash gifts received from someone other than the employer and costing no more than £250 per donor. The gift must not be in recognition of particular services by the employee in the course of employment.

- The provision of an annual private medical and/or a health screening.

- Private medical insurance for employees working overseas.

- Provision of eye care tests and/or corrective glasses for Visual Display Units use

- The provision of bicycles or cycling safety equipment to enable employees to get to and from work, provided they are available to staff generally.

- The occasional provision of a late night taxi where an employee is required to work later than usual.

- Works buses used to transport employees to/from work and available to employees generally. Employers can also provide subsidies to local bus companies to assist them in running services to help employees travel to/from work. In return the employees receive free or reduced fares.

- Parking spaces near place of work – for cars, bicycles or motorcycles.

- Scholarships provided by an employer to a family member of an employee are **not** exempt if the payment is provided by reason of the employment – that is the payment would not have been made if the employee did not work for the employer. However, scholarships can be exempt if they meet the following conditions:

  - The scholarship would still have been awarded even if the employee had not worked for the employer.

  - The recipient is in full time education.

  - The payment is made from a trust fund or a special scheme.

  - No more than 25% of the fund is used to provide scholarships linked to employment.

3 Benefits assessable on all employees and directors

3.1 Summary of benefits

The following benefits are assessable on all employees and directors, irrespective of the level of their earnings.

Type of benefit	Amount assessable
The gift of an asset convertible into money (i.e. the gift of an asset the employee could sell, for example, a computer or television)	Cash equivalent (i.e. the price the employee could obtain if he converted the benefit into cash). Special rules may apply to P11D employees.
The payment by an employer of an employee's liabilities (e.g. telephone bill).	The amount paid by the employer.

Type of benefit	Amount assessable
Cash vouchers.	Cash receivable when cashed in.
Non-cash vouchers (includes transport vouchers, cheque vouchers).	Cost of voucher to the employer.
Credit cards.	Whatever the employee charges to the card but does not reimburse (but not interest and annual fee).
Accommodation.	See below (parts 1 and 2 only).

3.2 Accommodation

The assessable benefit amount depends on whether or not the accommodation is 'job related'.

Accommodation is 'job related':

(a) if **necessary** for the proper performance of employment duties.

(b) if provided for **better performance** of duties and it is **customary** to provide accommodation in such circumstances.

(c) if there is a **special security** threat and the accommodation is part of the arrangements to counter the threat.

'Job related' therefore includes accommodation provided for caretakers, hotel staff, clergy and certain members of the government.

A director can only claim exemption under (a) or (b) if:

• he has no material interest in the company and,

• he is a full time working director or the company is a non-profit making organisation.

The calculation of the assessable benefit is split into three parts.

3.2.1 Part 1 – Basic Charge

The basic charge for being provided with accommodation is:

Not job related	Job related
Higher of (i) Annual value of the property (also known as gross rateable value or market rental value), and (ii) rent paid by employer (if property is rented rather than owned by the employer)	Exempt benefit

Example

Harry is provided with a flat to live in by his employer (it is not job related accommodation).

The flat has an annual value of £2,000 and the employer pays rent of £200 per month.

Harry contributes £50 per month towards the private use of the flat.

Required:

What is his taxable benefit in 2013/14?

Solution

	£	£
Basic charge		
Higher of (i) annual value; and	2,000	
(ii) rent paid by employer (12 × £200)	2,400	
	———	2,400
Less: Contribution by employee (as mentioned in 1.2 above) (12 × £50)		(600)
		———
Taxable benefit		1,800
		———

3.2.2 Part 2 – Expensive Accommodation Charge

If the accommodation provided is purchased by the company and cost more than £75,000, it is deemed to be 'expensive'.

An additional benefit may apply as follows:

Not job related	Job related
(Cost – £75,000) × Official rate of interest	Exempt benefit

The official rate of interest is set annually by HMRC and will be given to you in the exam.

Cost includes any improvements made to the property before 6 April in the tax year for which the benefit is being calculated. So if the benefit is being calculated for 2013/14, then all improvement costs incurred up to 5 April 2013 must be included in the 'cost' figure.

Example

Jack was provided with a house to live in by his employer (not job related). It cost his employer £150,000 in June 2008. An extension was added in May 2011 costing £50,000. The house has an annual value of £3,000.

Required:

Assuming the official rate of interest is 4%, what is the taxable benefit?

Solution

		£	£
Basic charge			
Higher of (i) annual value; and		3,000	
(ii) rent paid by employer (owned)		Nil	
		———	3,000
Expensive accommodation			
((£150,000 + £50,000) – £75,000) × 4%			5,000
			———
Taxable benefit			8,000
			———

If the accommodation was purchased by the company more than 6 years before the employee moves in, then a different rule applies.

Cost is replaced by the market value of the property at the date the employee moves in, plus the cost of any improvements made after the employee moves in but before the 6 April in the tax year of calculation.

 Example

Sanjay was provided with a house to live in by his employer. It is not job related accommodation. The house cost £100,000 when the company bought it in December 2003.

Sanjay moved in during March 2011 when the property was worth £210,000. In July 2013 an extension was built on the house costing £32,000.

Assuming the official rate of interest is 4%, what is the 'expensive' accommodation charge in Sanjay's benefit calculation for 2013/14?

A £1,000

B £2,280

C £5,400

D £6,680

Solution

The answer is C.

(£210,000 – £75,000) × 4% = £5,400

Since the employer bought the house more than 6 years before Sanjay moves in, the cost is replaced by market value at March 2011.

The cost of the extension in July 2013 is ignored for 2013/14. It will be included in the 'expensive' accommodation benefit calculation for 2014/15 and thereafter.

3.2.3 Part 3 – Provision of Services

This part of the benefit is only applicable to employees earning more than £8,500 per annum (and all directors) – so called P11D employees

You may like to return to this section after you have studied Section 4 below.

Not job related	Job related
Use of furniture – 20% per annum of market value when first provided (usually cost). Household expenses (e.g. heating, maintenance, decorating, but not capital improvements) – cost to employer	Same – but restricted to: 10% of **other** employment income.

  Example

Amy is a hotel manager and is provided with accommodation on the site of the hotel (job related). Her annual salary is £25,000. She has other benefits of £500 and makes payments into her employer's registered occupational pension scheme of £2,000 per annum.

The accommodation has an annual value of £1,500 and cost her employer £90,000 four years ago. The accommodation contains furniture which cost her employer £10,000 four years ago (when she first got the accommodation). The employer pays all of her household bills totalling £1,000.

Required:

Calculate the taxable accommodation benefit for 2013/14.

Solution

	£
Basic charge (exempt)	Nil
Expensive accommodation charge (exempt)	Nil
Provision of services – furniture (20% × £10,000)	2,000
– household bills	1,000
	———
Total	3,000
	———
Restricted to (10% × other employment income)	
(10% × £23,500) (W)	2,350
	———

Working: **Other employment income**

	£
Salary	25,000
Other benefits	500
Less: Allowable expenses	(2,000)
	———
	23,500
	———

There are many places to go wrong in calculating the accommodation benefit.

Before starting to calculate consider all the factors that can impact (e.g. does it cost more than £75,000, is it owned or rented by the employer, is it job related, and was it bought by the employer more than 6 years before the employee moved in?).

 Activity 1

Mr X

Mr X has a salary of £30,000 and lives in a furnished company flat that cost his employers £105,000 in June 2008.

The annual value of the flat is £2,400 and Mr X pays his employer rent of £100 a month. The accommodation is not job related. Furniture costing £6,500 was first provided in June 2008.

The official rate of interest is 4%.

Required:

Which of the following is the correct figure for Mr X's taxable benefit for 2013/14?

A   £4,900

B   £3,700

C   £2,500

D   £6,700

 Activity 2

Read the following statements which relate to the provision of accommodation for an employee which is not job related.

Mark each statement as true or false.

		True	False
1	Furniture provided by an employer for use by an employee is taxed at 20% per annum of the market value when first made available.		
2	Furniture provided by an employer for use by an employee is taxed on the cost to the employer in the year of purchase.		
3	The running costs of the accommodation which are paid for by the employer are taxed on the employee at 20% of their total cost.		
4	The running costs of the accommodation which are paid for by the employer are taxed on the employee at their total cost.		

4 Benefits assessable on P11D employees

4.1 P11D employees

The benefits covered in this section apply only to those employees earning at a rate of at least £8,500 a year and to directors, irrespective of their level of earnings.

If an individual fits this definition then a Form P11D will be required for them.

Directors are taxed in the same way as employees earning at a rate of £8,500 a year (including benefits).

Most employees are P11D employees.

4.2 The main benefits taxed on P11D employees

The main additional benefits taxable on P11D employees are:

- Company cars
- Fuel provided for company cars
- Vans
- Beneficial loans
- Gifts and use of assets.

Where any other benefits are provided to P11D employees the taxable amount is the cost to the employer of providing the benefit less any amount contributed towards the cost by the employee.

These rules apply where, for example, an employer pays for private health insurance or for membership of a sports club for an employee.

4.3 Company cars

This benefit will be tested in the exam.

When a car is made available by an employer for *private* use, a taxable benefit arises as a result of the private use of the car.

The benefit is calculated as a percentage of the list price of the car when first registered.

$$\text{Benefit} = (\% \times \text{List price when new})$$

List price

The list price may be different to the price paid for the car by the employer. Take care to select the correct figure.

The cost of any extra accessories provided with the car must be added to the list price. In addition, the cost of any accessories acquired subsequently must also be added to the list price, but only if the accessory cost more than £100.

The list price can be reduced by any capital contribution made by the employee towards the purchase of the car, subject to a maximum deduction of £5,000.

Determining the percentage

The usual minimum percentage is 11% and the maximum is 35%.

The percentage depends on the rate at which the car emits carbon dioxide (CO_2). This is usually recorded on the car's registration document (and is supplied in the exam).

If the emission rate is 95 grams per kilometre travelled (for 2013/14), the percentage of 11% applies to petrol cars.

This is increased by 1% for every extra complete 5 grams emitted.

Diesel engine vehicles are surcharged an extra 3% to reflect the additional pollutants compared to petrol engines for the same carbon dioxide level of emission.

However, for both petrol and diesel the maximum percentage is 35%.

 Example

Louise is provided with a company car with a carbon dioxide emission rate of 122 g/km.

What percentage is to be applied assuming the car runs on:

(a)   Petrol

(b)   Diesel?

Solution

(a)   **122 g/km petrol**

Ignore the extra 2 g/km (always round down to the next 0 or 5).

∴ 120g/km

95 g/km	11%
120 g/km = extra 25 g/km	
Therefore 25 × $^1/_5$	5%
	___
Appropriate percentage	16%
	___

(b) **122 g/km diesel**

As above	16%
Diesel supplement	3%
Appropriate percentage	19%

Always look out for the type of fuel.

The emission rate of 95 g/km is given in the exam.

There are lower percentages for cars with very low carbon dioxide emissions.

Emissions	Petrol	Diesel
75 g/km or less	5%	8%
Between 76 and 94 g/km	10%	13%

Where a car emits no carbon dioxide, the percentage is zero, such that there is no benefit.

 Activity 3

What percentage would be applied for petrol cars with the following CO_2 emissions?

1   84 g/km

2   72 g/km

3   143 g/km

4   233 g/km

Non-availability

Where a car is unavailable to the employee for 30 consecutive days or more during any part of the tax year, the benefit is reduced proportionately.

Temporary non-availability of less than 30 days is ignored.

Where a car is unavailable for part of the tax year, the benefit should be calculated on a daily basis but in the assessment you should do calculations to the nearest month unless you are told otherwise.

Running costs

Running expenses (for example servicing, insurance) are deemed to be included in the benefit figure and **do not** produce an additional benefit.

However, the provision of a **chauffeur** is counted as an additional benefit valued at the **private use portion** of the chauffeur's employment costs.

Contributions for private use

Employees are commonly required to make a monthly payment towards the cost of private use. Such contributions made by the employee are deducted from the taxable benefit.

Remember that where the employee contributes towards the cost of purchasing the car, the treatment is different; such a contribution reduces the list price used in calculating the benefit.

Cars used only for business

Where an employee is specifically forbidden from using his company car for private purposes and, as a matter of fact, does not so use it, there will be no taxable car benefit.

There is also no benefit where there is provision of a company car (and associated services) which is a 'pool' car.

A pool car is one which is not exclusively used by any one employee, and which is not available for travel from home to work, being garaged at company premises, and is only used for business travel.

Activity 4

1   Sue is provided with a 2,000 cc petrol driven car by her employer that cost £15,400. The emission rate shown on the registration document is 181 grams of carbon dioxide per kilometre and the list price of the car when new was £16,000.

During 2013/14 Sue drove 3,000 business miles and paid her employer £2,000 in respect of her private use of the car.

Required:

What is the benefit taxable on Sue for 2013/14?

> 2 Paul is provided with a 2,300 cc diesel powered car by his employer that cost £34,000. The list price of the car when new was £39,000. Paul paid £3,000 towards the purchase of the car.
>
> During 2013/14 Paul drove 28,000 business miles. The emission rating of the car is 212 g/km.
>
> **Required:**
>
> What is the benefit taxable on Paul for 2013/14?

4.4 Fuel provided for private purposes

The provision of petrol or diesel in a company car for **private use** is the subject of a benefit charge which is in addition to the charge for the provision of the car itself.

The benefit is calculated as £21,100 multiplied by the same percentage used for calculating the car benefit.

The figure of £21,100 is given in the exam.

The fuel benefit is £Nil if either:

- the employee has to pay his employer for *all* fuel provided for private use; or

- the fuel is only provided by the employer for business use.

There is no reduction in the fuel benefit if the employee only **partially** reimburses his employer for private fuel. This is a common source of error in exam questions.

Where the car is unavailable to the employee for 30 consecutive days or more during any part of the tax year, both the car and fuel benefit are reduced proportionately.

In these circumstances, the benefit should be calculated on a daily rather than a monthly basis, however for exams work to the nearest month.

Temporary non-availability of less than 30 days is ignored.

If private use fuel is withdrawn during the year, the fuel benefit figure is reduced pro rata. However, this only applies if the withdrawal is permanent.

For example, if the car is provided throughout the year but the provision of private use fuel is only suspended between 1 November 2013 and 31 January 2014, a full year's charge will still apply.

Example

From 1 November 2013 Joan's employer provided her with an 1,800 cc car, the list price of which was £15,000 with an emission rate of 144 g/km. Up to 5 April 2014 she drove 6,000 miles of which 4,500 were private. The company paid for all running expenses.

Between 1 November 2013 and 31 January 2014 the company paid for all petrol usage including private use. Joan made a contribution to her employer of £15 per month towards the provision of the petrol for her private use. From 1 February 2014 her employer only paid for business use petrol.

Required:

Calculate Joan's taxable benefits for 2013/14.

Solution

	£
Car benefit (£15,000 × 20% × $^5/_{12}$)	1,250
Fuel benefit (£21,100 × 20% × $^3/_{12}$)	1,055
	―――――
Taxable benefits	2,305

The percentage is 20% = 11% + (140 – 95) × $^1/_5$.

The car was available for 5 months (1 November 2012 to 5 April 2013).

Fuel for private use was only available for 3 months (1 November 2013 to 31 January 2014).

The contribution towards the cost of private petrol does not reduce the fuel benefit, as the cost of the private petrol was not reimbursed in full.

4.5 Company vans

In the case of a company van with private use the assessable benefit is as follows:

- £3,000 per annum for unrestricted private use of the van.

- £564 per annum if private fuel is provided by the employer.

Taking the van home at night is not treated as private use.

Incidental private use, such as the occasional trip to the rubbish tip, is ignored. However, this would not extend to regular shopping trips.

Both benefits are time apportioned if the van is unavailable to the employee for 30 consecutive days or more during any part of the tax year.

4.6   Beneficial loans

Where by reason of employment an employee or a relative is provided with an interest free or cheap loan, the benefit derived from such an arrangement is taxable.

There is no taxable benefit where:

- the total loans to an employee do not exceed £5,000 at any time during the tax year; or

- the loan is used by the employee to purchase equipment required for the purposes of his employment; or

- the loan is used by the employee to pay for expenditure incurred wholly, exclusively and necessarily in the performance of the duties of the employment.

The assessable benefit is calculated as follows:

	£
Loan outstanding × the official rate of interest (ORI)	X
Less: Interest actually paid by the employee	(X)
Taxable benefit	X

The ORI will be given in the exam.

Where the loan is provided or repaid part way through the year, the benefit is calculated using either the average or the precise method.

- *Precise method*

  Interest is calculated on the balance of the loan on a daily basis.

  The examiner has stated that a computation using the precise method will not be set in the assessment.

- *Average method*

	£
½ × (Balance outstanding at beginning of year + Balance outstanding at the end of the year) × ORI	X
Less: Interest actually paid by the employee	(X)
Taxable benefit	X

If the loan was provided or repaid during the tax year, the amount of the loan on those dates is used instead of the balance at the beginning or end of the tax year and the benefit is multiplied by the proportion of the year that the loan was available.

A taxable benefit arises in respect of any amount of loan written off by the employer, even if the loan was for less than £5,000.

 Example

Bob was loaned £10,000, interest free, by his employer on 6 August 2012. He repaid £2,000 on 6 September 2013.

Required:

Calculate the amount taxable on Bob in 2013/14. Assume an official rate of interest of 4.00%.

Solution

The assessable benefit using the average method is:

	£
½ × (£10,000 + £8,000) × 4.00%	360
Less: Interest paid by employee	(Nil)
Taxable benefit	360

 Example

Bob was loaned £10,000, interest free, by his employer on 6 August 2013 and repaid £2,000 on 6 September 2013.

Required:

Calculate the amount taxable on Bob in 2013/14. Assume an official rate of interest of 4.00%.

Solution

The assessable benefit using the average method is:

	£
½ × (£10,000 + £8,000) × 8/12 × 4.00%	240
Less: Interest paid by employee	(Nil)
Taxable benefit	240

4.7   Gifts and use of assets

If an asset (for example, a television) is owned by the company but the employee is allowed to use it privately, the taxable benefit is calculated as:

20% of the open market value when the asset was first made available (usually 20% of the cost).

This has been seen already as part of the accommodation benefit.

If the employer does not own the asset, but rents it, the benefit is the greater of 20% of the value of the asset and the rent paid by the employer.

If an asset which is new is gifted to the employee, the benefit will be the cost to the company.

If an asset has been used and is then subsequently gifted to an employee, the benefit is the higher of:

- market value (MV) at the date of the gift (less the amount paid by employee).

- original market value less benefit amounts assessed to date (less the amount paid by the employee).

- This rule does not apply for cars or bicycles, the gift of these assets will just be the market value (MV) at the date of the gift (less the amount paid by employee.

Example

A suit costing £300 was purchased for Bill's use by his employer on 6 April 2012. One year later Bill purchased the suit for £20. Its market value at that time is estimated to be £30.

Required:

Calculate the amounts taxable on Bill.

Solution

The assessable benefits are computed as follows:

	£
2012/13 – Use of suit	
Annual value (20% × £300)	60
	——
2013/14 – Purchase of suit	
Suit's current market value	30
Less: Price paid by employee	(20)
	——
	10
	——

KAPLAN PUBLISHING

Suit's original market value		300
Less: Taxed in 2012/13 in respect of use		(60)
Less: Price paid by employee		(20)
		———
		220
		———

Thus the taxable benefit in 2013/14 is £220, being the greater of £10 and £220.

4.8 General charging section

This covers any other benefits not listed above.

The assessable benefit will be the **cost to the employer** of providing the benefit (e.g. package holiday, medical insurance, etc).

This is the case even if, thanks to the employer's buying power, this is less than the price an employee would have to pay.

 Activity 5

June gives you the following information about her employment.

- She belongs to a private medical insurance scheme and the company paid the required premium of £1,270 (including £650 for her family).

- June took meals in the fully subsidised staff canteen, the cost for the year being £335.

- June was paid a round sum expense allowance of £1,870, out of which she paid £800 on entertaining customers and £550 on business travel.

Required:

What is the total of June's assessable benefits in respect of these items?

A   £1,790

B   £2,925

C   £2,590

D   £1,940

Activity 6

1   Raider is employed by Coliseum Ltd.

When at the company premises Raider has use of a car owned by the company for business journeys only. It had a list price of £62,000 and an emission rating of 223 g/km, is 3,500 cc, costs £4,800 a year to run and the chauffeur's salary is £17,500. It is garaged at the company's head office and is used in addition by all the directors.

Required:

What is the assessable benefit?

A   £21,700

B   £26,500

C   £44,000

D   £Nil

2   Raider is also provided with a two-year-old 3.5 litre Rover car. Coliseum Ltd paid £16,100 for the car, which had a list price of £17,000. However, Raider prefers to use his own car, a Lotus, and therefore lets his wife use the Rover.

The company pays for all of the running costs of the Rover car, including petrol for private use.

The carbon dioxide emission rate of the Rover is 242 g/km. Raider's business mileage in his own car is 12,000 miles. Both cars run on petrol.

Required:

What is the total assessable employment income in respect of these two vehicles?

A   £8,335

B   £8,020

C   £13,335

D   £950

Activity 7

Read the following statements and mark each one as true or false.

		True	False
1	Howie is loaned a new computer costing £1,000 by his employer on 6 April 2013. The taxable benefit for 2013/14 is £200.		
2	If the computer had been given to Howie on 6 April 2013 there would be no assessable benefit.		
3	Dale is a housemaster at a boarding school and is required to live on the premises. This is an example of job related accommodation.		
4	Ken drives a company van. He is required to take it home every night ready for work in the morning as he frequently drives from home straight to the customer's premises. He does not use it for any other private purposes. The taxable benefit is £3,000.		

5 Summary

You should be prepared for any/all of the assessable benefits to be tested. There will be a task on company car benefits and another task on other taxable and exempt benefits.

Company cars

Employees are taxed on a percentage of the vehicle's list price.

The percentage used is dependent upon the level of carbon dioxide emissions normally ranging from 11% to 35% moving up in increments of 1% for every 5 g/km in excess of the base figure of 95 g/km.

There is also a 3% supplement for diesel engines (although the maximum percentage is still 35%).

Do not forget the lower rates of 5% and 10% for cars with low emissions.

The fuel benefit uses the same percentage as calculated for the car, applied to a figure of £21,100.

Accommodation

Employees are taxed in 3 areas in relation to non-job related accommodation provided by the employer.

These are:

- Annual value: Always given in the exam

- Extra Benefit: For accommodation costing more than £75,000, an additional benefit of ((Cost – £75,000) × 4%) is also charged.

- Use of furniture: Furniture is treated in the same way as an employee using an employer's assets (i.e. MV when provided × 20%).

Beneficial loan

Employees are taxed on the interest they would normally pay on a loan, when provided by an employer at below normal rates of interest.

The calculation is: (Loan amount × 4%) – interest rate paid

Exempt benefits

These are always tested and detailed knowledge is required.

KAPLAN PUBLISHING

6 Test your knowledge

 Workbook Activity 8

Ethelred is the finance director of Buttercup Limited. The company provided him with benefits in the year ended 5 April 2014 as follows:

	£
Season ticket from home to office	292
Car owned by the company:	
Citroen CX 2000 (1985 cc)	
List price when new	13,800
First registered on 1 October 2010	
Emission rating: 157 g/km	
Private medical insurance	1,628

Ethelred advises you that during the year his car did 16,800 miles, of which 3,360 miles represented private use, and that the company paid £1,848 in respect of all of the petrol for the car.

Ethelred paid £800 towards the cost of purchasing the car.

He also paid £1,000 to Buttercup Ltd for his wife and family to be included on the private medical insurance.

Required:

1   What is the assessable benefit in respect of the season ticket?

2   What is the total assessable benefit in respect of the car?

3   What is the assessable benefit in respect of the private medical insurance?

✍ Workbook Activity 9

William Makepeace has the following employment income for 2013/14:

(a) Salary as an area manager.   £25,000

(b) As area manager, William has the use of a 1,600 cc company car throughout the year, all the costs being met by the employer.

The details for the year ended 5 April 2014 are:

	£
List price of car when new in 2011	8,000
Cost of car in 2011	7,800
Emission rating: 141 g/km	
Contribution made by William for:	
Private use of car	600
Private use petrol	480

The total mileage for the year was 20,000 miles of which 15,000 miles were for private motoring.

During the year, however, William had two accidents and the car was incapable of being used for 12 days in July 2013 and 40 days in November and December 2013, whilst repairs were being carried out.

No replacement car was provided during these periods.

(c) William had a loan of £50,000 from his employer throughout the year on which he paid interest of 1%. The loan had been used to purchase a yacht. The official rate of interest is 4% for the tax year 2013/14.

Required:

1   What is William's assessable car benefit for 2013/14?

2   What is William's fuel benefit for 2013/14?

3   What is William's loan benefit for 2013/14?

Workbook Activity 10

Gordon is the managing director of a large manufacturing company. He receives the following benefits in addition to his salary.

- School fees totalling £10,000 are paid direct to a school in respect of his two children.

- He is provided with a petrol engine car (2,200 cc, list price £25,000 when new in April 2009) with emission rating of 240 g/km.

- Gordon paid £1,300 towards the cost of purchasing the car. He also paid £150 per month towards the cost of his private use of the car.

- A car parking space is provided for him in a multi-storey car park near his office at a cost of £600 per annum. He is not provided with fuel for private use.

- He was provided with a laptop computer for personal use which cost £750 on 6 September 2013. Ownership of the laptop is retained by the company.

Required:

1   The school fees are not an assessable benefit. TRUE or FALSE?

2   What is Gordon's car benefit?

    A   £6,495

    B   £8,295

    C   £6,950

    D   £7,680

3   What is the benefit in respect of the car parking space?

    A   £600

    B   £Nil

4   What is the benefit in respect of the laptop computer?

    A   £150

    B   £87

    C   £75

    D   £62

Workbook Activity 11

Gina is the sales director of a large manufacturing company. She receives the following benefits in addition to her salary.

- The company supplied Gina with a mobile telephone which she used for making private and business calls. The phone cost £250.

- The company paid £1,420 in January 2014 as the annual premium for private medical insurance cover for Gina and her family. She contributed £750 to her employer to include her husband in the scheme.

- An interest free loan of £10,000 made on 1 May 2013 to enable Gina to purchase a boat. The official rate of interest for 2013/14 is 4%.

Required:

Show the total taxable benefit in respect of each of the above items for 2013/14.

 Workbook Activity 12

Marianne was employed by Logistics Ltd at an annual salary of £52,000.

Throughout the year she was provided with a rent-free furnished flat which had an annual value of £1,500. Logistics Ltd paid £150,000 for the flat in 2012. The official rate of interest for 2013/14 is 4%.

The furniture in the flat was paid for by Logistics Ltd in 2012 and had cost £20,000.

Logistics Ltd paid heating and lighting bills for the flat amounting to £3,000 during 2013/14.

Other benefits for 2013/14 amounted to £3,600.

Required:

Calculate the amount of employment income chargeable on Marianne for 2013/14 assuming:

(a) the occupation of the flat was job related.

(b) the occupation of the flat was not job related.

Workbook Activity 13

Merlin's annual salary from Shalot Limited is £50,000. He was relocated by Shalot Limited on 6 April 2013 and was reimbursed relevant relocation expenditure incurred of £10,000.

Shalot Limited provided Merlin with a loan of £30,000 on 6 April 2013 on which annual interest of 1.25% was payable. The official rate of interest is 4%.

Required:

What is the amount of employment income taxable on Merlin for 2013/14?

 Workbook Activity 14

Joseph, age 24 years, has been employed by Rock Radio in central London for several years as a producer.

On 1 January 2012 he was provided with a company flat which has an annual value of £5,000 and was let at an annual rent of £8,500 paid for by Rock Radio on a five year tenancy from the same date. The occupation of the flat was not 'job-related'.

The furniture in the flat had cost £40,000 when first provided by Rock Radio.

Rock Radio paid £7,000 for utility services, decorating and repairs for the flat.

Required:

What is the amount of Joseph's taxable accommodation benefit for 2013/14?

A £55,500

B £52,000

C £23,500

D £20,000

Workbook Activity 15

Worf Limited provided Marina with the following benefits.

A loan of £32,300 on 6 April 2013 on which annual interest of 1.5% was payable. The official rate of interest is 4%.

A bicycle costing £400 and cycle safety equipment costing £100 was provided for Marina on 6 April 2013 and was to be used mainly for travel to and from work. All employees are entitled to this benefit.

Worf Limited provided group membership of a nearby gymnasium. The cost of Marina's membership was £350 per annum although the normal annual membership fee was £750.

Required:

1   What is the amount of the loan benefit taxable on Marina for 2013/14?

2   What is the total of the assessable benefits for the bicycle and cycle safety equipment and the gym membership?

 Workbook Activity 16

Mr F Darcy is paid an annual salary of £36,000 and also bonuses based on his company's performance. The accounting year ends on 31 December each year and the bonuses are normally determined and paid on 31 May thereafter. In recent years bonuses have been:

Year to 31 December 2012   £8,000

Year to 31 December 2013   £4,000

Mr Darcy pays 7% of his basic salary to the company's registered occupational pension scheme.

Required:

Calculate Mr Darcy's employment income for 2013/14.

Workbook Activity 17

On 6 July 2013, Kate was provided with a company loan of £25,000 on which she pays interest of 1.4% per annum. The official rate of interest is 4%.

Required:

What is the assessable benefit for 2013/14?

A   £650

B   £1,000

C   £750

D   £487

 Workbook Activity 18

When accommodation is purchased by an employer, what is the cost of the property above which an additional benefit is applied?

A   £50,000

B   £70,000

C   £75,000

D   £100,000

 Workbook Activity 19

Would the following situations be treated as being job related, such that no accommodation benefit arises?

1   Accommodation provided for a caretaker of a school   YES/NO

2   Accommodation provided for a hotel worker   YES/NO

3   Accommodation provided for security reasons   YES/NO

Workbook Activity 20

Complete the following sentences so that the benefit is exempt from tax.

1   Childcare paid for by an employer on behalf of a basic rate taxpayer is exempt up to the first……per week

    A   £25

    B   £28

    C   £55

    D   £60

2   Provision of mobile telephones is limited to…… per employee

    A   1

    B   2

    C   3

3   Long service awards are restricted to…….per year of service

    A   £25

    B   £50

    C   £75

    D   £100

4   Relocation expenses up to……are not taxable

    A   £6,000

    B   £7,000

    C   £8,000

    D   £9,000

5   Staff parties are tax free provided the total cost of all parties does not exceed……per tax year

    A   £125

    B   £150

    C   £175

    D   £200

Workbook Activity 21

Budget Ltd is an estate agency and provided the following benefits to a number of its employees during 2013/14.

Required:

Which of the following is NOT assessable employment income for 2013/14?

A   Medical insurance provided to a key member of staff

B   Free membership of the gym situated next door to the company headquarters

C   A second mobile phone provided to the chief executive of the company

D   Child care vouchers of £25 per week to the sales director, a higher rate taxpayer, who chose to redeem them with an approved child carer, rather than taking advantage of the on-site facilities

 Workbook Activity 22

Jacob earns a salary of £40,000 per annum and was provided with a computer for private use on 1 October 2013. The market value of the computer when first provided was £4,300 and at 5 April 2014 the market value was £3,000.

Required:

What is the value of the benefit in respect of this computer for 2013/14?

A   £600

B   £860

C   £430

D   £300

Workbook Activity 23

Leo was provided with a house to live in by his employer. The employer rented the house from a local resident and paid rent of £32,000 per year. Leo paid rent of £12,000 per year to his employer. The property has an annual value of £9,750 p.a.

What is the assessable value of this benefit, assuming the accommodation is not job related?

A   £9,750

B   £32,000

C   £20,000

D   Nil

Employment income – supplementary pages

Introduction

In the exam you will be asked to complete part of a tax return.

The tax return includes a number of supplementary pages.

The employment pages are considered in this chapter.

SKILLS
Make computations and submissions in accordance with current tax law (5.1 S)

CONTENTS
1   Employment supplementary pages

1 Employment supplementary pages

1.1 The individual tax return

The individual tax return comprises:

- the main return (form SA100); and

- a series of supplementary pages.

HM Revenue and Customs will usually send a taxpayer the supplementary pages that they expect them to need.

Form SA102 is the employment supplementary page, and can be found on HM Revenue and Customs website (www.hmrc.gov.uk).

1.2 Completing the employment supplementary page

This is one of the three supplementary pages that are examinable in this paper. The others are the property income pages (SA105) and capital gains pages (SA108). They are dealt with in Chapters 7 and 15 respectively.

The assessment will require one of these forms to be completed. Hence the accurate completion of tax return forms is an important aspect of the assessment.

In the assessment you will be given most of the information to enter into the tax return but may have to calculate some items for inclusion. In real life the information is taken from an employer's PAYE forms. Salary, bonus and tax paid details are taken from forms P45 or P60. Details of benefits and expenses are included on form P11D.

There are two pages to the form which allow an employee to fill in details of two separate employments. In the assessment you will only be asked to complete one page.

The following is important in connection with the completion of forms in the exam.

- When completing the form in the exam, figures must be entered in the correct boxes.

- You will normally be asked to complete just one page of any form.

- Commas need not be entered for numbers of four digits or more.

- You do not need to fill in every box, only relevant ones.

Working through the form, the main boxes to be used are:

Name and taxpayer reference		– This relates to the employee's details
1	Pay from employment	– Total salary/wages and bonus from P45/P60.
2	Tax taken off 1	– From P45/P60.
3	Tips and other payments	– These are possible but unlikely.
4, 5	Details of employer	– If these details are provided in the assessment you must include them on the form.

Benefits

You may need to complete any of the following boxes:

9	Cars and vans	– Chapter 4, 4.3 and 4.5
10	Fuel	– Chapter 4, 4.4
11	Medical and dental insurance	– Chapter 4, 4.8
12	Vouchers, credit cards, mileage	– Includes private expenditure on company credit cards and travel season tickets
13	Assets provided by employer	– Includes assets transferred or on loan – Chapter 4, 4.7.
14	Accommodation	– Chapter 4, 3.2
15	Other benefits	– Includes money on loan, subscriptions, professional fees and payment of bills in respect of accommodation
16	Expenses received from employer	– Including travelling, subsistence and entertainment – Chapter 3, section 3.

Employment expenses

17	Travel and subsistence	– Tax allowable expenses incurred by employee – Chapter 3, section 3.
19	Professional fees and subscriptions	– Tax allowable payments made.
20	Other expenses	– Includes tax allowable entertaining expenditure.

HM Revenue & Customs

Employment
Tax year 6 April 2013 to 5 April 2014

Your name

Your Unique Taxpayer Reference (UTR)

Complete an *Employment* page for each employment or directorship

1. Pay from this employment – the total from your P45 or P60 - *before tax was taken off*

   £ . 0 0

2. UK tax taken off pay in box 1

   £ . 0 0

3. Tips and other payments not on your P60 - *read the Employment notes*

   £ . 0 0

4. PAYE tax reference of your employer (on your P45/P60)

   /

5. Your employer's name

6. If you were a company director, put 'X' in the box

7. And, if the company was a close company, put 'X' in the box

8. If you are a part-time teacher in England or Wales and are on the Repayment of Teachers' Loans Scheme for this employment, put 'X' in the box

Benefits from your employment - use your form P11D (or equivalent information)

9. Company cars and vans - *the total 'cash equivalent' amount*

   £ . 0 0

10. Fuel for company cars and vans - *the total 'cash equivalent' amount*

    £ . 0 0

11. Private medical and dental insurance - *the total 'cash equivalent' amount*

    £ . 0 0

12. Vouchers, credit cards and excess mileage allowance

    £ . 0 0

13. Goods and other assets provided by your employer - *the total value or amount*

    £ . 0 0

14. Accommodation provided by your employer - *the total value or amount*

    £ . 0 0

15. Other benefits (including interest-free and low interest loans) - *the total 'cash equivalent' amount*

    £ . 0 0

16. Expenses payments received and balancing charges

    £ . 0 0

Employment expenses

17. Business travel and subsistence expenses

    £ . 0 0

18. Fixed deductions for expenses

    £ . 0 0

19. Professional fees and subscriptions

    £ . 0 0

20. Other expenses and capital allowances

    £ . 0 0

Shares schemes, employment lump sums, compensation, deductions and Seafarers' Earnings Deduction are on the *Additional information* pages enclosed in the tax return pack.

SA102 2013 Page E 1 HMRC 12/12

John Stentz who works for COGM plc as an accountant has the following income assessable in 2013/14.

	Box	£	Tax £
Salary	1/2	25,000	5,514
Bonus	1/2	10,000	3,700
Car benefit	9	3,640	–
Private health insurance	11	500	–
Low interest loan	15	1,020	–
Employer pension contribution (exempt benefit)	–	2,000	

He has also made the following payments in the year:

	Box	£
Own contributions into occupational pension scheme	1 (deduction)	1,500
AAT membership fees	19	100
Health club membership fees (not allowable)	–	200

Complete John's employment supplementary pages.

Note that there are two possible treatments of the employee pension scheme contributions.

If the contributions are made under the 'net pay' scheme, then the employee contributions reduce the salary figure shown in Box 1.

This is the approach used in the examples in this text. This also means that the total of gross pay shown on an employee's form P60 will be after the deduction of the employee's contributions. Hence it is important to read the question to see whether the salary is given before or after deduction of pension scheme contributions. Normally it is given gross before deductions.

If the net pay scheme does not apply, then the salary is entered gross in Box 1 and the pension contributions are included elsewhere in the tax return and not on the employment supplementary pages.

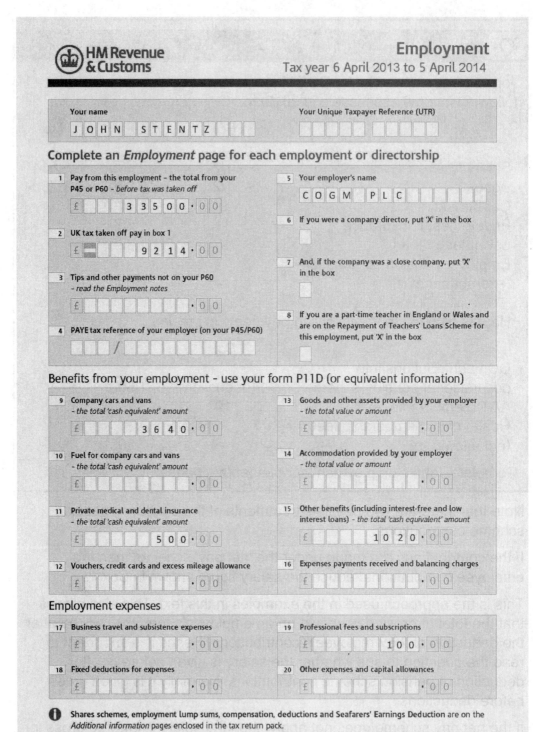

Activity 1

Complete the employment supplementary page for LA Raider with the information which follows the form.

HM Revenue & Customs

Employment
Tax year 6 April 2013 to 5 April 2014

Your name

Your Unique Taxpayer Reference (UTR)

Complete an *Employment* page for each employment or directorship

1 Pay from this employment – the total from your P45 or P60 - *before tax was taken off*

£ ⬚ · 0 0

2 UK tax taken off pay in box 1

£ ⬚ · 0 0

3 Tips and other payments not on your P60 - *read the Employment notes*

£ ⬚ · 0 0

4 PAYE tax reference of your employer (on your P45/P60)

⬚ / ⬚

5 Your employer's name

6 If you were a company director, put 'X' in the box

7 And, if the company was a close company, put 'X' in the box

8 If you are a part-time teacher in England or Wales and are on the Repayment of Teachers' Loans Scheme for this employment, put 'X' in the box

Benefits from your employment – use your form P11D (or equivalent information)

9 Company cars and vans
- *the total 'cash equivalent' amount*

£ ⬚ · 0 0

10 Fuel for company cars and vans
- *the total 'cash equivalent' amount*

£ ⬚ · 0 0

11 Private medical and dental insurance
- *the total 'cash equivalent' amount*

£ ⬚ · 0 0

12 Vouchers, credit cards and excess mileage allowance

£ ⬚ · 0 0

13 Goods and other assets provided by your employer
- *the total value or amount*

£ ⬚ · 0 0

14 Accommodation provided by your employer
- *the total value or amount*

£ ⬚ · 0 0

15 Other benefits (including interest-free and low interest loans) - *the total 'cash equivalent' amount*

£ ⬚ · 0 0

16 Expenses payments received and balancing charges

£ ⬚ · 0 0

Employment expenses

17 Business travel and subsistence expenses

£ ⬚ · 0 0

18 Fixed deductions for expenses

£ ⬚ · 0 0

19 Professional fees and subscriptions

£ ⬚ · 0 0

20 Other expenses and capital allowances

£ ⬚ · 0 0

ℹ **Shares schemes, employment lump sums, compensation, deductions and Seafarers' Earnings Deduction** are on the *Additional information* pages enclosed in the tax return pack.

SA102 2013   Page E 1   HMRC 12/12

L.A Raider is employed by Coliseum Ltd.

He receives a salary of £50,000 plus a bonus of £14,200. He pays a pension contribution of £1,500 under the net pay scheme.

He is provided with a company car for which the car benefit is £5,950 and the fuel benefit £5,915

Raider is provided with the use of a company video camera for which the benefit is £600.

His employer pays private medical insurance of £1,270.

Raider receives a round sum allowance of £1,850 of which he spends £550 on business travel.

Raider also uses his own car for business for which he can make a mileage claim of £4,500 as he receives no reimbursement from his employer.

2   Summary

The employment supplementary page summarises the taxable employment income.

In Chapter 9 it can be used to help calculate the income tax liability.

3 Test your knowledge

 Workbook Activity 2

Maurice Knight

Maurice has provided the following details of his employment income for the year to 5 April 2014.

	£
Salary including bonus (tax deducted £4,301)	18,100
Car benefit	3,200
Car fuel benefit	3,600
Interest free loan	450
Medical insurance	840
Expenses payments	5,210

You establish that the expenses reimbursed comprised:	£
Business travel	3,750
Subscription to professional body	510
Entertaining customers	950

Required:

Complete the employment supplementary page for Maurice's tax return for 2013/14.

HM Revenue & Customs

Employment
Tax year 6 April 2013 to 5 April 2014

Your name

Your Unique Taxpayer Reference (UTR)

Complete an *Employment* page for each employment or directorship

1 Pay from this employment – the total from your P45 or P60 - *before tax was taken off*

£ . 0 0

2 UK tax taken off pay in box 1

£ . 0 0

3 Tips and other payments not on your P60 - *read the Employment notes*

£ . 0 0

4 PAYE tax reference of your employer (on your P45/P60)

/

5 Your employer's name

6 If you were a company director, put 'X' in the box

7 And, if the company was a close company, put 'X' in the box

8 If you are a part-time teacher in England or Wales and are on the Repayment of Teachers' Loans Scheme for this employment, put 'X' in the box

Benefits from your employment - use your form P11D (or equivalent information)

9 Company cars and vans - *the total 'cash equivalent' amount*

£ . 0 0

10 Fuel for company cars and vans - *the total 'cash equivalent' amount*

£ . 0 0

11 Private medical and dental insurance - *the total 'cash equivalent' amount*

£ . 0 0

12 Vouchers, credit cards and excess mileage allowance

£ . 0 0

13 Goods and other assets provided by your employer - *the total value or amount*

£ . 0 0

14 Accommodation provided by your employer - *the total value or amount*

£ . 0 0

15 Other benefits (including interest-free and low interest loans) - *the total 'cash equivalent' amount*

£ . 0 0

16 Expenses payments received and balancing charges

£ . 0 0

Employment expenses

17 Business travel and subsistence expenses

£ . 0 0

18 Fixed deductions for expenses

£ . 0 0

19 Professional fees and subscriptions

£ . 0 0

20 Other expenses and capital allowances

£ . 0 0

ℹ **Shares schemes, employment lump sums, compensation, deductions and Seafarers' Earnings Deduction** are on the *Additional information* pages enclosed in the tax return pack.

SA102 2013   Page E 1   HMRC 12/12

Property income

Introduction

In recent years many more people have been buying properties to let out.

This is reflected in the importance that the computation of property income has in the syllabus.

This chapter explains how taxable property income is calculated and how losses can be relieved.

KNOWLEDGE

Explain the main current legislation relating to personal taxation (1.1 K)

Identify the main legislative features relating to property income from furnished and unfurnished rented property, rent a room scheme, holiday lets and buy to let investments (1.9 K)

SKILLS

Prepare schedules of income from land and property determining profits and losses (2.3 S)

Describe types of relief which are available on property income including allowable expenses, wear and tear allowance, loss relief – and the circumstances in which each apply (3.6 S)

Make computations and submissions in accordance with current tax law (5.1 S)

CONTENTS

1   Property income
2   Allowable expenditure
3   Losses
4   Furnished holiday lettings
5   Rent a room relief

1 Property income

1.1 Property letting

All income from letting property in the UK is added together.

It includes:

- rental income from land.
- rental income from commercial property.
- rental income from residential property.

1.2 Basis of assessment

It is critical to ensure that the correct amount of property income is taxed in a tax year. There are two main issues to deal with.

(i) The taxable amount is the **profit** from all land and buildings being let out.

	£
Rental income receivable (less any non-recoverable amounts)	X
Less: Allowable expenses (Section 2)	(X)
Taxable property income	X

In the assessment, where there is more than one property being let out, you may be asked to calculate the profit on each property separately, or the total from all properties together.

(ii) Property income and expenses are dealt with on an **accruals** basis for the tax year.

Note this is different to employment income which you will recall is assessed on a **receipts** basis.

1.3 Accruals basis

The accruals basis means that we deal with income and expenses that **relate to the tax year**, not necessarily those paid and received in the year.

Any apportionment of income and expenses should be carried out to the nearest month.

Example

In the tax year 2013/14, Mr Jenkins let out a property, beginning on 6 October 2013, at £2,000 per month.

Rent for the first 5 months was received on time. However, rent for the last month was not received until 20 April 2014.

What is the rental income assessable in 2013/14?

Solution

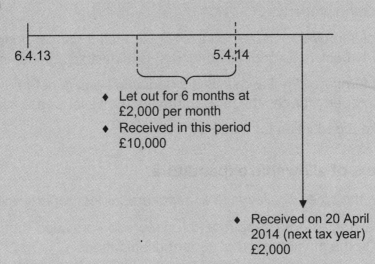

- Let out for 6 months at £2,000 per month
- Received in this period £10,000

- Received on 20 April 2014 (next tax year) £2,000

On the accruals basis, ignore amounts actually received and instead tax what is due.

The amounts relating to 2013/14 and therefore taxable are £12,000 (6 × £2,000).

2 Allowable expenditure

2.1 'Wholly and exclusively'

Expenditure which may be deducted in computing the profit from property income is that which is incurred 'wholly and exclusively' for the purposes of letting.

Note: This rule is similar to that for allowable expenditure for employment income, but omits the 'necessarily' condition.

2.2 Capital expenditure

Capital expenditure is not an allowable deduction in calculating property income.

It will normally be dealt with as part of the cost of the property and will be an allowable deduction when the property is sold.

This will be dealt with in later chapters under chargeable gains.

Capital expenditure will include the following:

- Cost of the property.

- Cost of improvements, although ongoing maintenance (bringing the property back to its original condition) is allowable against income.

The cost of furniture is not an allowable deduction and is not part of the cost of the property for capital gains purposes (however see 2.4 below).

Do not make a deduction for these items.

2.3 Items of allowable expenditure

Specifically, the types of allowable expenditure for let property will include:

(a) internal and external repairs and redecoration provided that they relate to the making good of current dilapidations.

   Note that the cost of initial repairs necessary in order to make a property usable is not deductible (e.g. repairs to a roof which had been damaged prior to the purchase of the property).

(b) gardening;

(c) cleaning;

(d) agent's commission;

(e) costs of collecting rents (legal costs), including unpaid rents;

(f) advertising for new tenants;

(g) insurance premiums against damage to the structure of the property;

(h) legal and accountancy costs for preparing claims, accounts and tax computations in respect of the property;

(i) maintenance of common parts of blocks, offices and flats;

(j) interest on loans taken out to buy or improve the property;

(k) council tax and water rates;

(l) irrecoverable rents;

(m) an allowance for the wear and tear (depreciation) of furniture (see 2.4 below) if the property is let furnished.

Example

Strudwick has four properties in Gasholder Street, London SE11 (numbers 63, 65, 67 and 69) which he lets on a commercial basis.

Each property is let for a rental of £1,500 per quarter paid in advance at the end of each quarter.

During 2013/14 Strudwick has the following expenses and allowances:

Mortgage interest	£5,000
Agent's commission	£750
Repairs to premises	£480

Calculate Strudwick's taxable property income for 2013/14.

Solution

	£
Rentals (4 × 4 × £1,500)	24,000
Expenses: Mortgage interest	(5,000)
Agent's commission	(750)
Repair to premises	(480)
	_____
Taxable property income	17,770
	_____

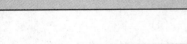 Activity 1

Jane lets out two properties at an annual rental of £5,000 each. She incurs agent's fees of £1,200 on property 1 and £700 on property 2. She also incurs expenses of £6,000 repairing and redecorating property 2 during the year.

Required:

What is her taxable property income?

2.4　Wear and tear allowance

Where a landlord provides furniture:

- he cannot deduct the cost of the furniture from the letting profits as it is capital (Section 2.2 above), but

- he would like to make a deduction against letting income for the 'wearing out' of the furniture. This would then allow for replacements in the future.

The deduction that can be made each year calculated as:

> **10% × (rental income –**
> **[council tax and water rates if paid by the landlord])**

The amounts deducted from the rental income are payments that would normally be the tenant's responsibility; council tax and water rates are the two most important examples.

💡 Example

During 2013/14 Mr Lord let out a furnished property at a rent of £10,000 per annum. The expenses incurred for the year are as follows:

	£
Repairs (on maintenance) (no capital items)	2,000
Council tax and water rates	500
Gardening and cleaning	250
Buildings insurance	300
New chairs for kitchen	200

What is Mr Lord's taxable property income for 2013/14?

Solution

	£	£
Rental income		10,000
Less: Allowable expenditure		
Repairs and maintenance	2,000	
Council tax and water rates	500	
Gardening and cleaning	250	
Buildings insurance	300	
Chairs for kitchen (capital)	–	
Wear and tear allowance (W)	950	
		(4,000)
Taxable property income		6,000

(W)　Wear and tear allowance = 10% × (£10,000 – £500) = £950

It is easy to miss the wear and tear allowance in the assessment. Look out for the word 'furnished'.

If the landlord has not paid any council tax or water rates, the wear and tear allowance is simply (10% × rental income).

If the landlord has had to write off some rents as irrecoverable, these should be deducted from the rental income before calculating the allowance.

3 Losses

3.1 Treatment of a loss

A loss arises if allowable expenses are more than the rental income. For example in 2013/14:

	£
Rental income	10,000
Less: Allowable expenses	(10,500)
Loss	(500)

If this happens:

(i)   the tax computation will show property income = NIL.

Never show a negative figure in the tax computation; and

(ii)   the loss is carried forward and set off against the next available profit from property letting in future years (i.e. the £500 above is carried forward to the 2014/15 computation).

 Activity 2

Are the following statements true or false?

1   Income from property is taxed on a receipts basis.

2   Wear and tear allowance is calculated on net rents after deducting irrecoverable rents, and after deducting council tax and water rates paid by the landlord.

3   Where the allowable expenses exceed the rental income, the loss arising can be deducted from the individual's other taxable income.

Activity 3

Bernard Marks

Bernard Marks has presented you with a statement of income and expenditure on the three furnished properties that he lets out.

Property number	1	2	3
	£	£	£
Rental income	3,000	3,500	2,500
Less: Expenses			
Agent's commission	(300)	(350)	(250)
Buildings insurance	(120)	(120)	(120)
Repairs and maintenance (Note 1)	(560)	(660)	(3,560)
Council tax	(400)	(450)	(380)
Accountancy fees	(50)	(50)	(50)
Mortgage interest	(100)	(130)	(90)
Net income for year = £1,260	1,470	1,740	(1,950)

Note 1

Repairs and maintenance is as follows:

	£	£	£
Gardening	260	260	260
General repairs (allowable)	300	400	800
New kitchen			2,500
	560	660	3,560

Required:

Calculate Bernard's taxable property income for 2013/14.

4 Furnished holiday lettings

4.1 Introduction

Profits arising from the commercial letting of 'furnished holiday accommodation' are assessable as property business income. However, special rules and reliefs apply to such properties (section 4.3).

As a result, separate records regarding these properties have to be kept.

4.2 Qualifying conditions

The letting will only be treated as 'furnished holiday accommodation' if it meets the following conditions:

- The property is situated in the UK or in a country within the EEA (the European Economic Area).

- It is let furnished.

- The letting is let on a commercial basis with a view to the realisation of profits.

- It is available for commercial letting, to the public generally, as holiday accommodation for not less than 210 days a year.

- The accommodation is actually let for at least 105 days a year (excluding periods of 'long-term occupation' – see below).

- Where a taxpayer owns more than one property, the 105 days test is satisfied if the average number of days for which the properties are let in the year is at least 105.

- The property must not be let for periods of 'long-term occupation' in excess of 155 days in a year.

Long-term occupation is defined as a period of more than 31 consecutive days when the property is let to the same person.

It is possible for the property to be let to the same person for more than 31 days, however, when aggregating all such periods of longer term occupation (which could be a few periods of letting to different persons); the total must not exceed 155 days.

4.3 Tax treatment of furnished holiday accommodation

Any profits from commercially let 'furnished holiday accommodation' remain assessable as property income.

However, the profits are treated as arising from a separate trade carried on by the landlord, and are not pooled with other rental property.

The following advantages and reliefs thereby become available:

- The profits are treated as relevant earnings for the purposes of relief for personal pension scheme contributions (see Chapter 10).

- Capital gains tax rollover relief and Entrepreneurs' relief are available. These reliefs are not examined in this unit; they are covered in Business tax.

- Normal capital allowances will be available in respect of plant and machinery. Capital allowances are dealt with in the Business tax unit.

Any losses from commercially let 'furnished holiday accommodation' are carried forward and deducted from future profits of the furnished holiday accommodation business.

 Activity 4

The following statements are all on the topic of furnished holiday lettings rules. Mark each statement as true or false.

		True	False
1	The property must be located in a recognised holiday location.		
2	Furnished property which is available for letting from 1 April to 31 October each year may qualify as furnished holiday letting provided other conditions are met.		
3	If the taxpayer owns more than one furnished property then each one must be let for at least 105 days per year.		
4	If a furnished property is let to the same person for two months at a time, then it cannot qualify as furnished holiday accommodation.		

5 Rent a room relief

5.1 Introduction

If an individual lets furnished accommodation in his or her main residence (i.e. has a lodger renting a room in his house), and the income is liable to tax as property income or trading income, a special scheme applies.

Note that the scheme can still apply where:

- the taxpayer does not own his or her main residence but rents it, and

- the lodger occupies more than one room in the property.

5.2 Gross annual rental receipts do not exceed £4,250

- If the gross annual rental receipts do not exceed £4,250 they will automatically be exempt from tax.

- The individual's limit of £4,250 is reduced by half to £2,125 if, during a particular tax year, any other person also received income from letting accommodation in the property while the property was the first person's main residence.

- This rule allows a married couple taking in lodgers to either have all the rent paid to one spouse (who will then have the full limit of £4,250), or to have the rent divided between the spouses (and each spouse will then have a limit of £2,125).

- An individual may elect to ignore the exemption for a particular year, for example, if a loss is incurred when taking account of expenses.

- An election to ignore rent a room relief for 2013/14 must be made by 31 January 2016.

5.3 Gross annual rental receipts exceed £4,250

- If the gross annual rental receipts exceed £4,250, an individual may choose between:
  - paying tax on the excess of his gross rent over £4,250. This must be claimed by 31 January 2016 for 2013/14.
  - being taxed in the normal way on the profit from letting (rent less expenses and wear and tear allowance).

Summary: Assess lower of:

Method 1 – Normal assessment		Method 2 – Rent a room relief	
	£		£
Rental income	X	Rental income	X
Less Expenses	(X)	Less Rent a room relief	(4,250)
Less Wear and tear allowance	(X)		
	───		───
Profit	X	Profit	X
	───		───

Activity 5

Rio lets out a room in his own house to a lodger throughout 2013/14.

The lodger pays rent of £90 per week. Rio incurs expenses of £2,100 in respect of the room.

What is Rio's taxable property income for 2013/14 assuming he elects for the most tax efficient treatment?

 6 **Summary**

Property income is an important aspect of preparing an income tax computation. The main issues to beware of are:

- Capital items   – disallow.
- Furnished property   – wear and tear allowances.
- Losses   – carry forward to the next year.
- Furnished holiday accommodation   – definition.
- Rent a room relief   – rents above or below the limit.

7 Test your knowledge

Workbook Activity 6

Mrs Shah bought a house in January 2013 as an investment.

She rented it out furnished to students from 1 June 2013. She charged rent of £500 per month payable in advance. In August 2013, she paid £700 for the windows in the house to be repainted.

What is her taxable property income for 2013/14?

Workbook Activity 7

Alan owns a house which is let furnished throughout the year to 5 April 2014 at a rent of £650 per month, payable in advance.

Alan incurred the following expenditure during the year: water rates £300, council tax £850, property insurance £500, purchase of new cooker £400. He also incurred loan interest of £2,500 on a loan taken out to purchase the property. Alan claims wear and tear allowance for the property.

What is Alan's taxable property income for 2013/14?

Workbook Activity 8

Rachman

On 1 December 2012, Rachman purchased a freehold block of flats for £200,000. All the flats were let unfurnished on monthly tenancies.

In the year to 5 April 2014, his receipts and payments were as follows:

	Year ended 5 April 2014 £
Receipts	
Rents collected (see (a))	26,280
	———
Payments	
Repairs and maintenance (see (b))	2,380
Caretaker's wages	5,800
Insurance and incidentals (all allowable)	269
Mortgage interest (see (c))	15,400
	———
	23,849
	———

(a) Rents

	£
Rents owing at beginning of period	240
Rents due	26,850
	———
	27,090
Less: Rent owing at end of period	(810)
	———
Cash received for rents	26,280
	———

(b) Repairs and maintenance

	£
Garden maintenance	500
Lift maintenance	180
Normal decorations and incidental repairs	800
Asphalting drive (in April 2013)	
(the drive was in a dangerous state at the time of purchase)	900
	———
	2,380
	———

(c) The mortgage interest was paid on a loan of £145,000 taken out to purchase the flats.

Required:

Compute the amount of the taxable property income for 2013/14.

 Workbook Activity 9

James

During 2012, James purchased a freehold flat for £150,000. The flat was let furnished for a monthly rent of £700 until 31 July 2013. Unfortunately the tenant disappeared still owing the July rent.

The property was re-let from 1 October 2013 for a monthly rent of £750. Outgoings for the year to 5 April 2014 were:

	£
Agent's commission	1,163
Redecoration between tenants	1,745
Installation of central heating	1,980
Insurance and incidentals (all allowable)	547
Professional charges (see (a))	880
Mortgage interest (see (b))	3,400
	———
	10,135
	———

(a) Professional charges

Legal charges for new lease	150
Accountancy	420
Valuation for insurance purposes	310
	880

(b) The mortgage interest was paid on a loan of £75,000 taken out to purchase and furnish the flat.

Required:

Compute the amount of the property income profit or loss for 2013/14.

📝 Workbook Activity 10

The amount of rent that can be received tax free under the rent a room scheme is ....?

A £4,000

B £4,250

C £4,750

D £5,000

Workbook Activity 11

Mark the following statements as true or false.

		True	False
1	You cannot use the rent a room scheme if you yourself live in rented accommodation.		
2	If a lodger occupies an entire floor, the rent a room scheme can still apply.		
3	The scheme applies to both furnished and unfurnished accommodation.		
4	Charges for additional services, such as laundry, do not count in the annual exempt income limit for rent a room.		
5	When working out the profit made from renting out a room, capital costs such as furniture cannot be taken into account.		

 Workbook Activity 12

Arthur

Arthur has two shops which he lets.

Shop 1.

The annual rent was £3,000 on a lease which expired on 30 June 2013. Arthur took advantage of the shop being empty to carry out repairs and decorating. The shop was let to another tenant on a five-year lease at £4,000 per annum from 1 October 2013.

Shop 2.

The shop was purchased on 10 April 2013 and required treatment for dry-rot. Arthur also undertook some normal re-decorating work before the shop was let on 1 October 2013 on a seven-year lease at an annual rental of £6,000.

The rent for both shops was due in advance on the first day of each month.

The following expenditure was incurred in 2013/14:

	Shop 1		Shop 2	
	£		£	
Insurance	190		300	
Ground rent	10		40	
Repairs and decorating	3,900	(Note 1)	5,000	(Note 2)
Accountancy	50		50	
Advertising for tenant	100		100	

Notes:

(1)   Includes £2,500 for re-roofing the shop following gale damage in February 2013. Because the roof had been badly maintained the insurance company refused to pay for the repair work.

(2)   Includes £3,000 for dry rot remedial treatment. The dry rot was present when the shop was bought in April 2013.

Required:

Using the following pro forma calculate the property income or loss made on each property for 2013/14

	Shop 1	Shop 2
	£	£
Income		
Expenses		
	_____	_____
Net profit/loss		
	_____	_____

Property income – supplementary pages

7

Introduction

In Chapter 5 we looked at the employment income supplementary pages.

In the assessment it is possible that you may instead be required to complete a property page.

SKILLS
Make computations and submissions in accordance with current tax law (5.1 S)

CONTENTS
1   Land and property supplementary pages

1 Land and property supplementary pages

1.1 Contents of the form

Form SA105 contains the land and property supplementary pages. It can be found on the website www.hmrc.gov.uk.

In the assessment you will only be required to complete page 2 of the form.

1.2 Completion of the form

This is one of the three supplementary pages that are examinable in this paper. The others are the employment income pages (SA102) and capital gains pages (SA108). They are dealt with in Chapters 5 and 15 respectively.

The assessment will require one of these forms to be completed. Hence the accurate completion of tax return forms is an important aspect of the assessment.

In the assessment you will be given most of the information to enter into the tax return but you may have to calculate some of the figures e.g. wear and tear allowance.

The following is important in connection with the completion of forms in the exam.

- When completing the form in the exam, figures must be entered in the correct boxes.

- You will normally be asked to complete just one page of any form.

- Commas need not be entered for numbers of four digits or more.

- You do not need to fill in every box, only relevant ones.

Working through the form, the main boxes to complete on page UKP 2 are:

Property income

20   is the only box that you will use in the income section.

          It is the total of all relevant properties including furnished holiday letting profit calculated on page 1. Deduct any irrecoverable rent from this figure.

Boxes 21, 22 and 23 will not be used.

Property expenses

24 – 29   will show the total of all allowable expenses (except wear and tear – see below) categorised as appropriate.

Calculating your taxable profit or loss

30 – 35   will not be used.

36   is the remaining allowable expense of 'wear and tear allowance'.

37   is for the Rent a room exempt amount.

38   is for total property income less expenses and 10% wear and tear allowance.

39   if the task mentions a loss brought forward it goes here.

41   Recall that if there is an overall loss, the taxable property income is nil (box 38 will show 0) and the loss is carried forward.

The only other boxes to complete are the sub-totals and totals in boxes 40 and, in a net loss position, 43.

Property income

Do not include furnished holiday lettings, Real Estate Investment Trust or Property Authorised Investment Funds dividends/distributions here.

20 Total rents and other income from property

£ · 0 0

21 Tax taken off any income in box 20

£ · 0 0

22 Premiums for the grant of a lease – from box E on the Working Sheet - *read the notes*

£ · 0 0

23 Reverse premiums and inducements

£ · 0 0

Property expenses

24 Rent, rates, insurance, ground rents etc.

£ · 0 0

25 Property repairs, maintenance and renewals

£ · 0 0

26 Loan interest and other financial costs

£ · 0 0

27 Legal, management and other professional fees

£ · 0 0

28 Costs of services provided, including wages

£ · 0 0

29 Other allowable property expenses

£ · 0 0

Calculating your taxable profit or loss

30 Private use adjustment – *read the notes*

£ · 0 0

31 Balancing charges – *read the notes*

£ · 0 0

32 Annual Investment Allowance

£ · 0 0

33 Business Premises Renovation Allowance (Assisted Areas only) – *read the notes*

£ · 0 0

34 All other capital allowances

£ · 0 0

35 Landlord's Energy Saving Allowance

£ · 0 0

36 10% wear and tear allowance – *for furnished residential accommodation only*

£ · 0 0

37 Rent a Room exempt amount

£ · 0 0

38 Adjusted profit for the year – from box O on the Working Sheet - *read the notes*

£ · 0 0

39 Loss brought forward used against this year's profits

£ · 0 0

40 Taxable profit for the year (box 38 minus box 39)

£ · 0 0

41 Adjusted loss for the year – from box O on the Working Sheet - *read the notes*

£ · 0 0

42 Loss set off against 2013–14 total income – *this will be unusual – read the notes*

£ · 0 0

43 Loss to carry forward to following year, including unused losses brought forward

£ · 0 0

SA105 2013   Page UKP 2

Example

Complete the land and property supplementary page in respect of the following income and expenditure for Mr Lord. The property is let furnished.

Taxable property income – 2013/14

	£	£	Box
Rental income		10,000	20
Less: Allowable expenditure			
Repairs and maintenance	2,000		25
Council tax and water rates	500		24
Gardening and cleaning	250		28
Buildings insurance	300		24
		(3,050)	
Property income		6,950	

In the assessment you will probably have to calculate the wear and tear allowance from the information given.

In this example the wear and tear allowance is £950.

(10% (£10,000 – £500))

Property income

Do not include furnished holiday lettings, Real Estate Investment Trust or Property Authorised Investment Funds dividends/ distributions here.

20 Total rents and other income from property

£ 1 0 0 0 0 · 0 0

21 Tax taken off any income in box 20

£ · 0 0

22 Premiums for the grant of a lease - from box E on the Working Sheet - *read the notes*

£ · 0 0

23 Reverse premiums and inducements

£ · 0 0

Property expenses

24 Rent, rates, insurance, ground rents etc.

£ 8 0 0 · 0 0

25 Property repairs, maintenance and renewals

£ 2 0 0 0 · 0 0

26 Loan interest and other financial costs

£ · 0 0

27 Legal, management and other professional fees

£ · 0 0

28 Costs of services provided, including wages

£ 2 5 0 · 0 0

29 Other allowable property expenses

£ · 0 0

Calculating your taxable profit or loss

30 Private use adjustment - *read the notes*

£ · 0 0

31 Balancing charges - *read the notes*

£ · 0 0

32 Annual Investment Allowance

£ · 0 0

33 Business Premises Renovation Allowance (Assisted Areas only) - *read the notes*

£ · 0 0

34 All other capital allowances

£ · 0 0

35 Landlord's Energy Saving Allowance

£ · 0 0

36 10% wear and tear allowance - *for furnished residential accommodation only*

£ 9 5 0 · 0 0

37 Rent a Room exempt amount

£ · 0 0

38 Adjusted profit for the year – from box O on the Working Sheet - *read the notes*

£ 6 0 0 0 · 0 0

39 Loss brought forward used against this year's profits

£ · 0 0

40 Taxable profit for the year (box 38 minus box 39)

£ 6 0 0 0 · 0 0

41 Adjusted loss for the year - from box O on the Working Sheet - *read the notes*

£ · 0 0

42 Loss set off against 2013–14 total income – *this will be unusual - read the notes*

£ · 0 0

43 Loss to carry forward to following year, including unused losses brought forward

£ · 0 0

SA105 2013　　　　　Page UKP 2

Activity 1

Complete the land and property supplementary page for Bernard Marks in Activity 3 of Chapter 6.

Property income

Do not include furnished holiday lettings, Real Estate Investment Trust or Property Authorised Investment Funds dividends/distributions here.

20 Total rents and other income from property

£ _____ . 0 0

21 Tax taken off any income in box 20

£ _____ . 0 0

22 Premiums for the grant of a lease – from box E on the Working Sheet – *read the notes*

£ _____ . 0 0

23 Reverse premiums and inducements

£ _____ . 0 0

Property expenses

24 Rent, rates, insurance, ground rents etc.

£ _____ . 0 0

25 Property repairs, maintenance and renewals

£ _____ . 0 0

26 Loan interest and other financial costs

£ _____ . 0 0

27 Legal, management and other professional fees

£ _____ . 0 0

28 Costs of services provided, including wages

£ _____ . 0 0

29 Other allowable property expenses

£ _____ . 0 0

Calculating your taxable profit or loss

30 Private use adjustment – *read the notes*

£ _____ . 0 0

31 Balancing charges – *read the notes*

£ _____ . 0 0

32 Annual Investment Allowance

£ _____ . 0 0

33 Business Premises Renovation Allowance (Assisted Areas only) – *read the notes*

£ _____ . 0 0

34 All other capital allowances

£ _____ . 0 0

35 Landlord's Energy Saving Allowance

£ _____ . 0 0

36 10% wear and tear allowance – *for furnished residential accommodation only*

£ _____ . 0 0

37 Rent a Room exempt amount

£ _____ . 0 0

38 Adjusted profit for the year – from box O on the Working Sheet – *read the notes*

£ _____ . 0 0

39 Loss brought forward used against this year's profits

£ _____ . 0 0

40 Taxable profit for the year (box 38 minus box 39)

£ _____ . 0 0

41 Adjusted loss for the year – from box O on the Working Sheet – *read the notes*

£ _____ . 0 0

42 Loss set off against 2013–14 total income – *this will be unusual - read the notes*

£ _____ . 0 0

43 Loss to carry forward to following year, including unused losses brought forward

£ _____ . 0 0

SA105 2013   Page UKP 2

2 Summary

Land and property supplementary page 2 summarises profits from lettings.

In Chapter 9 it can be used to help calculate the income tax liability.

3 Test your knowledge

 Workbook Activity 2

Brian Finlay (1)

Brian Finlay owned a house which he let, furnished, to students at a monthly rental of £1,000 until 31 July 2013. The property was redecorated in August and let again from 1 September 2013 for £1,200 per month.

Details of expenditure during 2013/14 were:

	£
Running expenses whilst empty	150
Redecoration	2,010
New washing machine (August 2013)	250
Gardening	520
Legal fee for tenancy agreement	75
Mortgage interest	3,700
Insurance	305

On 1 May 2013, Brian had acquired a buy-to-let flat. He paid service charges of £25 per month and mortgage interest of £500 per month. The property was let unfurnished from 1 August 2013 at a monthly rent of £600.

Required:

Calculate Brian's taxable property income for 2013/14.

Workbook Activity 3

Brian Finlay (2)
Required:

Using the details given in the previous question, complete the land and property page 2 for Brian Finlay.

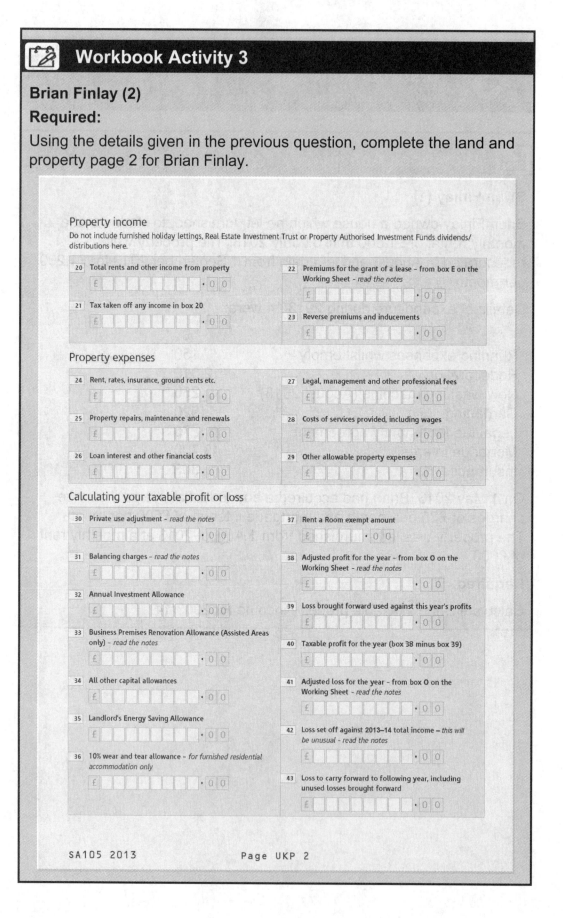

Investment income

Introduction

Investment income of some type will form part of most individuals' income tax computations. It will feature in the assessment.

This chapter considers interest and dividends received. It explains how they are taxed and when they are not taxable.

KNOWLEDGE	CONTENTS
Explain the main current legislation relating to personal taxation (1.1 K)	1 Investment income
	2 Savings income
Explain the main legislative features relating to savings income, including exempt savings income (1.2 K)	3 Dividend income
Identify the main legislative features relating to dividend income from UK registered companies (1.8 K)	
Describe taxable and non-taxable savings income (2.5 K)	

SKILLS

List non-savings, savings and dividend income and check for completeness (2.2 S)

Make computations and submissions in accordance with current tax law (5.1 S)

1 Investment income

1.1 Types of investment income

Investment income can generally be separated into two categories.

1.2 Income received net

Some investment income is received net of tax (10% or 20%). However, the gross amount of such income must be included in an income tax computation.

The income is grossed up using the formula:

$$\text{Gross} = \text{Amount received} \times \frac{100}{100 - \text{Rate of tax deducted}}$$

The types of investment income received net will be discussed in detail throughout the chapter.

🔆 Example

Frances has received the following net amounts during 2013/14.

(a) £600 – net of 20% tax.

(b) £405 – net of 10% tax.

Calculate the gross investment income for 2013/14.

Solution

		£
(a)	Gross = £600 × $\dfrac{100}{100-20}$ = £600 × $\dfrac{100}{80}$	750
(b)	Gross = £405 × $\dfrac{100}{100-10}$ = £405 × $\dfrac{100}{90}$	450
	Gross investment income	1,200

1.3 Basis of assessment

All investment income is taxed on a **cash received basis**.

It does not matter to which period the income relates.

 Example

Bank interest of £1,000 (gross) for the year to 30 June 2013 is received on 30 June 2013.

In which tax year is the income taxed?

Solution

The interest is received on 30 June 2013 which is in the tax year 2013/14. Hence, it is taxed in 2013/14.

2 Savings income

2.1 Types of savings income

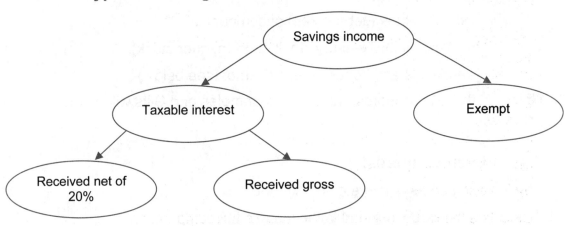

There are three possible treatments of savings income (interest).

- If received net of 20% tax:

    (i)   Gross up.

    $$\text{Taxable interest} = \text{Amount received} \times \frac{100}{80}$$

    (ii) Put the gross amount in the tax computation.

- If received gross:

  Simply put the amount received in the tax computation.

- If exempt:

  Do not put in the tax computation, but make a note in your answer to state that it is exempt.

2.2 Interest received net of 20% tax

This type of savings income includes the following.

Interest received on:

- Bank accounts.

- Building society accounts.

- Unquoted loan notes (debentures) of companies

There is usually one of these included in the assessment.

2.3 Interest received gross

This includes the following.

Interest received on:

- Quoted loan notes (debentures) of companies

- Gilts (for example, Treasury stock or Exchequer stock).

- NS&I accounts and bonds unless exempt (see below)

Note that the rate of interest quoted for loan notes and Gilts will be the gross rate.

2.4 Exempt interest

The following types of interest are exempt.

These should not be included in the income tax computation.

- Interest on National Savings Certificates.

- Interest on Save As You Earn (SAYE) sharesave accounts.

- Interest on delayed repayments of income tax.

- Interest on ISAs (see 2.5 below).

These types of exempt interest were considered in Chapter 2, but are repeated here to reinforce that they are likely to be included amongst a list of other (taxable) interest received.

Interest on individual savings accounts (ISAs) is an example of exempt income which will almost certainly appear in the exam.

2.5 Individual Savings Accounts (ISAs)

An investment of up to £11,520 per tax year can be made into an ISA by a UK individual aged at least 18 (or 16 in the case of cash only ISAs). ISAs are offered by many financial institutions who must comply with rules administered by HMRC.

Of the £11,520:

- it can all be invested in shares. This will generate exempt dividend income; or

- up to £5,760 of the investment can be invested in a bank or building society (the balance can be invested in shares). The cash component will generate exempt interest.

2.6 Tax rates to apply to taxable savings income

The normal tax rates (as previously considered in Chapter 2) are:

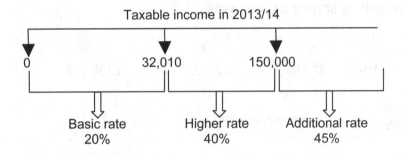

Taxable income in 2013/14

| 0 | 32,010 | 150,000 |

| Basic rate 20% | Higher rate 40% | Additional rate 45% |

These are the rates of tax to apply to non-savings income.

When calculating tax on savings income (interest), any amount which falls within the first £2,790 of taxable income is taxed at 10%.

Accordingly, the tax rates are:

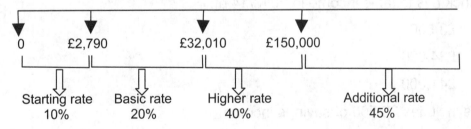

| 0 | £2,790 | £32,010 | £150,000 |

| Starting rate 10% | Basic rate 20% | Higher rate 40% | Additional rate 45% |

Activity 1

Joseph has taxable savings income of £5,000 for 2013/14. He has no other income.

What is his tax liability for 2013/14?

A   £500

B   £1,000

C   £721

D   £779

Where an individual has non-savings and savings income, the non-savings income is taxed first and then the savings income, to work through the different rate bands.

Assuming an individual has other taxable income of £1,100, the effect on savings income is shown as follows:

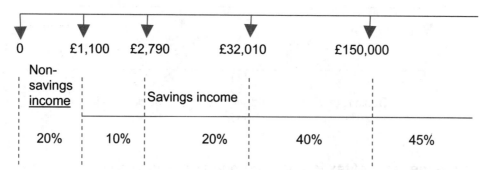

| 0 | £1,100 | £2,790 | £32,010 | £150,000 |

| Non-savings income | | Savings income | | |
| 20% | 10% | 20% | 40% | 45% |

 Example

Patrick has taxable income in 2013/14 of:

(i)   £3,500

(ii)   £34,000

(iii)   £41,000

This includes £2,500 of savings income.

What is his income tax liability for the year?

Solution

(i) £3,500 taxable income (£1,000 non-savings (N-S) and £2,500 savings (S).

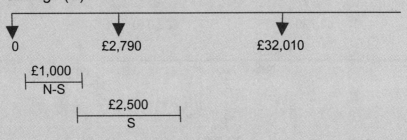

	£		£
Non-savings	1,000	× 20%	200.00
Savings	1,790	× 10%	179.00
	710	× 20%	142.00
	―――		
	3,500		
	―――		―――
Income tax liability			521.00
			―――

(ii) £34,000 taxable income (£31,500 non-savings and £2,500 savings).

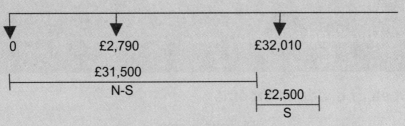

	£		£
Non-savings	31,500	× 20%	6,300.00
Savings	510	× 20%	102.00
	―――		
	32,010		
Savings	1,990	× 40%	796.00
	―――		
	34,000		
	―――		―――
Income tax liability			7,198.00
			―――

(iii) £41,000 taxable income (£38,500 non-savings and £2,500 savings).

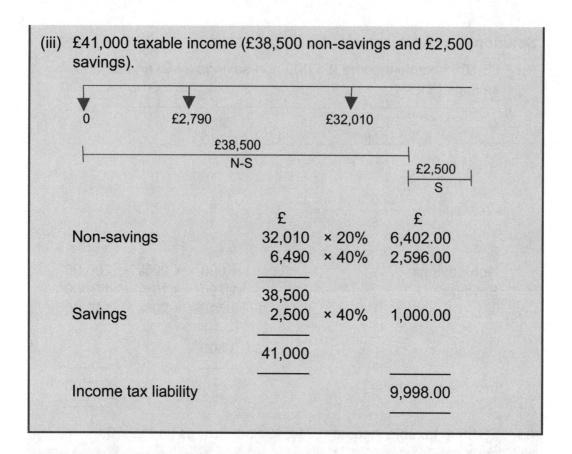

	£		£
Non-savings	32,010	× 20%	6,402.00
	6,490	× 40%	2,596.00
	─────		
	38,500		
Savings	2,500	× 40%	1,000.00
	─────		
	41,000		
	─────		─────
Income tax liability			9,998.00
			─────

3 Dividend income

3.1 Types of dividend income

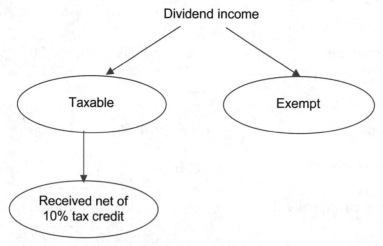

Dividend income is usually taxable (only dividends from ISA investments are exempt).

Dividends may be paid by:

- companies, or

- unit trusts and open-ended investment companies.

Dividends that are taxable are received net of a notional 'tax credit'. This is not actually tax deducted at source but is treated as if it is.

As dividend income received is treated as if received net of a 10% tax credit, we must:

(i) Gross up.

$$\text{Taxable amount} = \text{Amount received} \times \frac{100}{90}$$

(ii) Put the gross amount on the tax computation.

3.2 Tax rates

The tax rates for dividend income are:

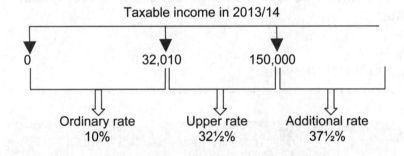

Where an individual has a mixture of all different types of income, we work through the different rate bands in the order:

(i) Non-savings income

(ii) Savings income

(iii) Dividend income.

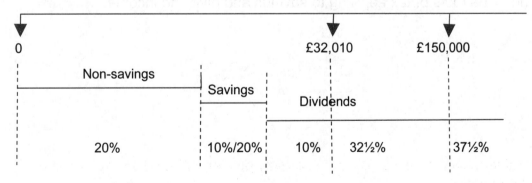

Activity 2

Emily

Emily has taxable income in 2013/14 as follows:

£34,110 of which £2,000 (gross) is bank interest and £3,000 (gross) is dividend income.

Required:

Calculate her tax liability for the year.

 Activity 3

Simon

Simon has taxable income in 2013/14 as follows:

£158,400 of which £26,300 (gross) is bank interest and £46,200 (gross) is dividend income.

Required:

Calculate his tax liability for the year.

4 Summary

It is essential to be aware of:

(i)   whether savings income is received net or gross;
and

(ii)   the rates of tax applying to savings and dividend income.

5 Test your knowledge

Workbook Activity 4

Mr Bundy

Mr Bundy has sent you a list of his investment income in 2013/14.

	£
Dividend income received	600
Bank interest credited to his account	51

Mr Bundy also has a holding of £10,000 4% Barwest Bank Ltd loan notes. The interest is paid six-monthly, on 31 March and 30 September each year. Barwest Bank Ltd is an unquoted company.

Required:

Complete the following schedule for Mr Bundy's investment income for 2013/14 showing the gross and net amounts, and the amounts of tax deducted or tax credits. Calculate to the nearest pound.

	Net	Gross	Tax deducted
	£	£	£
Dividends	_____	_____	_____
Bank interest	_____	_____	_____
Loan note interest	_____	_____	_____

Workbook Activity 5

Mrs Gubbins

Mrs Gubbins has given you the following information to assist you in preparing her income tax return for the year to 5 April 2014.

	£
Bank interest credited to her account	76
Building society interest credited to her account	124
Dividend income received: ABM Ltd	64
ICF Ltd	121
CRP Ltd	157

Required:

Prepare a summary of Mrs Gubbins' investment income for 2013/14, showing the gross and net amounts, and the amount of tax deducted/tax credits.

	Net	Gross	Tax deducted/ tax credit
	£	£	£
Bank interest			
	_____	_____	_____
Building society interest			
	_____	_____	_____
Dividends			
	_____	_____	_____

Workbook Activity 6

Place a tick in the correct column against the following types of investment income to indicate whether they are normally received net or gross.

	Net	Gross
Bank interest		
Building society interest		
Interest from NS&I investment accounts		
Interest from gilts		
Loan stock interest from unquoted companies		

Calculating income tax payable

Introduction

This chapter brings together all of the types of income considered in the earlier chapters. It then works towards calculating income tax payable.

This is an important chapter as calculation of taxable income and income tax liability is always tested.

KNOWLEDGE
Explain the main current legislation relating to personal taxation (1.1 K)

SKILLS
List non-savings, savings and dividend income checking for completeness (2.2 S)
Apply allowances that can be set against non-savings income (3.1 S)
Apply deductions and reliefs and claim loss set-offs (3.2 S)
Account for personal allowances (3.3 S)
Calculate income tax payable (3.4 S)
Make computations and submissions in accordance with current tax law (5.1 S)

CONTENTS

1 Proforma income tax computation
2 Calculation of taxable income
3 Income from self employment
4 Reliefs
5 Personal allowance (PA)
6 Calculation of income tax payable
7 Approach to computations in the assessment

1 Proforma income tax computation

The income tax computation is completed in two stages:

(i)   Calculation of taxable income.

(ii)   Calculation of income tax payable.

Each of these is looked at in turn in this chapter.

2 Calculation of taxable income

2.1   Overview of the calculation of taxable income

In Chapter 2 there was a proforma income tax computation. It is repeated here with more detail added. This proforma should be learned.

A Person

Income tax computation – 2013/14

	£	£
Earned income		
Employment income		X
Pension income		X
Income from self employment		X
		——
		X
Savings income		
Building society interest (amount received × 100/80)	X	
Bank interest (amount received × 100/80)	X	
Quoted loan note interest (received gross)	X	
Treasury stock interest (received gross)	X	
NS&I interest (usually received gross)	X	
	——	
		X
Dividends (amount received × 100/90)		X
Property income		X
		——
Total income		X
Less: Reliefs		(X)
		——
Net income		X
Less: Personal allowance (PA)		(X)
		——
Taxable income		X
		——

All the entries in the proforma have been considered in detail in Chapters 3 to 8 with the exception of:

- income from self employment;
- reliefs; and
- personal allowance.

These are covered in sections 3 to 5 of this chapter.

2.2 Expanded proforma income tax computation

The proforma is expanded as set out below in order to assist in the calculation of the income tax liability.

'Other' income is all income apart from savings income (interest) and dividends. Accordingly, it includes employment income, property income and income from self employment.

A Person

Income tax computation – 2013/14

	Total £	Other £	Savings £	Dividends £
Earned income	X	X		
Savings income	X		X	
Dividends	X			X
Property income	X	X		
Total income	X	X	X	X
Less: Reliefs	(X)	(X)*		
Net income	X	X	X	X
Less: Personal allowance	(X)	(X)*		
Taxable income	X	X	X	X

* Reliefs and the personal allowance are deducted primarily from other income. If the other income is reduced to nil, any remaining deduction is then made from savings income and finally dividend income.

You may also find 'other' income referred to as non-savings income.

3 Income from self employment

The computation of income from self employment is covered in Business tax, and is outside the scope of Personal tax.

It does, however, form part of an individual's total income.

If given in the assessment, you simply need to include the taxable trade profit that will be given to you in the income tax computation as earned income.

4 Reliefs

Relief is available for losses, certain types of expenditure incurred by the tax payer and certain assets gifted to charity by the tax payer.

The loss relief rules are not examinable in this unit but are covered in Business tax.

4.1 Other reliefs

If an individual gives certain assets to charity, tax relief is available by deduction from total income.

The amount of the deduction is the value of the asset gifted.

The assets available for this treatment are:

(a) Listed shares and securities (i.e. where the company's name ends in 'plc').

(b) Units in an authorised unit trust.

(c) Land and buildings which the charity agrees to accept.

There are other types of reliefs (e.g. certain interest payments). These are not in the Personal tax syllabus.

5   Personal allowance (PA)

5.1   Availability

All individuals are entitled to a personal allowance of £9,440 for 2013/14.

The personal allowance is deducted from net income (i.e. total income less reliefs) in arriving at taxable income.

The personal allowance can only be relieved against income of the current tax year. Any unused amount cannot be carried forward or carried back, nor can it be offset against capital gains.

> **Example**
>
> Mavis has a salary of £23,000 in 2013/14 which is her only source of income.
>
> Calculate her 2013/14 taxable income and tax liability.
>
> **Solution**
>
> | | £ |
> |---|---|
> | Total income | 23,000 |
> | Less: Reliefs | (Nil) |
> | Net income | 23,000 |
> | Less: Personal allowance | (9,440) |
> | Taxable income | 13,560 |
> | Mavis' income tax liability is: (£13,560 × 20%) | £2,712.00 |

5.2   Age allowance

Taxpayers born prior to 6 April 1948 are entitled to a higher rate of personal allowance.

- Those born between **6 April 1938 and 5 April 1948 (**i.e. aged at least 65 but no more than 74 at the start of 2013/14) are entitled to an increased personal allowance of £10,500 in 2013/14.

- Those born before **6 April 1938 (**i.e. aged at least 75 at the start of 2013/14) get the highest rate personal allowance of £10,660 in 2013/14.

- The allowance is given to attempt to provide some protection for those on lower incomes.

- An income restriction operates to reduce the level of the allowances, where the taxpayer's net income reaches a certain level. This is set at £26,100 for 2013/14.

- The reduction in allowances is calculated as:

  - **50% × (Net income – £26,100)**

  - this formula gives a progressive reduction in the personal age allowance.

    However, this reduction can never cause the allowance to fall below the basic personal allowance of £9,440 for 2013/14.

Example

Calculate the age allowance in the following situations:

- Dennis was born on 1 May 1946 and has net income of £26,950

- Nora was born on 1 July 1930 and has net income of £28,600

- Peter is aged 78 and has net income of £34,100

Solution

	Dennis £	Nora £	Peter £
Personal age allowance	10,500	10,660	10,660
Less: Restriction			
50% × (£26,950 – £26,100)	(425)		
50% × (£28,600 – £26,100)		(1,250)	
50% × (£34,100 – £26,100)			
= £4,000 restricted			(1,220)
	———	———	———
Personal age allowance	10,075	9,410	9,440
	———	———	———

5.3 Restricted personal allowance

The personal allowance and the age allowance are restricted if an individual's net income exceeds £100,000.

The reduction is half of the amount by which the individual's net income exceeds £100,000. The allowance remaining is rounded up to the next whole pound.

Once an individual's net income exceeds £118,880 (£100,000 + (2 × £9,440)) they will not receive a personal allowance or an age allowance.

The personal allowance is never reduced to a negative number.

Example

Dan has net income in 2013/14 of £111,475.

Calculate Dan's personal allowance for 2013/14.

Solution

	£
Personal allowance	9,440.00
Less: Restriction	
50% × (£111,475 – £100,000)	(5,737.50)
	————
	3,702.50
	————
Restricted allowance (rounded up)	3,703.00
	————

Note: Where an individual's net income exceeds £100,000, the individual's date of birth is irrelevant as their personal age allowance will be reduced to the basic personal allowance due to the excess of their income over £26,100.

Activity 1

Identify the personal allowances available to the following individuals in 2013/14.

Taxpayer	Date of birth/age at 6.4.2013	Net income
Vera	4 June 1938	£105,000
Agatha	15 March 1935	£27,100
Henry	20 August 1925	£28,100
Leon	70	£32,100

6 Calculation of income tax payable

6.1 Tax rates

In Chapter 8 the different rates of income tax were considered in detail.

These are shown below using the limits for 2013/14.

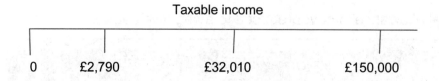

Taxable income

0   £2,790   £32,010   £150,000

Types of income (in order of calculation)

Other	20%	20%	40%	45%
Savings	10%	20%	40%	45%
Dividends	10%	10%	32½%	37½%

Pence should be shown when calculating income tax; it is not correct to round calculations to the nearest pound.

However, in your assessment you must follow the rule you are given for a particular task.

6.2 Proforma calculation of income tax payable

A Person

Income tax payable – 2013/14

	Total £	Other £	Savings £	Dividends £
Taxable income (from first part of proforma)	X	A	B	C
Income tax				£.pp
Other income A × 20%/40%/45%				X
Savings income B × 10%/20%/40%/45% (Note 1)				X
Dividend income C × 10%/32.5%/37.5%				X
Income tax liability				X
Less: Tax deducted at source				(X)
Income tax payable				X

Note:

1   Savings income that is part of the first £2,790 of taxable income (after taking account of other income) is taxed at 10%.

It is important to be able to distinguish between income tax liability and income tax payable (as per the proforma).

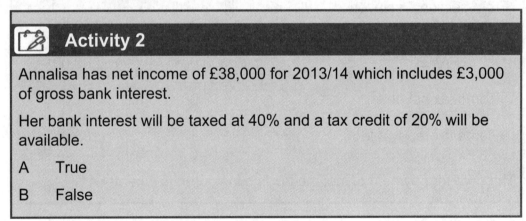

Activity 2

Annalisa has net income of £38,000 for 2013/14 which includes £3,000 of gross bank interest.

Her bank interest will be taxed at 40% and a tax credit of 20% will be available.

A   True

B   False

6.3 Tax deducted at source

The income tax **liability** is the total amount of income tax that an individual must pay to HM Revenue and Customs (HMRC) for a tax year.

Most individuals have already paid some tax at source (known as tax credits).

- Salaries – have tax deducted under the PAYE system at all relevant rates (20%, 40% and 45%).

- Bank interest – has 20% tax deducted at source.

- Building society interest – has 20% tax deducted at source.

In all of these situations the payer (employer, bank, etc) pays over the withheld tax to HMRC on behalf of the taxpayer.

These tax credits can reduce the tax liability leaving a smaller amount of tax still owed to HMRC (or possibly even a tax repayment).

⚙ Example

From the example in section 5, Mavis had PAYE deducted from her salary.

What is her income tax payable/repayable if the PAYE deducted was:

(a)   £2,500; or

(b)   £3,000?

Solution

	(a)	(b)
From section 5 solution		
Income tax liability	2,712.00	2,712.00
Less: Tax deducted at source		
PAYE	(2,500.00)	(3,000.00)
Income tax payable	212.00	
Income tax repayable		(288.00)

The date for payment of income tax is considered in Chapter 11.

6.4   Dividend tax credits

Dividends are deemed to have a tax credit of 10%. This is not actually withheld tax but is treated in the same way.

There is one difference between this and the other tax credits. A dividend tax credit cannot generate a tax repayment (it can only reduce a liability down to nil).

However, if there are a number of tax credits, the dividend tax credit can be set off first, allowing the others to generate a repayment if available.

 Activity 3

The only income Jane received during 2013/14 was dividends of £9,360.

What is Jane's income tax liability for 2013/14?

A   Nil

B   £936.00

C   £96.00

D   £1,040.00

 Example

Stephanie is paid a gross salary in 2013/14 of £30,405. Her employer deducted income tax under PAYE of £5,060 in respect of 2013/14.

Stephanie also receives the following amounts of investment income in 2013/14.

	£
UK dividends	16,470
Building society interest	400
Bank interest	640

In June 2013 Stephanie donated shares in a quoted company worth £1,100 to a registered charity.

Calculate Stephanie's income tax payable for 2013/14.

Solution

Stephanie – Income tax computation – 2013/14

	Total £	Other £	Savings £	Dividends £
Employment income	30,405	30,405		
Building society interest				
(£400 × 100/80)	500		500	
Bank interest (£640 × 100/80)	800		800	
Dividends (£16,470 × 100/90)	18,300			18,300
Total income	50,005	30,405	1,300	18,300
Less: Reliefs	(1,100)	(1,100)		
Net income	48,905	29,305	1,300	18,300
Less: PA	(9,440)	(9,440)		
Taxable income	39,465	19,865	1,300	18,300

Income tax

£			£
19,865	× 20%	(other)	3,973.00
1,300	× 20%	(savings)	260.00
10,845	× 10%	(dividends)	1,084.50
32,010			
7,455	× 32.5%	(dividends)	2,422.87
39,465			

Income tax liability		7,740.37
Less:	Tax deducted at source	
	Dividends (£18,300 × 10%)	(1,830.00)
	Savings (£1,300 × 20%)	(260.00)
	PAYE	(5,060.00)
Income tax payable		590.37

Activity 4

Stanley

The 2013/14 tax return of Stanley shows the following income for the year ended 5 April 2014:

	£
Salary from Dee Ltd	102,485
Bank deposit interest received	2,000
Dividends – amount received	26,100
Building society interest – amounts received	800

Dee Ltd paid Stanley a performance related bonus. On 9 September 2012 he was paid his first bonus of £43,280 relating to the year ended 30 June 2012 and on 17 September 2013 he was paid £38,480 relating to the year ended 30 June 2013.

Stanley has travelled 11,500 business miles in his own car in 2013/14. Dee Ltd paid him 47p per mile.

During 2013/14 the PAYE paid was £57,800.

Required:

Compute Stanley's income tax payable for 2013/14.

Approach to this question

The first step is to draw up an income tax computation proforma.

In this case, you will have to be careful when slotting in the figure for the bonus, as information is given for two tax years. You will also need to gross up any net amounts given using the correct grossing up fraction.

The income tax liability can then be calculated.

This question requires the calculation of tax payable, so you must then deduct from the tax liability any tax suffered at source, (i.e. tax credits on savings income received net), and also tax paid under PAYE (pay as you earn).

7   Approach to computations in the assessment

There will **normally** be at least one task in the assessment which requires you to prepare all or part of an income tax computation. However, the income tax computations in the assessment will not be as long as the example Stephanie or the Activity 4 above. These are included to give you an overview and it is important that you practise full computations to increase your understanding of how income tax works.

A grid is provided in the assessment to assist you when preparing income tax computations. This will have up to 5 columns:

*   the left hand column for descriptions

*   the other columns for numerical entry.

A 5 column grid will allow you to enter a full computation per the proforma in this chapter. The example below shows a suggested approach.

 Example

Arthur was born on 1 June 1936. He has a pension from his former employers of £18,235, a state pension of £5,200 and received dividends of £4,500.

Required:

Calculate Arthur's income tax liability using the grid below.

Approach

Step 1

Use the paper provided in your assessment to draw up a standard income tax computation. This need not be particularly neat as it will be thrown away at the end of the assessment!

	Total	Other	Dividends
	£	£	£
Employment Pension	18,235	18,235	
State pension	5,200	5,200	
Dividends (£4,500 × 100/90)	5,000		5,000
Net income	28,435	23,435	5,000
Less: PA (W)	(9,493)	(9,493)	
Taxable income	18,942	13,942	5,000

£			
13,942 × 20%	(other)		2,788.40
5,000 × 10%	(dividends)		500.00
18,942			
Income tax liability			3,288.40

Working:

	£
Personal age allowance	10,660
Less: Restriction	
50% × (£28,435 – £26,100)	(1,167)
	9,493

Step 2

Enter the figures into the assessment grid.

There is no need to put in lines marking totals and subtotals. Remember to check you have enough space before you start – if not abbreviate.

	Total	Other	Divis	
	£	£	£	
Employment pension	18,235	18,235		
State pension	5,200	5,200		
Dividends (4,500 × 100/90)	5,000		5,000	
Total = Net income	28,435	23,435	5,000	
Less Age PA				
(10,660 – ½ (28,435 – 26,100)	(9,493)	(9,493)		
Taxable income	18,942	13,942	5,000	
£13,942 × 20%	2,788.40			
£5,000 × 10%	500.00			
Income tax liability	3,288.40			

This will be manually marked so you need to include simple workings.

In some questions you may not have enough information to complete a full computation as the question may be more focused on calculating a restricted personal allowance.

In this case it is the figure of net income that you need without worrying what type of income is included. If there is doubt as to the source of income, always assume it is 'other income'.

 Activity 5

Hossam was born on 1 June 1962. For 2013/14 he has income of £50,000 plus he receives bank interest of £1,800 and dividends of £4,500.

Required:

Calculate the income tax liability using the grid below.

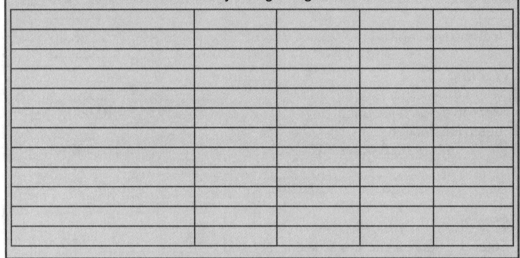

8 Summary

This chapter has set out the two stages of the income tax computation:

(a)   Calculation of taxable income.

(b)   Calculation of income tax payable.

It is worth noting that every individual is entitled to a personal allowance, irrespective of their age but this may be reduced depending on their income.

Older taxpayers receive a higher level of personal allowance but this is reduced if their net income exceeds a limit (£26,100 for 2013/14). All taxpayers have a reduced allowance if their net income exceeds £100,000.

9 Test your knowledge

 Workbook Activity 6

Mary

Mary is employed as a sales representative at an annual salary of £37,900. She is provided with a company car by her employer which gave rise to a taxable benefit for 2013/14 of £5,200.

Mary is in an occupational pension scheme into which she pays 6% of her basic salary.

Mary received dividends during 2013/14 of £1,350.

Required:

Calculate Mary's income tax liability for the year 2013/14 using this grid.

Note: You do not have enough columns here to set out a full columnar computation. You should still prepare a columnar computation in your workings. In your grid you can use the left hand columns for description and workings and simply enter your total column in the third column in the grid.

Workbook Activity 7

Artemis was born on 1 July 1935. His total income for 2013/14 is £110,750.

To what personal allowance is Artemis entitled for 2013/14?

 Workbook Activity 8

Briony

Until 31 December 2013 Briony was employed by JJ Gyms Ltd as a fitness consultant. Her taxable employment income was £39,295, from which PAYE of £6,700 was deducted.

On 1 January 2014 Briony commenced in self-employment running a music recording studio. Her taxable trade profit assessable for 2013/14 is £15,415.

During 2013/14, Briony received rental income from a buy-to-let property of £6,500 and dividend income of £1,710.

Required:

Calculate Briony's income tax payable for 2013/14.

 Workbook Activity 9

Sally has net income from employment and self employment for 2013/14 of £47,965. She suffered PAYE on her employment income of £4,500.

What is Sally's income tax liability for 2013/14?

A   £4,508.00

B   £9,008.00

C   £7,705.00

D   £12,784.00

Workbook Activity 10

Jon

Jon informs you of the following matters so that you can prepare his income tax computation.

- His salary for 2013/14 is £39,830 with tax deducted of £5,850.

- During June 2013 he cashed in his holding of National Savings Certificates for £2,340. These had been purchased in 2007 for £2,000 and had earned 4% per annum compound for five years.

- Jon has been very lucky with his bets on the horses this year, winning £500 on the Derby (June 2013) but he tells you that most years he loses more than he wins.

- He received building society interest of £320 in the year to 5 April 2014.

- He received bank deposit interest of £400 in the year to 5 April 2014.

- He received dividends of £1,890 in the year to 5 April 2014.

Required:

Calculate Jon's income tax payable for 2013/14.

 Workbook Activity 11

Marcel

Marcel is aged 71.

His income for 2013/14 was as follows:

	£
Interest on National Savings Certificates	1,250
Occupational pension (gross)	9,660
Dividends (net)	3,600
Interest on British Government stocks	9,400
Bank interest (net)	3,000

PAYE of £280 was deducted from the occupational pension.

Required:

Calculate the income tax payable by Marcel for 2013/14.

Workbook Activity 12

Mr Black

Mr Black gives you the following information for 2013/14.

	£
Salary (PAYE deducted £6,420)	43,000
Dividends received	297
Bank interest received	28

Required:

What is the income tax payable by Mr Black for 2013/14?

 Workbook Activity 13

Mark the following statements as true or false.

		True	False
1	The personal allowance for a taxpayer born before 6 April 1948 is never reduced below the standard personal allowance of £9,440.		
2	The first £2,790 of savings income is always taxed at 10%.		
3	The tax credit on dividends can never be repaid but can be used to reduce tax liability to nil.		
4	If a taxpayer has no taxable income for 2013/14 they can carry forward the benefit of their unused personal allowance to 2014/15.		

KAPLAN PUBLISHING

Workbook Activity 14

Louis

Louis has provided you with the following information for 2013/14.

	£
Salary (PAYE deducted £44,250)	146,400
Dividends received	3,060
Bank interest received	5,600

Required:

Calculate the income tax payable by Louis for 2013/14.

 Workbook Activity 15

Mr Ephraim was born on 1 August 1935 and has total income for 2013/14 of £28,100.

To what personal allowance is Mr Ephraim entitled for 2013/14?

A   £8,660

B   £10,660

C   £9,440

D   £9,660

Pension payments and Gift Aid

Introduction

Tax relief is available in respect of these two types of payment. This chapter considers how much tax relief is available and how it is given.

KNOWLEDGE

Explain the main current legislation relating to personal taxation (1.1 K)

SKILLS

Apply deductions and reliefs and claim loss set-offs (3.2 S)

Calculate income tax payable (3.4 S)

Describe taxation relief which can be given on income from employment including deductible (allowable) expenses, pensions relief and charitable donations (3.5 S)

Make computations and submissions in accordance with current tax law (5.1 S)

CONTENTS

1 Pension contributions
2 Donations to charity
3 Pension payments, Gift Aid and personal allowances

1 Pension contributions

1.1 Tax efficiency

A tax efficient way of providing for retirement is to make contributions into a registered pension scheme.

It is tax efficient for the following reasons:

- The individual gets tax relief on the contributions made.

- The employer gets tax relief on any contributions made, but without there being a taxable benefit for the employee.

- The income and capital gains generated by the funds in a pension scheme are exempt from income tax and capital gains tax.

- Part of the pension may be taken as a tax-free lump sum.

Registered pension schemes are available to all individuals.

Certain employed persons have a choice of provision so the full details are included in this section for all individuals.

1.2 Options available to employees

An OPS is an option only if the employer has a scheme available.

An OPS is also known as a company pension scheme. Such schemes were considered briefly in Chapter 3.

A PPS is an option for an employee who:

- has no OPS available from his employer.

- chooses the PPS in preference to his employer's OPS.

- also has an OPS.

1.3 Options available to other individuals

Other individuals may save through a PPS.

1.4 Tax relief for pension contributions

All registered pension schemes are governed by the same rules, regardless of whether they are occupational or personal pensions.

An individual may make a pension contribution of any amount into a registered pension scheme or may make contributions into a number of different schemes. Tax relief will however only be available for a maximum annual amount.

The maximum total annual contribution into *all* pension schemes that an individual can obtain tax relief for is the higher of:

- £3,600, and

- 100% of the individual's relevant earnings, chargeable to income tax in the tax year.

Relevant earnings include trading profits, employment income, but not investment income (although profits from furnished holiday lettings are specifically included in the definition of relevant earnings).

Note that an individual with no relevant earnings can still obtain tax relief on contributions of up to £3,600.

 Example

Rob has employment income of £2,500 and interest income of £10,000 (gross) in 2013/14.

What is the maximum pension contribution that Rob can get tax relief for in 2013/14?

Solution

The maximum pension contribution that Rob can get tax relief for in 2013/14 is £3,600 – being the higher of:

	£
– £3,600 and	3,600
– 100% of relevant earnings	
= employment income	2,500

1.5 Method of giving tax relief for pension contributions

The **amount of tax relief** that is given for pension contributions is the same whether the contributions are to a personal pension scheme or an occupational pension scheme.

However, the **method by which the tax relief is given** is different for the two types of scheme.

1.6 Tax relief for contributions to personal pension schemes

Personal pension contributions are paid net of basic rate tax (20%).

Higher rate and additional rate income tax relief is achieved by extending the basic rate and additional rate bands by the gross amount of the pension contribution.

For example, if an individual pays a premium of £8,000 (net) – equivalent to a gross premium of £10,000 (£8,000 × 100/80) – his higher rate threshold is extended to £42,010 (£32,010 + £10,000).

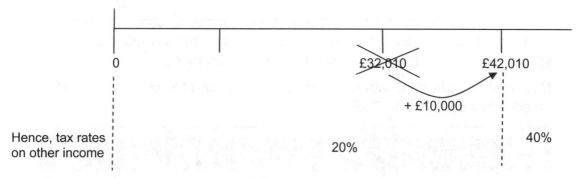

The limit at which he starts paying tax at the additional rates is also extended. The new limit is £160,000 (£150,000 + £10,000).

🔅 Example

Pauline is a bank employee. Her income for 2013/14 is as follows:

	£
Salary	39,000
Benefits	5,640
Bank interest received	4,800

She made a personal pension contribution of £3,200 (net) in 2013/14.

Calculate Pauline's income tax liability for 2013/14.

Solution

	Total £	Other £	Savings £
Employment income (£39,000 + £5,640)	44,640	44,640	
Bank interest (£4,800 × 100/80)	6,000		6,000
Net income	50,640	44,640	6,000
Less: PA	(9,440)	(9,440)	
Taxable income	41,200	35,200	6,000

Income tax

£			£
35,200	× 20%	(other)	7,040.00
810	× 20%	(savings)	162.00
36,010	(W)		
5,190	× 40%	(savings)	2,076.00
41,200			
Income tax liability			9,278.00

Working:

	£
Basic rate band	32,010
Add: Personal pension contribution (£3,200 × 100/80)	
(maximum contribution = 100% × £44,640)	4,000
Extended basic rate band	36,010

1.7 Method of giving tax relief for occupational pension scheme contributions

The pension contribution paid is deducted from employment income in the year of payment.

Relief for tax is obtained through the PAYE system, at all rates of tax, and no further tax adjustment is required in the income tax computation other than showing the deduction against employment income (i.e. it is an allowable expense).

Example

David received an annual salary of £42,667 and interest income of £12,000 (gross) in 2013/14.

Each year David pays 3% of his salary and his employer pays a further 5% into his employer's registered occupational pension scheme.

Explain how David will obtain tax relief for his pension contributions and calculate his income tax liability for 2013/14.

Solution

- David will pay a pension contribution of £1,280 (£42,667 × 3%) in 2013/14 on which he will obtain full tax relief, as it is less than the maximum available for tax relief of £42,667 (100% of earned income).

- David will obtain tax relief, at basic and higher rates, for the contribution through the PAYE system.

  His employer will deduct the pension contribution from David's taxable pay, in order to calculate the PAYE due.

David

Income tax computation – 2013/14

	Total £	Other £	Savings £
Employment income	42,667		
Less: Pension contributions (3%)	(1,280)		
	41,387	41,387	
Interest income	12,000		12,000
Net income	53,387	41,387	12,000
Less: PA	(9,440)	(9,440)	
Taxable income	43,947	31,947	12,000

Income tax

£			£
31,947	× 20%	(other)	6,389.40
63	× 20%	(savings)	12.60
32,010			
11,937	× 40%	(savings)	4,774.80
43,947			
Income tax liability			11,176.80

The pension contributions made by David's employer are an exempt benefit.

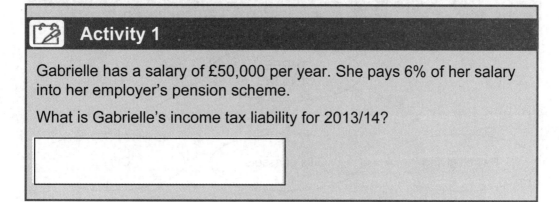

Activity 1

Gabrielle has a salary of £50,000 per year. She pays 6% of her salary into her employer's pension scheme.

What is Gabrielle's income tax liability for 2013/14?

1.8   Annual allowance

Contributions into a registered pension scheme can be made by the scheme member or any other party (e.g. employer).

If the total contributions paid into the pension scheme exceed the annual allowance then the individual member is charged income tax on the excess.

The annual allowance is not examinable.

1.9 Lifetime allowance

There is no restriction on the *total* contributions that an individual may make into a registered pension scheme. There is only a limit upon the annual contributions in respect of which *tax relief will* be available.

As funds in a registered pension scheme grow tax free there is also a limit, the 'lifetime allowance', which determines the maximum amount that an individual can accumulate in a pension scheme tax free.

The lifetime allowance is considered when a member becomes entitled to take benefits out of the scheme e.g. when he becomes entitled to take a pension.

The lifetime allowance is not examinable.

2 Donations to charity

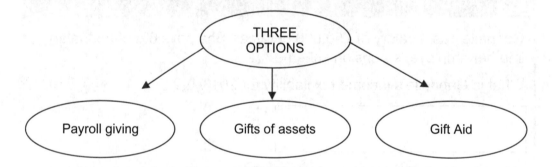

2.1 Options available to individuals

Payroll giving – an individual can have an amount deducted from salary/wages at each pay day.

This is treated as an allowable expense when calculating employment income (see Chapter 3).

Gifts of assets – an individual can make gifts of certain assets (mainly quoted shares and land and buildings).

The value of the asset gifted is treated as a relief against total income (see Chapter 9).

Gift Aid – an individual can make regular payments or one-off payments of cash directly to charity (see 2.2 below).

KAPLAN PUBLISHING

2.2 Gift Aid

If an individual declares a charitable payment of cash to be under 'Gift Aid', the amount of the donation is treated as paid net of basic rate tax which is then recoverable by the charity:

	£
Donation actually paid, say	80
Basic rate tax (20/80)	20
	——
Gross value of gift to charity	100
	——
Charity claims direct from HMRC	20
	——

If the individual is a basic rate taxpayer there is no effect on his personal taxation.

If the individual is a higher or additional rate taxpayer he will benefit from higher or additional rate relief by extending his basic rate band and additional rate band by the gross amount of the Gift Aid payment.

In the above example, the taxpayer would not be subject to the higher rates (40% or 32½%) until his taxable income exceeded £32,110 (£32,010 + £100 gross Gift Aid).

This is the same as the mechanism that gives tax relief for personal pension payments.

Taxpayers can elect to treat a Gift Aid donation as if it were paid in the previous tax year.

Example

John earns £70,000 p.a. and pays a total of £4,800 to a number of charities in 2013/14 under the Gift Aid scheme.

Calculate his income tax liability for 2013/14.

Solution

	£
Net income	70,000
Less: Personal allowance	(9,440)
	——
Taxable income	60,560
	——

Basic rate band: £32,010 + (£4,800 × 100/80) = 38,010

	£	
Income tax:	38,010 × 20%	7,602.00
	22,550 × 40%	9,020.00
	60,560	
Income tax liability		16,622.00

 Activity 2

Imogen

Imogen has given you the following details relating to her tax affairs for 2013/14.

	£
Employment income (PAYE = £57,180)	166,040
Dividends received	2,790
Payroll giving	2,500
Personal pension payment	6,320

Required:

Calculate Imogen's income tax payable or repayable for 2013/14.

Approach to a question

Step 1: Consider how to treat the gift to charity

- Payroll giving deduction against employment income; or

- Relief against total income for gifts of certain assets; or

- Gift Aid.

Step 2: Consider how to treat the pension payment:

- Allowable expense against employment income (OPS) or

- Extend basic rate band (PPS).

Step 3: Now continue with the income tax computation.

3 Pension payments, Gift Aid and personal allowances

We saw in Chapter 9 that taxpayers born before 6 April 1948 can receive a higher personal allowance but that it is reduced if the taxpayer has net income over £26,100.

We also saw that the personal allowance is reduced where a person's income exceeds £100,000.

When calculating these restrictions, the figure of net income should be reduced by the grossed up amount of any Gift Aid payment or personal pension contributions.

 Example

Rasheda was born on 1 September 1945. Her only source of income is £28,200 annual pension received from her former employers.

She makes a Gift Aid payment of £480 each year.

What is her personal age allowance for 2013/14?

Solution

Net income for calculating the age allowance restriction

	£
Pension	28,200
Less: gross Gift Aid (£480 × 100/80)	(600)
Adjusted net income	27,600

Age allowance

	£
Born between 6 April 1938 and 5 April 1948	10,500
Less: ½ (£27,600 – £26,100)	(750)
	9,750

Activity 3

Kieron was born on 1 May 1934. He receives a pension of £29,200 per year and pays £800 a year to Oxfam under Gift Aid.

What is Kieron's income tax liability for 2013/14?

A   £3,708

B   £3,918

C   £3,938

D   £3,952

Example

Rodney was born on 1 August 1962. His only source of income is an annual salary of £115,000.

He makes personal pension contributions of £7,200 each year.

What is his personal allowance for 2013/14?

Solution

Net income for calculating the personal allowance restriction

	£
Salary	115,000
Less: gross pension contributions	
(£7,200 × 100/80)	(9,000)
	———
Adjusted net income	106,000
	———

Personal allowance

Standard personal allowance	9,440
Less: ½ (£106,000 − £100,000)	(3,000)
	———
Reduced personal allowance	6,440
	———

Activity 4

Kurt was born on 1 January 1989. He receives a salary of £106,000 per year and pays £1,600 a year to Oxfam under Gift Aid.

What is Kurt's personal allowance for 2013/14?

A   £9,440

B   £5,440

C   £7,440

D   £7,240

4   Summary

- Pension contributions are a tax efficient way of providing for retirement.

- There are two types of pension scheme

Occupational Pension Schemes	Personal Pension Schemes
↓	↓
Tax relief given at source through the PAYE system	Paid net of basic rate tax Gross up by 100/80 Extend the basic rate band to obtain higher rate tax relief

- There are three tax efficient ways of giving to charity:

    – Payroll giving

    – Gift of assets

    – Gift Aid

    You must be able to deal with all of these.

- If a taxpayer born prior to 6 April 1948 makes a Gift Aid payment or personal pension payment, the gross amount of the payment is deducted from their net income for the purposes of calculating their age personal allowance.

- If a taxpayer with net income of £100,000 or more makes a Gift Aid payment or personal pension payment, the gross amount of the payment is deducted from their net income for the purposes of calculating their personal allowance.

5 Test your knowledge

 ## Workbook Activity 5

Mr Mars

Mr Mars has been self-employed for many years. His taxable trade profits assessable in 2013/14 were £43,765.

He has the following net investment income for 2013/14.

	£
Building society interest	480
Bank interest	1,400

Mr Mars paid a personal pension contribution of £2,800 on 13 December 2013.

Required:

Calculate Mr Mars' income tax liability for 2013/14.

 ## Workbook Activity 6

Proctor

The following information is relevant to Proctor's taxation position for the year ended 5 April 2014.

(1)   His salary as managing director of Peter Proctor (Engineers) Limited was £37,625 and his Form P11D showed his assessable benefits totalled £1,800. The company does not have an occupational pension scheme.

(2)   During the year, Proctor paid £3,200 (net) and Peter Proctor (Engineers) Limited paid £10,000 into Proctor's personal pension scheme.

(3)   Other income:

(i)	Building society interest (net)	£576
(ii)	Rental income	£5,410

Required:

Calculate Proctor's income tax liability for 2013/14.

Workbook Activity 7

Ming Lee

Ming Lee, born on 9 June 1957, is employed as a management consultant. For 2013/14 her taxable employment income is £47,600. Tax deducted under PAYE was £9,900.

Her only other income in 2013/14 is £6,300 of building society interest received.

Required:

(a) Calculate the maximum amount of tax deductible contributions that Ming could have made into a personal pension scheme for 2013/14.

(b) Calculate Ming's income tax payable/repayable for 2013/14 assuming she had contributed the maximum amount to her personal pension.

 Workbook Activity 8

Marjorie

Marjorie was employed at an annual salary of £17,000. PAYE of £1,700 was deducted in 2013/14. She was provided with a Peugeot car which gave rise to a taxable benefit of £2,330.

Other relevant information is as follows:

(1) Marjorie has an account with the Halifax Building Society and £200 interest was credited on 31 January 2014.

(2) Marjorie received dividends in 2013/14 of £1,350.

(3) Marjorie paid contributions of £78 per month into her employer's occupational pension scheme throughout 2013/14.

Required:

Calculate Marjorie's tax payable for 2013/14.

Workbook Activity 9

Peter

Peter is employed as a Sales Director by Neat Limited. He earned a salary of £157,350 in the year to 5 April 2014.

He makes personal pension contributions of £38,400 (net) each year. He also makes charitable payments under the Gift Aid scheme totalling £5,400.

He receives net bank and building society interest of £2,000.

Required:

Calculate Peter's income tax liability for 2013/14.

 Workbook Activity 10

Long Life

Long Life was born on 1 March 1942 and has been in business for many years. His taxable trade profits for 2013/14 were £31,100

He made a payment to Save the Children (a charity) of £2,800 (net) under the Gift Aid Scheme on 1 September 2013.

Required:

What is Long Life's income tax payable for 2013/14?

A   £4,340.00

B   £4,120.00

C   £4,270.00

D   £4,332.00

Workbook Activity 11

Mark the following statements as true or false.

		True	False
1	Jessica has a salary of £50,000 and pays £4,000 to her employer's occupational pension scheme. Her basic rate band will be extended by £5,000.		
2	Making a Gift Aid payment never affects the tax liability of a taxpayer whose taxable income falls under the basic rate threshold.		
3	Employer contributions to a personal pension scheme are paid net of 20% tax.		
4	Payroll giving is paid gross and is an allowable employment income expense.		

Payment and administration

Introduction

An essential element of any tax adviser's role is to ensure that a client's returns and tax payments are accurate and on time.

KNOWLEDGE

Explain the main current legislation relating to personal taxation (1.1 K)

Explain the responsibilities that individuals have for disclosure of income and payment of tax to the relevant tax authorities (1.3 K)

Explain the main features of the self assessment system of taxation (1.4 K)

Describe the duties and responsibilities of a tax practitioner (1.5 K)

Identify sources of taxation information for individuals (1.6 K)

Explain the tax authority's filing and payment process in relation to all personal income (1.7 K)

SKILLS

Make computations and submissions in accordance with current tax law (5.1 S)

Apply the due dates of payment of income tax by individuals, including payments on account (5.3 S)

CONTENTS

1   Self assessment
2   The payment of income tax and capital gains tax
3   Interest and penalties on payments of tax
4   HM Revenue and Customs enquiries

1 Self assessment

1.1 The self assessment return

Certain individuals are required to complete a return for every tax year.

This covers income and gains, reliefs and allowances and, in some cases, a calculation of the tax payable.

The key details to grasp concerning the return are the *filing dates.*

The taxpayer has the choice of filing a paper return or filing electronically online. The date by which a return must be filed depends on the method used.

All completed and signed *paper* returns must normally be filed by:

- *31 October* following the end of the tax year.

All on line (electronic) returns must be filed by:

- *31 January* following the end of the tax year.

The relevant dates for a 2013/14 return are therefore 31 October 2014 and 31 January 2015.

31 January following the end of the tax year is known as the 'filing date' regardless of whether the return is filed on paper or electronically.

When a return is issued less than 3 months before the due date, it must be filed within three months of the date of issue.

The return consists of a six page summary form with supplementary pages which vary according to an individual's income and gains position. Some of the supplementary pages were seen in Chapters 5 and 7.

The taxpayer is permitted to correct or 'repair' their self assessment return within 12 months of the filing date (i.e.by 31 January 2016 for a 2013/14 return).

HMRC can correct 'obvious errors' and anything else which they believe to be incorrect by reference to the information they hold in the period of nine months from the date the return was filed.

 Example

A 2012/13 return is filed on 14 December 2013.

HMRC can make corrections up to 14 September 2014.

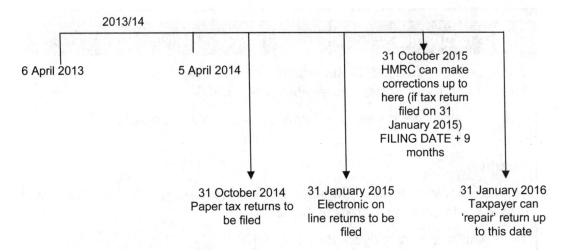

1.2 Penalties for late filing

Failure to submit a return by 31 January *following a tax year* will result in a penalty.

The system operates as follows:

Immediate penalty	£100
Delay of more than three months	£10 per day (maximum 90 days)
Delay of more than six months	5% of tax due

Delay of more than 12 months:

No deliberate withholding of information	5% of tax due
Deliberate withholding of information	70% of tax due
Deliberate withholding of information with concealment	100% of tax due

The penalties based on the tax due are each subject to a minimum of £300.

A penalty will not be charged if the taxpayer has a reasonable excuse for the late filing, for example a serious illness. A lack of knowledge of the tax system is not a reasonable excuse.

Example

Jag submitted his 2013/14 self assessment return on 31 August 2015. The outstanding income tax payable was £8,900.

What penalties will be levied in respect of the late submission of the return?

Solution

The return was due on 31 January 2015. Accordingly, it is more than six months but less than 12 months late.

There will be an immediate penalty of £100.

Because the return is more than three months late, a penalty of £10 per day will be charged for 90 days, i.e. £900.

Because the return is more than six months late there will also be a penalty of 5% of the tax due (subject to a minimum payment of £300), i.e. £445.

Accordingly, the total penalty will be £1,445 (£100 + £900 + £445).

 Activity 1

Required:

(a) State the latest date by which the taxpayer should submit his tax return if:

(i) he wishes to file his return online; or

(ii) he wishes to file a paper return.

(b) State:

(i) the penalties that will be charged where a tax return is submitted within six months of the due date;

(ii) the penalties that will be charged where a tax return is submitted more than 6 months late.

Approach to answering written questions

The chief assessor has written a guidance document to assist students with written answers. With the permission of AAT the full text of this document, updated by Kaplan to 2013/14, is included as an Appendix. Some of the key points from the advice are set out below.

Firstly, it's important you understand that the software in which you are answering the task is not Microsoft Word. So there's no:

- spell checker

- grammar checker

- automatic correcting of typos.

You **must** proofread what you've written and correct any obvious spelling and grammatical errors.

There's often a mark for presentation of the answer, and the assessor is looking for whether the way you've presented your work would be acceptable in the workplace. This mark is independent of the technical answer, and what we look for is whether a client would find the answer acceptable from a visual perspective.

Before you start to type:

You must read the question in detail. We've noticed that students often scan read a question, decide what it's about in an instant and then write the answer without giving any thought or consideration to the details. You should:

- read through once to get the general feel of the question

- read through again, slower this time, concentrating on key words or phrases

- plan your answer, ensuring all key areas are covered

- decide the structure of your answer, considering where you'll use things like an email, a memo or bullet points

- type up your answer

- proof read your answer, correcting any errors.

Too many times it would seem that students only follow the fifth of these points. If you do this it **will** affect your marks.

Consider exactly who you're writing to. Most likely it will be a client, so this needs to influence your approach.

Remember, if the client is writing to you for advice, they don't know the answer. We often see students give half answers which the assessor will understand, but which a client would not. As a result, they lose marks.

Similarly, be sure to avoid:

- abbreviations

- technical jargon

- SMS/text message speak.

1.3   Penalties for incorrect tax returns

If the taxpayer files an incorrect tax return, a penalty equal to a percentage of the tax under declared may be charged. The penalty may be waived for inadvertent errors, as long as the taxpayer notifies HMRC of the error as soon as possible.

The percentage depends on the reason for the error.

Taxpayer behaviour	Maximum penalty % of tax lost
Mistake	No penalty
Failure to take reasonable care	30%
Deliberate understatement	70%
Deliberate understatement with concealment	100%

The penalties may be reduced at HMRC discretion where the taxpayer discloses information to HMRC. The reduction depends on the circumstances of the penalty and whether the taxpayer discloses the information before HMRC discover the error (unprompted disclosure) or afterwards (prompted disclosure).

	Minimum penalties	
Taxpayer behaviour	Unprompted disclosure % of tax lost	Prompted disclosure % of tax lost
Failure to take reasonable care	Nil	15
Deliberate understatement	20	35
Deliberate understatement with concealment	30	50

Example

State the maximum and minimum penalties that may be levied on each of the following individuals who have submitted incorrect tax returns.

Lars   Deliberately understated his tax liability and attempted to conceal the incorrect information that he had provided. HMRC have identified the understatement and Lars is helping them with their enquiries.

Sven   Accidentally provided an incorrect figure even though he checked his tax return carefully. He realised his mistake a few days later and notified HMRC.

Jo   Completed his tax return too quickly and made a number of errors. The day after he had submitted the tax return he decided to check it thoroughly and immediately provided HMRC with the information necessary to identify the errors.

Solution

Penalties for incorrect tax returns are a percentage of the under declared tax.

Lars   The maximum percentage for a deliberate understatement with concealment is 100%. The minimum percentage for prompted disclosure of information (where the taxpayer provides information in response to HMRC identifying the error) in respect of deliberate understatement with concealment is 50%.

Sven   No penalty is charged where a taxpayer has been careful and has made a genuine mistake.

Jo   The maximum percentage for failing to take reasonable care is 30%. The minimum percentage for unprompted disclosure is nil.

2 The payment of income tax and capital gains tax

2.1 The instalment system

The submission of information to HMRC, and the penalties relating thereto, should not be confused with the fact that certain individuals will also need to make payments of tax.

In the UK tax system, many individuals pay the majority of their tax by 'deduction at source'.

For example, the most common forms of savings income (bank interest and building society interest) have 20% income tax deducted. Dividend income has a 10% tax credit. Both forms of tax credit cover the tax liability of a basic rate taxpayer.

Also, employees suffer tax at source through the PAYE system.

However, some individuals are subject to an instalment system based upon total liability.

The instalment system operates as follows:

- 31 January *in* the tax year: first payment on account.
- 31 July *following* the tax year: second payment on account.
- 31 January *following* the tax year: final payment.

For example, for the tax year 2013/14 the following dates are relevant:

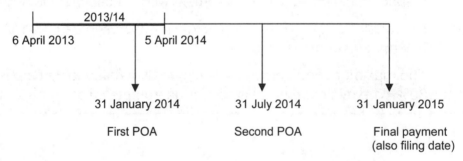

The payments on account are based on the previous year's tax payable (i.e. total income tax liability less tax deducted at source).

The taxpayer can claim to make reduced payments on account where this year's income tax payable is expected to be less than that of last year. The taxpayer will be charged a penalty if the claim to make reduced payments on account was made either fraudulently or negligently.

Example

Roderic is required to pay tax in instalments. His income tax payable for 2012/13 was £5,100.

His tax payable for 2013/14 is £7,629.

What are Roderic's payments in respect of his income tax payable for 2013/14?

Solution

Step 1: Determine the relevant dates.

31 January 2014	–	first payment on account
31 July 2014	–	second payment on account
31 January 2015	–	final payment

Step 2: Determine the amounts due:

- The amounts due for the 'payments on account' are based on an equal division of the previous year's tax payable, hence = £2,550.

- The final payment will be based on the final liability for 2013/14 less the payments on account already made.

	£
2013/14 IT liability	7,629
Payments on account	(5,100)
	———
Final payment	2,529
	———

```
                    2013/14
6 April 2013    |    5 April 2014
                |
                ▼              ▼              ▼
        31 January 2014    31 July 2014    31 January 2015
        First instalment   Second instalment   Final payment
         ½ × £5,100          ½ × £5,100         (balance)
          = £2,550            = £2,550          = £2,529
```

Step 3: Prepare a final summary.

	£	
31 January 2014	2,550	⎫
31 July 2014	2,550	⎬ Payments on account
31 January 2015	2,529	Balancing payment

On 31 January following the end of the tax year the taxpayer must pay the final payment on account for the year just ended, together with the first payment on account for the new tax year.

In Roderic's case this means that on 31 January 2015 he will start the instalment system all over again, by making the first payment on account of his 2014/15 liability based on 2013/14 tax payable.

Hence, his total 31 January 2015 payment is:

$$\frac{£7,629}{2} = £3,814 + £2,529 = £6,343.$$

2.2 No requirement for payments on account

Payments on account are not required in the following circumstances:

- The income tax payable for the previous tax year by self assessment is less than £1,000, or

- More than 80% of the income tax liability for the previous year was met through tax deducted at source.

It is this second exclusion which means that most employed people, even where they are higher rate taxpayers, will not have to make payments on account.

2.3 Capital gains tax

The payments on account system does not apply to capital gains tax (CGT) because, for most individuals, assessable capital gains do not routinely occur annually.

CGT is therefore paid in one instalment on 31 January following the tax year regardless of whether there was a CGT liability for the previous year.

The CGT liability is not taken into account when determining the payments on account for income tax (see Chapter 12).

Example

Brenda's income tax liability for 2013/14 is £31,200. She has tax credits in respect of PAYE and bank interest of £22,800.

Brenda's income tax liability for 2012/13 was £26,100. She had tax credits in that year of £18,700.

What are Brenda's payments in respect of her income tax payable for 2013/14?

Solution

Step 1: Determine the relevant dates.

31 January 2014	–	first payment on account
31 July 2014	–	second payment on account
31 January 2015	–	final payment

Step 2: Determine the amounts due:

- The 'payments on account' are equal to half of the previous year's tax payable of £7,400 (£26,100 – £18,700).

- Each payment on account will therefore be £3,700.

- The final payment will be based on the final liability for 2013/14 less the payments on account already made.

	£
2013/14 IT liability (£31,200 – £22,800)	8,400
Payments on account (£3,700 × 2)	(7,400)
	———
Final payment	1,000
	———

Step 3: Prepare a final summary.

	£	
31 January 2014	3,700	⎫
31 July 2014	3,700	⎬ Payments on account
31 January 2015	1,000	Balancing payment

2.4 Recovery of overpaid tax

A taxpayer who believes that he has paid too much income tax or capital gains tax can submit a claim in order to have the excess tax repaid. The claim must be submitted within 4 years of the end of the relevant tax year.

3 Interest and penalties on payments of tax

3.1 Interest

Failure to make payments, whether payments on account (POA) or final payments, by the due date will attract interest. This applies to CGT as well as income tax.

Interest is charged from the day the tax is due until the day before it is paid. The calculation of interest on tax paid late is not within the syllabus.

In addition to the interest charge there is also a penalty where tax is paid late.

3.2 Penalty for late payment of tax

A penalty will be charged where there is income tax or capital gains tax outstanding after the day on which the final payment of tax is due (31 January after the end of the tax year). This penalty is in addition to any interest that is charged.

- More than 30 days late   5% of tax overdue
- More than six months late   further 5% of tax overdue
- More than 12 months late   further 5% of tax overdue

A late payment penalty may be mitigated (i.e. reduced) where the taxpayer can provide a reasonable excuse, for example a serious illness.

Not having enough money to pay, or lack of knowledge of self assessment, are *not* reasonable excuses.

 Example

Cray submitted the final payment in respect of his 2012/13 self assessment return on 30 September 2014.

What penalties will be charged in respect of the late payment of the tax?

Solution

The final payment in respect of the 2012/13 self assessment return was due on 31 January 2014. The payment is more than six months but less than 12 months late.

Because the payment is more than 30 days late there will be a penalty of 5% of the tax outstanding.

Because the payment is more than six months late there will be a further penalty of 5% of the tax outstanding.

4 HM Revenue and Customs enquiries

4.1 Time limit

HMRC can enquire into an individual's tax return under their compliance check powers.

They have to issue a written notice to initiate an enquiry and they cannot issue a notice more than 12 months after the date the return was submitted by the taxpayer to HMRC.

HMRC may choose a return for enquiry if they suspect that it is incomplete or inaccurate in some respect or it may be selected at random. Their own internal instructions forbid an officer from giving any reason for the enquiry.

4.2 Enquiry procedure

Once the enquiry notice is given HMRC can request relevant documents and written particulars. This means HMRC is entitled to full answers to any specific questions.

At the end of the enquiry a completion notice is issued stating the outcome of the enquiry (for example, no amendment made or tax liability increased by £10,000!).

If HMRC issue an amended assessment on completion, the taxpayer has 30 days from completion to appeal to the Tribunal against HMRC's amendment.

4.3 Discovery assessments

Although HMRC usually only have 12 months from the date a return is filed to open an enquiry, they can replace a self assessment at a later date by making a discovery assessment.

A discovery assessment can be made where tax has been lost (i.e. under self assessed) even though there has been no careless or deliberate behaviour on the part of the taxpayer or his agent.

This usually means that there was insufficient information in the tax return or contentious items in the tax return had not been brought to HMRC's attention for them to choose to open an enquiry within the time limit.

The taxpayer can appeal to the Tribunal against a discovery assessment.

4.4   Appeals procedure

The taxpayer can request an informal review of the disputed decision.

Formal appeals are made to the Tax Tribunal.

Appeals from the Tax Tribunal on a point of law (but not on a point of fact) may be made to the Court of Appeal and from there to the Supreme Court.

The Tribunal is independent of HMRC.

Activity 2

Mark the following statements as true or false.

		True	False
1	Paper tax returns must normally be filed by 31 December.		
2	If a taxpayer files their 2013/14 return on 16 February 2015, they will be charged a late filing penalty of £300.		
3	Payments on account are not required for capital gains tax.		
4	Fred pays his balancing payment of £1,250 for 2013/14 on 15 October 2015. HMRC will charge a penalty of £62.50.		

---

5   Summary

Most income tax is collected at source either through PAYE or by deduction on interest and dividend income.

If collection at source has not resulted in the payment of the correct final liability – e.g. where a higher rate taxpayer has savings/dividend income – the deficit is collected by 'self assessment'.

Payment dates

31 January – Final payment of IT due for tax year to previous 5 April.

– CGT due for disposals in tax year to previous 5 April.

– First POA for current tax year (based on previous year's payable).

31 July – Second POA for current tax year.

Filing returns (2013/14 return)

Paper return   –   31 October 2014

Electronic return   –   31 January 2015 (the 'filing date')

Main penalties

Miss the filing date (i.e. 31 January)   –   £100 penalty

Tax unpaid by 30 days after 31 January –   5% penalty

Incorrect return   –   penalties ranging from 0 to 100% of tax underpaid

If no enquiry notice issued by anniversary of the submission date, taxpayer can assume that his tax liabilities are agreed.

However, if HMRC are able to show they had insufficient information supplied in the tax return, they can make a 'discovery' assessment at a later date.

6 Test your knowledge

Workbook Activity 3

Megan

Megan's income tax payable for 2013/14 is £6,487.12

Income tax payments on account for 2013/14 are £2,097 each, based on 2012/13 liabilities.

Required:

State the amounts and due dates of all payments using the above information.

Workbook Activity 4

Lewis

Lewis submitted his 2013/14 self assessment return on 31 March 2015 and made a final payment of the tax outstanding for the year of £2,000 on that date.

Mark the following statements about Lewis as true or false.

		True	False
1	Lewis will be charged a penalty of £100 for late filing.		
2	Lewis will be charged a 10% late payment penalty.		
3	No interest is payable by Lewis if he has to pay a late payment penalty.		

Workbook Activity 5

Enquiries

HM Revenue and Customs must give written notice before starting an enquiry into a self assessment personal tax return.

Required:

(a) State the date by which the written notice must normally be given.

(b) State the main reasons for the commencement of an enquiry.

(c) Explain the choices available to a taxpayer who is notified of an additional tax liability as a result of an enquiry.

 Workbook Activity 6

Income tax self assessment

You are required to state:

(a) The latest date by which paper income tax returns for the year 2013/14 should be returned to HM Revenue and Customs.

(b) The date by which on-line (electronic) income tax returns for the year 2013/14 should be submitted.

(c) The penalties for the late submission of income tax returns and when they apply.

 Workbook Activity 7

Ruby Chan (1)

Ruby Chan has been self-employed for many years. Her income tax liability for 2013/14 is £17,042. Ruby has tax credits in respect of building society interest of £800.

In 2012/13, Ruby's income tax liability was £10,320. She had tax credits in that year of £520.

Required:

Calculate Ruby's payments on account and balancing payment in respect of her 2013/14 income tax liability and her payments on account for 2014/15. Your answer should include the relevant due dates.

Workbook Activity 8

Ruby Chan (2)

Ruby Chan (see the previous activity) did not file her 2013/14 tax return until 31 May 2015.

Required:

Write to Ruby and advise her of the consequences of:

(i)   not filing her tax return for 2013/14 until 31 May 2015.

(ii)   not making the balancing payment for 2013/14 until 31 May 2015.

 Workbook Activity 9

Self assessment

State:

(i)   the normal dates for payment of income tax in respect of the tax year 2013/14 and

(ii)   how the amounts of these payments are arrived at.

Introduction to capital gains tax

12

Introduction

In the assessment there will be a number of tasks covering various aspects of capital gains tax (CGT).

This chapter determines when we need to perform a CGT computation and how to calculate the CGT payable.

The following chapters will describe how to calculate chargeable gains.

KNOWLEDGE
Explain the main current legislation relating to personal taxation (1.1 K)
Identify the main features of the capital gains tax system (4.1 K)
Describe chargeable and exempt assets (4.2 K)
Describe the process for relief of current year allowable losses, and for losses unrelieved in the current year (4.3 K)
Identify the current annual exempt amount and describe the effect of this on an individual's capital gains tax liability (4.4 K)

SKILLS
Identify and value chargeable personal assets and shares that have been disposed of (4.5 S)
Apply reliefs and exemptions (4.7 S)
Calculate capital gains tax payable (4.8 S)
Make computations and submissions in accordance with current tax law (5.1 S)

CONTENTS

1   Capital gains tax computation
2   Chargeable disposal
3   Chargeable person
4   Chargeable asset
5   Calculating CGT

1 Capital gains tax computation

1.1 The three essential elements

A capital gains tax (CGT) computation is only required if there is a:

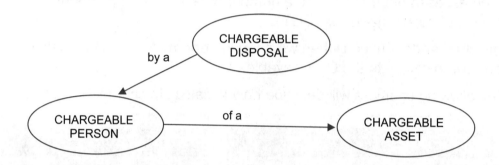

2 Chargeable disposal

2.1 Disposals

A chargeable disposal includes:

- a sale of an asset (whole or part of an asset),

- a gift of an asset,

- an exchange of an asset,

- the loss or destruction of an asset.

Where a gift is made the sale proceeds are deemed to be its market value.

Where an asset is lost or destroyed the sale proceeds are likely to be nil or insurance proceeds.

2.2 Exempt disposals

The following occasions are exempt disposals and so no CGT computation is required:

- Disposals on the death of a taxpayer.

- Gifts of assets to charities.

3 Chargeable person

3.1 Chargeable person

A chargeable person is:

- an individual; or
- a company (only dealt with in the Business Tax paper).

3.2 Exempt persons

Charities do not pay capital gains tax on their disposals.

4 Chargeable asset

4.1 Exempt assets

All assets are chargeable unless they are in the list of exempt assets.

The main types of exempt asset are listed below.

Those most likely to be in an assessment are marked *.

(a) *Principal private residences (see Chapter 13).

(b) Gilts and qualifying corporate bonds (e.g. Treasury stock and debentures).

(c) *Wasting chattels – a wasting asset is one with an expected life of not more than 50 years, a chattel is tangible moveable property (e.g. a racehorse) (see Chapter 13). All animals in the assessment are wasting chattels.

(d) *Other chattels sold at a gain where the consideration is £6,000 or less (see Chapter 13). (e.g. an antique costing £4,000 sold for £4,500)

(e) *Private motor cars, including vintage and veteran cars.

(f) National Savings Certificates, Premium Bonds and SAYE certificates.

(g) Shares held in an ISA (individual savings account).

(h) Cash, legal tender in the UK.

(i) Foreign currency bank accounts.

(j) Medals awarded for valour, unless acquired by purchase.

(k)   Betting and lottery winnings.

(l)   Compensation or damages for any wrong or injury suffered by an individual in his person or in his profession or vocation.

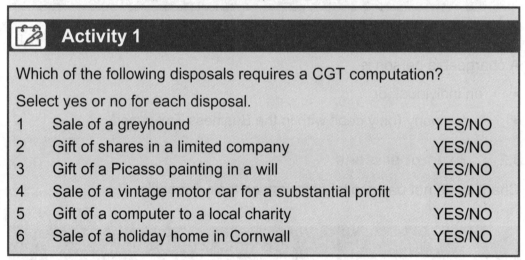

Activity 1

Which of the following disposals requires a CGT computation?

Select yes or no for each disposal.

1	Sale of a greyhound	YES/NO
2	Gift of shares in a limited company	YES/NO
3	Gift of a Picasso painting in a will	YES/NO
4	Sale of a vintage motor car for a substantial profit	YES/NO
5	Gift of a computer to a local charity	YES/NO
6	Sale of a holiday home in Cornwall	YES/NO

5 Calculating CGT

5.1   Introduction

Capital gains tax (like income tax) is calculated for the tax year.

For each individual we must undertake the following steps.

Step 1 (Chapters 13 and 14)

Calculate the gains or losses on disposals of individual assets for 2013/14 (i.e. disposals between 6 April 2013 and 5 April 2014).

For example, if four chargeable assets are disposed of, four calculations of gains or losses must be made.

Step 2

Bring together all gains and losses of the tax year and deduct the annual exempt amount to determine the taxable gains.

Step 3

Calculate the capital gains tax payable.

5.2   The annual exempt amount

An individual has an annual exempt amount which is applied to net chargeable gains after deduction of capital losses. The annual exempt amount for 2013/14 is £10,900.

The annual exempt amount can only be relieved against chargeable gains of the current tax year. Any unused amount cannot be offset against taxable income or carried forward or back.

5.3 Calculation of taxable gains

The proforma shows how chargeable gains and capital losses are brought together to calculate taxable gains.

The calculation of individual gains and losses is covered in the next chapter.

	£
Chargeable gains for the year	X
Less: Current year capital losses	(X)
Net chargeable gains for the year	X
Less: Capital losses brought forward	(X)
Net chargeable gains	X
Less: Annual exempt amount	(10,900)
Taxable gains	X

The treatment of capital losses is explained below.

 Activity 2

Manuel made chargeable gains and allowable losses for 2013/14 as set out below:

Gain of £60,000

Gain of £12,000

Capital loss of £4,000

Required:

Calculate Manuel's taxable gains for 2013/14.

A £57,100

B £61,100

C £68,000

D £72,000

5.4   Treatment of capital losses

There is a difference in the treatment of current year capital losses and brought forward capital losses.

Current year capital losses are automatically deducted from the chargeable gains of the year. Where there are net capital losses for the year, they will be carried forward for relief in the future.

Capital losses brought forward are automatically deducted from the net chargeable gains for the year.

However, the maximum amount of brought forward losses that will be offset is restricted to the amount required to reduce the net chargeable gains to the level of the annual exempt amount.

Accordingly, brought forward losses are not used to the extent that this would lead to wastage of the annual exempt amount.

Finally, a capital loss arising on a disposal to a connected person (Chapter 13) can only be used against a gain on a disposal to that same connected person.

⦿ Example

Mica has the following chargeable gains and losses for the two years ended 5 April 2014.

	2012/13	2013/14
	£	£
Gains	12,500	13,300
Losses	(14,000)	(2,000)

What gains (if any) are chargeable after considering all reliefs and exemptions?

KAPLAN PUBLISHING

Solution

	2012/13 £	2013/14 £
Current gains	12,500	13,300
Current losses	(12,500)	(2,000)
		11,300
Brought forward losses*		(400)
	Nil	10,900
Annual exempt amount	Wasted	(10,900)
		Nil
Loss carried forward		
(£14,000 – £12,500)	1,500	
(£1,500 – £400)		1,100

*Utilised to reduce gains to annual exempt amount.

Activity 3

Gabi has the following chargeable gains and losses for the two years ended 5 April 2014.

	2012/13 £	2013/14 £
Gains	15,000	16,300
Losses	(17,000)	(4,000)

1   What are the losses carried forward (if any) at the end of 2012/13?

   A   £Nil

   B   £2,000

   C   £12,900

   D   £17,000

2   What are the losses carried forward (if any) at the end of 2013/14?

   A   £21,000

   B   £11,500

   C   £600

   D   £Nil

5.5   Calculation of CGT payable

Taxable gains are treated as an additional amount of income in order to determine the rates of CGT. However, the gains must not be included in the income tax computation.

Where the taxable gains fall within any remaining basic rate band they are taxed at 18%.

The balance of the taxable gains is taxed at 28%.

 Example

Basil has taxable gains of £14,600 in 2013/14. His taxable income for the year, after deducting the personal allowance, is £31,000.

Calculate Basil's capital gains tax liability for 2013/14.

Solution

	£
£1,010 (£32,010 – £31,000) × 18%	181.80
£13,590 (£14,600 – £1,010) × 28%	3,805.20
Capital gains tax liability	3,987.00

5.6   Payment of CGT

- CGT is payable by 31 January following the end of the tax year (31 January 2015 for 2013/14).

- There are no instalment payments for CGT.

- Interest and late payment penalties apply to late paid CGT (Chapter 11).

6 Summary

6.1 Essential elements

There are three essential elements for CGT to apply:

- Chargeable disposal, by a
- Chargeable person, of a
- Chargeable asset.

6.2 Order of calculation

To calculate CGT for the tax year:

Step 1 Calculate individual gains and losses.

Step 2 Calculate the CGT payable.

7 Test your knowledge

 Workbook Activity 4

Which of the following transactions carried out by an individual may give rise to a chargeable gain? Select yes or no for each disposal.

1	Sale of shares	YES/NO
2	Sale of a motor car	YES/NO
3	Gift of a holiday home	YES/NO
4	Sale of an antique (which cost £4,000) for £5,000	YES/NO
5	Gift of an antique (which cost £4,000) when it was valued at £15,000.	YES/NO

 Workbook Activity 5

Read the following statements and state whether they are true or false.

1 Capital losses are deducted before the annual exempt amount.

2 Excess capital losses can be offset against taxable income.

3 Any available capital losses must always be relieved in full.

4 Capital gains are taxed at 40% for higher rate taxpayers.

Workbook Activity 6

1   Mary made a capital loss of £4,000 in 2012/13. In 2013/14 she made a chargeable gain of £12,500 and a capital loss of £3,000.

How much capital loss is carried forward at the end of 2013/14?

A   £Nil

B   £4,000

C   £5,400

D   £7,000

2   What would your answer be if Mary had only made the chargeable gain of £12,500 in 2013/14 and not the capital loss?

A   £Nil

B   £1,600

C   £2,400

D   £4,000

 Workbook Activity 7

Carl sold three assets in 2013/14 and made two chargeable gains of £9,900 and £11,400 and a capital loss of £2,500. Carl has capital losses brought forward as at 6 April 2013 of £3,400.

Required:

What are Carl's taxable gains for 2013/14?

A   £4,500

B   £18,800

C   £15,400

D   £7,900

Workbook Activity 8

Misha has sold two assets in 2013/14 and made two chargeable gains of £16,800 and £11,400. Her taxable income for the year, after deducting the personal allowance, is £23,900.

Required:

What is Misha's capital gains tax liability for 2013/14?

A   £3,114.00

B   £4,033.00

C   £7,085.00

D   £4,844.00

Calculation of individual gains and losses

Introduction

It is likely that one of the CGT tasks will require a calculation of gains on assets other than shares.

This chapter looks at the standard calculations, followed by some special rules. At least one of the special rules is likely to be included in the exam.

KNOWLEDGE
Explain the main current legislation relating to personal taxation (1.1 K)
Describe chargeable and exempt assets (4.2 K)

SKILLS
Identify and value chargeable personal assets and shares that have been disposed of (4.5 S)
Calculate chargeable gains and allowable losses (4.6 S)
Apply reliefs and exemptions (4.7 S)
Make computations and submissions in accordance with current tax law (5.1 S)

CONTENTS

1   Proforma calculation of gains and losses
2   Special rules
3   Principal private residence exemption

1 Proforma calculation of gains and losses

1.1 Proforma

The following proforma is used to calculate a chargeable gain:

	Notes	£
Gross sale proceeds	(a)	X
Less: Selling costs	(b)	(X)
Net sale proceeds		NSP
Less: Allowable cost	(c)	(X)
Chargeable gain	(d)	X

1.2 Notes to the proforma

(a) Sale proceeds are usually obvious. However, where a transaction is not at arm's length (e.g. a gift) then market value will be substituted.

(b) Selling costs incurred on the disposal of an asset are an allowable deduction. Examples of such costs include valuation fees, advertising costs, legal fees, auctioneer's fees.

(c) The allowable cost of an asset is its purchase price plus any incidental purchase costs (for example legal fees) together with any capital expenditure incurred in the future that increases the value of the asset.

   If the asset was received as a gift then its cost = market value at the date of the gift.

   If the asset was inherited on someone's death then the cost = probate value (market value at the date of the death)

(d) The gain after deducting the costs above is known as a chargeable gain.

Activity 1

Paul

On 23 April 2013, Paul sold a property that was not his main residence for £145,000. He had purchased the property on 3 June 2005 for £108,000. The seller incurred fees in June 2005 of £2,000.

Required:

What is the chargeable gain arising on this disposal?

A   Nil

B   £37,000

C   £35,000

D   £26,100

2   Special rules

2.1   Variation on the proforma

There are a number of reasons why the proforma may be varied.

Each of the following is considered in turn:

- Part disposals (2.2 below).

- Chattels (2.3 below).

- Connected persons (2.4 below).

- Husband and wife and civil partners (2.5 below).

2.2   Part disposals

When there is a disposal, it is necessary to match costs with proceeds in order to calculate the gain.

When **part of an asset is disposed of** we need some method of deciding how much of the initial purchase cost relates to the part just disposed of, so that we can calculate a gain.

Example

Graham disposes of part of a field which cost £6,000 as a whole. He sold one corner of the field for £8,000 incurring £200 legal costs. We need to calculate the gain.

```
                          ┌──────────────┐
                          │  Proceeds    │
                          │  £8,000      │
                          │              │
     Cost of entire field │              │
          £6,000          └──────────────┘
```

We know the sale proceeds but not the cost of the part sold.

To calculate the gain it is necessary to **apportion part of the overall cost to the part disposed of.**

This could be done in a number of ways, e.g. based on the area of the land sold.

However, in order to make the calculation standard for all types of disposal, the following proportion of the cost is used for tax purposes:

$$\frac{A}{A+B}$$

where   A = the value of the part sold (if a sale then use sale proceeds **before** deducting selling expenses)

    B = the value of the unsold remainder

Solution

Thus, if the remainder of the land was worth £15,000 then the chargeable gain would be calculated as follows:

	£
Proceeds	8,000
Less: Selling expenses	(200)
Net sale proceeds	7,800
Less: Cost (£6,000) × $\dfrac{£8,000}{£8,000 + £15,000}$	(2,087)
Chargeable gain	5,713

2.3 Chattels

Chattels are tangible, moveable property; for example a picture or a table.

A building is not a chattel as it is not moveable. Similarly, shares are not chattels – a share certificate may be tangible and moveable but the asset of value is the underlying rights conferred by the certificate.

Wasting chattels (expected life not exceeding 50 years) are exempt.

Machinery is always treated as wasting. However, it will only be a wasting chattel if it is moveable.

All animals which appear in the assessment are regarded as wasting chattels.

Non-wasting chattels (expected life of more than 50 years) are likely to be items such as antiques, works of art, jewellery, etc.

The treatment of non-wasting chattels is based on the £6,000 rules.

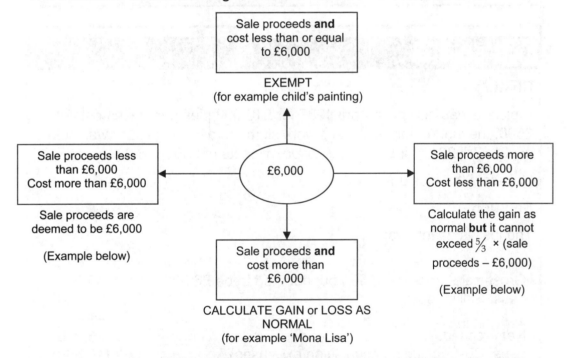

| | Sale proceeds **and** cost less than or equal to £6,000 |
| | EXEMPT (for example child's painting) |

Sale proceeds less than £6,000
Cost more than £6,000

Sale proceeds are deemed to be £6,000

(Example below)

£6,000

Sale proceeds more than £6,000
Cost less than £6,000

Calculate the gain as normal **but** it cannot exceed $\frac{5}{3}$ × (sale proceeds – £6,000)

(Example below)

Sale proceeds **and** cost more than £6,000

CALCULATE GAIN or LOSS AS NORMAL
(for example 'Mona Lisa')

 Example

Chattels 1

Marjory bought two antique tables in March 1989 for £1,000 each. She sold them both in June 2013 for £6,400 and £13,600 respectively.

Calculate the chargeable gains on the disposals.

Solution

	Table A £	Table B £
Proceeds (June 2013)	6,400	13,600
Less: Cost (March 1989)	(1,000)	(1,000)
Chargeable gain	5,400	12,600

The gains calculated above cannot exceed:

	Table A	Table B
5/3 × (£6,400 – £6,000)	667	
5/3 × (£13,600 – £6,000)		12,667
Chargeable gain	667	12,600

💡 Example

Chattels 2

A picture was bought in April 1987 for £10,000 plus purchase costs of £500; the market for the artist's work slumped and the picture was sold on 10 April 2013 for £500, less disposal costs of £50.

Calculate the loss on disposal.

Solution

The loss is as follows:

	£
Gross sale proceeds (£500 but deemed to be £6,000)	6,000
Less: Selling costs	(50)
Net proceeds	5,950
Less: Cost (including acquisition expenses)	(10,500)
Allowable loss	(4,550)

Notice that it is the gross sale proceeds **before** deducting selling costs that are deemed to be £6,000.

Activity 2

Mr Windsor

Mr Windsor has made the following disposals in 2013/14.

(1) A painting was sold in July 2013 for £6,600. He originally bought it in February 1995 for £3,500.

(2) A house which he bought in April 1988 for £5,000 (an investment property) was sold in September 2013 for £75,000. In June 1993 an extension costing £10,000 was built.

(3) He sold a car for £20,000 in June 2013 that had originally cost him £43,000 in June 2004.

(4) He bought a plot of land for £8,000 in August 1997. He sold part of the land for £20,000 in January 2014. At that time the remaining land was worth £60,000.

Required:

Calculate his chargeable gains.

2.4 Connected persons

Where a disposal is between connected persons:

(i) sale proceeds are deemed to be market value (any real sale proceeds are ignored); and

(ii) if a loss arises on a disposal to a connected person it can only be offset against a gain made on a disposal to the **same** connected person.

Connected persons are mainly relatives and their spouses/civil partners or relatives of your spouse/civil partner.

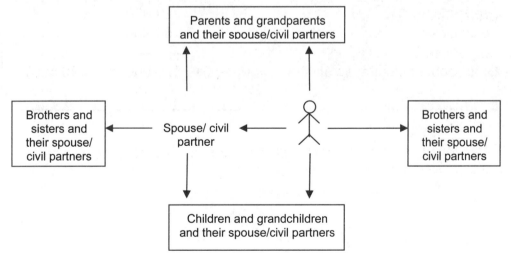

An individual is also connected with a company he controls and a partner is connected with his other business partners.

2.5 Husband and wife and civil partners

Whilst husband and wife are clearly connected persons, the tax treatment of assets disposed of by one to the other is different.

On disposals between husband and wife, sales proceeds are deemed to be equal to the seller's cost such that no gain or loss arises.

This figure is also used for the purchaser's cost when calculating a gain on a future sale by the purchaser.

This treatment also applies to disposals between civil partners.

Example

David purchased some jewellery in August 2003 for £50,000. In June 2012 he gave the jewellery to his wife Victoria when it was worth £200,000. Victoria sold the jewellery in May 2013 for £220,000.

Calculate Victoria's chargeable gain.

Solution

Disposal by David

	£
Deemed proceeds (equal to cost)	50,000
Less: Cost	(50,000)
No gain or loss arises	Nil

Sale by Victoria

	£
Proceeds	220,000
Less: Cost	(50,000)
Chargeable gain	170,000

Activity 3

For each statement below, tick the appropriate treatment.

		Actual proceeds used	Market value used	No gain or loss basis
1	Jamie gives an asset to his sister in law			
2	Husband sells an asset to his wife at market value			
3	Eloise sells an asset on EBay for £8,000 when the market value is £12,000			

3 Principal private residence exemption

3.1 General exemption

Other than business reliefs (which we do not need to consider for the Personal tax paper) the main CGT relief available to individuals is the *principal private residence* (PPR) exemption.

If the owner occupies his PPR throughout his period of ownership, the gain is exempt.

If there have been periods where the owner has not lived in the property, part of the gain may be taxable.

An individual who lives in more than one residence may elect for one of them to be treated as his main residence. This election must be made to HM Revenue and Customs within two years of commencing to live in the second residence.

3.2 Principal private residence relief

Where there has been a period of absence, the procedure is as follows:

(a)   Calculate the gain on the sale of the house.

(b)   Compute the total period of ownership in months.

(c)   Calculate periods of occupation in months.

(d)   PPR exemption = $\dfrac{\text{(c)}}{\text{(b)}} \times$ (a)

The PPR exemption must be given before deducting capital losses.

 Example

Jim bought a house on 1 January 1996. Initially the house remained empty. He started to live in the house on 1 October 2003, and lived in it until he sold it on 30 September 2013.

The gain on disposal before deduction of principal private residence relief was £167,500.

Calculate the chargeable gain after principal private residence relief.

Solution

Step 1: Calculate the gain before relief

Given = £167,500.

Step 2: Identify the total period of ownership and the period the house was occupied (lived in by Jim).

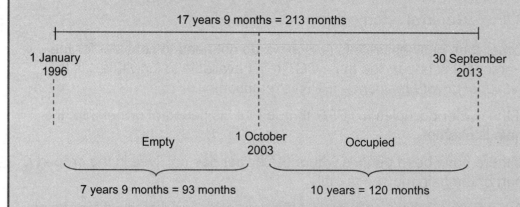

Step 3: Apply the PPR exemption.

		£
Gain before relief		167,500
Less: PPR exemption $\dfrac{120}{213} \times £167,500$		(94,366)
Chargeable gain		73,134

3.3 Periods of deemed occupation

Exemption is also available for the following periods of 'deemed occupation':

(a)   The last three years of ownership.

(b)   Up to three years of absence for any reason.

(c)   Any period spent working abroad.

(d)   Up to four years of absence while working elsewhere in the UK.

To be allowed, the absences in (b), (c) and (d) above must be preceded and followed by a period of actual occupation. No such condition applies to absence under (a) above.

Even for (c) and (d) the condition of actual occupation after a period of absence is relaxed where an employer requires the owner to work elsewhere immediately, thus making it impossible to resume occupation.

 Example

Arthur bought a house on 1 January 1995 and sold it on 30 September 2013 making a gain before deduction of reliefs of £167,500.

During this time:

1 January 1995	– 31 December 1996	Lived in house
1 January 1997	– 30 June 2003	Employed overseas
1 July 2003	– 31 December 2007	Travels the world
1 January 2008	– 30 September 2013	Lived in house

Solution

Step 1: Calculate the gain before relief

Given = £167,500.

Step 2: Identify:

*   **Period of ownership.**

*   **Periods of actual occupation.**

*   **Periods of deemed occupation (remember preceded and followed by actual occupation).**

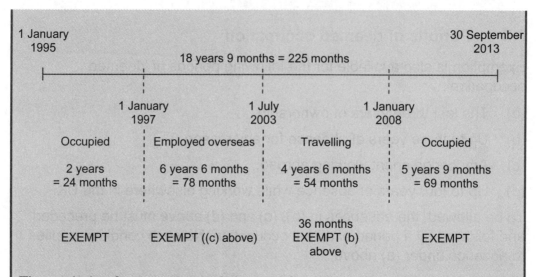

The periods of occupation before and after deemed occupation do **not** need to be **immediately** before and after (for example the employment overseas ended on 30 June 2003 and is followed by actual occupation which did not start until 1 January 2008).

Step 3: Apply PPR exemption.

			£
Gain before relief			167,500
PPR exemption			
	Months		
Occupied	24		
Employed overseas	78		
Any reason	36		
Occupied	69		
	———		
	207	out of 225	
	———		

$$\frac{207}{225} \times £167,500 \qquad\qquad (154,100)$$

| Chargeable gain | | | 13,400 |

Activity 4

Mr Rialto

Mr Rialto sold a house in London on 31 August 2013 and realised a gain of £144,000.

He purchased the house on 1 July 2001. He lived in the house until 31 October 2004 when he moved to Scotland for the purposes of his employment. He returned to the house on 1 January 2006.

On 1 July 2008 he left the house in order to travel around South America. He did not return to the house prior to its sale.

Required:

Calculate Mr Rialto's chargeable gain on the sale of the house.

4 Summary

In this chapter we have considered the proforma calculation of the chargeable gain for an individual asset.

	£
Sale proceeds	X
Less: Allowable cost	(X)
Chargeable gain	X

Additionally there are situations where the calculation should be varied slightly.

For part disposals, the cost must be apportioned on the basis of the formula: A / (A+B).

For chattel disposals special rules may apply depending on whether the asset is wasting and whether the cost or proceeds are less than £6,000.

For connected persons market value must be used for disposal proceeds and there are restrictions on the loss relief available.

If a taxpayer has only one house at any one time and occupies it throughout, the gain is fully exempt. Certain periods of non-occupation can still be deemed to be occupation.

5 Test your knowledge

Workbook Activity 5

Alfie bought a chargeable asset in August 2010 for £120,000. He spent £25,000 on improving the asset in February 2012. He sold the asset for £170,000 in February 2013.

The gain on this asset is:

Workbook Activity 6

Lisa bought a chargeable asset in November 2002 for £32,500, selling it in October 2013 for £56,250. She paid auctioneers commission of 2% when she bought the asset and 6% when she sold the asset.

The gain on this asset is:

Workbook Activity 7

Read the following statements and state whether they are true or false.

1 Brian sold a quarter of a plot of land. A quarter of the original cost should be deducted when calculating the chargeable gain.

2 Advertising costs are not an allowable deduction as they are revenue expenses.

3 Market value should be substituted for disposal proceeds when an asset is gifted to someone other than the spouse.

4 If Sally bought a picture for £8,000 and sold it for £3,000 her allowable loss will be £2,000.

Workbook Activity 8

Match the following statements to the correct asset details. All of the assets are chattels and none have a life of less than 50 years.

Match these statements below with the assets disposed of.

Asset	Sale proceeds	Cost	Statement
1	£8,000	£4,000	
2	£14,000	£20,000	
3	£16,000	£7,000	
4	£4,000	£9,000	
5	£3,000	£2,000	

Statements:

Exempt asset

Calculate gain as normal

Calculate loss as normal

Sale proceeds to be £6,000

Gain restricted to 5/3 rule

 Workbook Activity 9

Whahid bought 20 acres of land on 3 May 2001 for £28,000. On 12 December 2013 he sold 10 acres for £45,000. The market value of the remaining land at that time was £15,000.

What is the chargeable gain arising on the disposal of the land in December 2013?

A £31,000

B £13,100

C £24,000

D £32,000

Workbook Activity 10

Lionel disposes of a house which he had owned for 20 years making a gain of £200,000.

What would be the chargeable gain assuming:

1   he had always lived in the house,

2   he had never lived in the house,

3   he had lived in the house for three years, moved away for 8 years whilst he was working elsewhere in the UK, and then lived in it for the final 9 years of ownership?

 Workbook Activity 11

Mitch bought a house on 1 July 2003 for £100,000.

He lived in the house until 30 June 2009 when he decided to travel the world. The house remained empty until he sold it on 30 September 2013 for £170,000. The house was Mitch's only property.

Which periods are treated as occupied and which are not?

Occupation	Non-occupation

Shares and securities

Introduction

As part of the assessment you will be required to calculate a gain on the disposal of some shares.

There are special rules applying to share disposals as it is necessary to determine which particular shares have been sold.

KNOWLEDGE
Explain the main current legislation relating to personal taxation (1.1 K)

SKILLS
Identify and value chargeable personal assets and shares that have been disposed of (4.5 S)
Calculate chargeable gains and allowable losses (4.6 S)
Make computations and submissions in accordance with current tax law (5.1 S)

CONTENTS

1   The matching rules
2   Same day and next 30 days
3   Share pool
4   Bonus issues and rights issues
5   Approach to assessment questions

1 The matching rules

What distinguishes a share disposal from other asset disposals is the need for matching rules.

The main reason why matching rules are needed is because the same type of shares in a company may be bought at different times and at different prices.

Hence, if only some of the shares are sold we need to know which they are in order to identify their cost.

The matching rules for companies making disposals are different to those for individuals and are covered in Business Tax.

In relation to individuals, we match shares disposed of in the following order:

- first, with shares acquired on the same day as the disposal

- second, with shares acquired within the following 30 days (using the earliest acquisition first, i.e. on a FIFO basis)

- third, with the share pool (all the shares bought by the individual before the date of disposal)

Example

Frederic had the following transactions in the shares of DEF plc, a quoted company.

1 June 1991	Bought	4,000 shares for	£8,000
30 July 1998	Bought	1,800 shares for	£9,750
20 May 2006	Bought	1,000 shares for	£8,500
15 March 2014	Sold	3,500 shares for	£36,000
20 March 2014	Bought	400 shares for	£3,900

You are required to match the shares sold with the relevant acquisitions.

Solution

	Number	Number
Shares sold		3,500
(1) Shares acquired on same day		Nil
(2) Shares acquired in following 30 days		(400)
		3,100
(3) Share pool		
1 June 1991	4,000	
30 July 1998	1,800	
20 May 2006	1,000	
	6,800	
The disposal from the pool is therefore 3,100 out of 6,800		(3,100)
		Nil

Activity 1

Petra sold 200 shares in Red plc on 13 December 2013. She had acquired her shares in the company as follows:

	Number of shares
1 January 2004	650
14 February 2005	250
5 January 2014	50

In accordance with the share matching / identification rules the 200 shares sold by Petra are correctly identified as follows:

A   The 50 shares acquired on 5 January 2014 and then 150 of the remaining 900 shares in the pool.

B   The 50 shares acquired on 5 January 2014 and then 150 of the shares acquired on 14 February 2005.

C   200 of the shares acquired on 1 January 2004.

D   200 shares in the share pool which includes all 950 shares acquired.

Once the correct acquisition is identified, then the computation of the gains can be carried out. This is looked at in detail over the next few sections.

2 Same day and next 30 days

2.1 Calculation of the gain

The calculation of the gain on disposal is straightforward.

	£
Sale proceeds or market value	X
Less: Allowable cost	(X)
Chargeable gain	X

Example

Using the example details above (Frederic) calculate the gain on the sale of the shares acquired in the 30 days following the sale.

Solution

This consists of the sale of 400 shares.

Sale proceeds of £36,000 relates to 3,500 shares so must be apportioned. The proceeds relating to 400 shares will be:

$$\frac{400}{3,500} \times £36,000 = £4,114$$

	£
Sale proceeds	4,114
Cost	(3,900)
Chargeable gain	214

The balance of the proceeds (£36,000 − £4,114 = £31,886) will be applied to shares sold from the share pool.

3 Share pool

3.1 Calculation of the pooled cost

The share pool consists of all shares in a particular company purchased before the date of disposal. It is used to calculate the cost of shares sold by reference to the average cost of all shares purchased.

The pool is set up with two columns; number (of shares) and cost. Shares purchased are added to the pool and shares sold are deducted.

- For a purchase, add the number of shares acquired to the number column and the cost to the cost column.

- For a sale, deduct the number of shares sold from the number column and an appropriate proportion of the cost from the cost column.

Example

Using the example details above (Frederic), calculate the cost to be eliminated from the pool.

Solution

Share pool

	Number	Cost £
June 1991 purchase	4,000	8,000
July 1998 purchase	1,800	9,750
20 May 2006 purchase	1,000	8,500
	6,800	26,250
March 2014 disposal 3,100 out of 6,800 (Note 1)	(3,100)	(11,967)
Pool balance carried forward	3,700	14,283

Note:

(1) To calculate the amount to eliminate on disposal, multiply the total cost by $\dfrac{\text{Number of shares sold}}{\text{Total shares in pool}}$

3.2 Calculation of the gain on the share pool

The gain is calculated as normal:

	£
Sale proceeds	X
Less: Allowable cost	(X)
Chargeable gain	X

 Example

Using the details from the example Frederic, what is the gain on the share pool disposals?

Solution

Sale proceeds are £31,886 (from Frederic example above).

	£
Sale proceeds	31,886
Less: Allowable cost (above)	(11,967)
Chargeable gain on share pool shares	19,919

Hence, the total chargeable gain on disposal of the 3,500 shares = (£214 + £19,919) = £20,133

Activity 2

Ken has carried out the following transactions in shares in CYZ plc.

	Number	Cost £
Purchase (8 February 1997)	1,800	3,100
Purchase (12 September 2006)	1,200	4,400
Purchase (10 October 2013)	400	6,000
	Number	Proceeds
Sale (10 October 2013)	2,000	33,000

Required:

What is the chargeable gain?

4 Bonus issues and rights issues

4.1 Principles of bonus issues and rights issues

A bonus issue is the distribution of free shares to existing shareholders based on existing shareholdings.

The number of shares acquired is added to the number column but there is no cost to add to the cost column.

A rights issue involves shareholders acquiring new shares in proportion to their existing shareholdings. The shares are not free but are usually priced at a rate below the market price.

The number of shares acquired is added to the number column and the cost to the cost column. Accordingly, a rights issue is no different from any other purchase of shares.

 Example

Alma acquired shares in S plc, a quoted company, as follows.

2,000 shares acquired in June 1992 for £11,500.

In October 2002 there was a 1 for 2 bonus issue.

In December 2004 there was a 1 for 4 rights issue at £3 per share.

Alma sold 1,350 shares in November 2013 for £30,000.

What is the chargeable gain?

Solution

	£
Sale proceeds	30,000
Less: Cost (W)	(4,950)
	———
Chargeable gain	25,050
	———

Working: Share pool

	Number	Cost £
June 1992 purchase	2,000	11,500
October 2002 bonus issue (1 for 2)		
No cost so simply add in new shares	1,000	–
	3,000	11,500
December 2004 rights issue (1 for 4) (£3 × 750)	750	2,250
	3,750	13,750
November 2013 disposal $\dfrac{1,350}{3,750} \times £13,750$	(1,350)	(4,950)
Pool carried forward	2,400	8,800

 Activity 3

Mr Jones

In October 2013 Mr Jones sold 3,000 shares in Smith plc for £36,000. He had purchased 4,200 shares in June 1990 for £11,600. In August 2004 there was a 1 for 3 rights issue at £5.60 per share.

Required:

Calculate the chargeable gain on disposal.

5 Approach to assessment questions

In the assessment you will normally be asked to calculate a gain on shares. If so, this question will be manually marked. Hence it is important that you enter your answer into the table supplied correctly and show your workings.

In the specimen assessment a four column table is supplied. The first column is for description and narrative whilst the three other columns are for numerical entry.

This should allow you to enter your answer in the same layout as used throughout this chapter although with a little less detail. For example, you do not need to include lines marking totals and subtotals.

 Example

Jason bought 1,000 shares in VZ plc for £4.20 each in December 2003.

In July 2012 he received a 1 for 5 rights issue at £6.52 each.

In May 2013 he sold 400 shares for £45,000.

What is the chargeable gain? Your answer should clearly show the balance of shares carried forward. Show all workings.

Solution

		£	
Proceeds		45,000	
Less cost (pool)		(1,835)	
Gain		43,165	
Pool		Number	Cost (£)
12.03 Purchase		1,000	4,200
7.12 Rights issue	1,000/5 × £6.52	200	1,304
		1,200	5,504
5.13 Sale	400/1,200 ×	(400)	
	£5,504		(1,835)
Balance c/f		800	3,669

6 Summary

Share disposals require special matching rules.

Shares sold are matched with:

- purchases on the same day

- purchases within the following 30 days

- share pool.

- Bonus issues increase the number of shares held in the pool.

- Rights issues affect both the number of shares held in the pool and the pool cost.

7 Test your knowledge

Workbook Activity 4

Ben bought 1,000 shares in XYZ plc on 1 May 2004 and a further 500 shares on 5 September 2013. He sold 750 shares on 25 August 2013.

Which shares are the shares sold identified with?

A   750 of the shares acquired on 1 May 2004

B   500 of the shares acquired on 1 May 2004 and 250 of the shares acquired on 5 September 2013

C   The 500 shares acquired on 5 September 2013 and then 250 of the remaining 1,000 shares in the pool.

D   750 shares in the share pool which includes 1,500 shares acquired

Workbook Activity 5

Tony bought 15,000 shares in Last Chance Ltd for £6 per share in August 2002. He received a bonus issue of 1 for 15 shares in January 2005.

In November 2013 Tony sold 9,000 shares for £14 per share.

Required:

Calculate the gain made on the sale of the shares and show the balance of shares and their cost to carry forward.

All workings must be shown in your calculations.

Workbook Activity 6

Canrad sold all of his 2,145 ordinary shares in Turnip plc on 19 November 2013 for net sale proceeds of £8,580.

His previous dealings in these shares were as follows:

July 2009 purchased 1,750 shares for £2,625

May 2010 purchased 200 shares for £640

June 2011 took up 1 for 10 rights issue at £3.40 per share

What is the amount of the chargeable gain / allowable loss arising on the disposal?

A   (£6,248) loss

B   £4,652

C   £Nil

D   £5,315

 Workbook Activity 7

David bought 2,000 shares in PQR plc for £4,000 on 6 October 2000 and a further 1,000 shares for £3,000 in March 2006.

PQR plc made a rights issue of 1 new share for every 5 held at £4 per share in February 2008. David sold 400 shares in September 2013 for £7,000.

What is the cost of the shares sold?

A   £800

B   £2,400

C   £5,956

D   £1,044

Capital gains tax summary pages

Introduction

We have seen how to calculate chargeable gains and the exemptions and reliefs which are available.

We now consider how chargeable gains are shown on the tax return.

KNOWLEDGE
Identify the main features of the capital gains tax system (4.1 K)
SKILLS
Record relevant details of gains and the capital gains tax payable in the tax return (5.2 S)
Make computations and submissions in accordance with current tax law (5.1 S)

CONTENTS
1   Capital Gains Tax supplementary pages

1 Capital Gains Tax supplementary pages

1.1 Contents of the pages

There are two capital gains supplementary pages on Form SA108. In the assessment you will only ever be required to complete page 1.

The Form SA108 can be found on the website www.hmrc.gov.uk.

1.2 Completion of the form

This is one of the three supplementary pages that are examinable in this paper. The others are the employment income pages (SA102) and property income pages (SA105). These other pages were dealt with in Chapters 5 and 7 respectively.

The assessment will require one of these forms to be completed. Hence the accurate completion of tax return forms is an important aspect of the assessment.

In the assessment you will be given most of the information to enter into the tax return but you may have to calculate some figures.

The following is important in connection with the completion of forms.

- When completing the form in the exam, figures must be entered in the correct boxes.

- You will normally be asked to complete just one page of any form.

- Commas need not be entered for numbers of four digits or more.

- You do not need to fill in every box, only relevant ones.

1.3 When the form must be completed

If an individual has made chargeable gains which are less than the annual exempt amount, the capital gains summary pages do not need to be completed provided the total proceeds from all disposals are less than four times the annual exempt amount.

Accordingly, for 2013/14 the pages do not need to be completed if gains are less than £10,900 and proceeds less than £43,600.

If there are net capital losses for the year, the pages should be completed so that the losses can be carried forward.

1.4   Page CG1

The top half of the page is used to record gains and losses in the year, losses brought forward and the annual exempt amount for the year.

Summary of gains information:

Box 1   enter taxpayer's name (if given)

Box 3   enter the total gains in the year before losses but after PPR relief

Box 6   enter the total losses in the year

Box 7   enter any losses brought forward and used in the year (remember that brought forward losses do not reduce the net chargeable gains below the annual exempt amount of £10,600)

Box 10   if all losses are not offset in the year, enter the amount of losses remaining to be carried forward to set against future net chargeable gains.

You will not have to complete boxes 2, 4, 5, 8, 9, or 11 to 15.

Summary of information about quoted shares and securities:

Box 16   enter the number of disposals of quoted shares and securities in the year. For these purposes count the disposal of the same class of shares in the same company on the same day as a single disposal.

Box 17   enter the sale proceeds received on the disposals

Box 18   enter the total allowable costs on the disposal of all of the shares

Box 19   enter the chargeable gain made on the disposals before deducting losses.

You will not have to complete boxes 20 and 21.

HM Revenue & Customs

Capital gains summary
Tax year 6 April 2013 to 5 April 2014

1 Your name

2 Your Unique Taxpayer Reference (UTR)

Summary of your enclosed computations

Please read the *Capital gains summary notes* on pages CGN 10 to CGN 13 before filling in this section. **You must enclose your computations, including details of each gain or loss, as well as filling in the boxes.**

3 Total gains *(Boxes 19 + 25 + 31 + 32)*

£ · 0 0

4 Gains qualifying for Entrepreneurs' Relief (but excluding gains deferred from before 23 June 2010) - *read the notes on page CGN 11*

£ · 0 0

5 Gains invested under Seed Enterprise Investment Scheme and qualifying for exemption - *read the notes on page CGN 11 and 12*

£ · 0 0

6 Total losses of the year - *enter '0' if there are none*

£ · 0 0

7 Losses brought forward and used in the year

£ · 0 0

8 Adjustment to Capital Gains Tax - *read the notes*

£ · 0 0

9 Additional liability for non-resident or dual resident trusts

£ · 0 0

10 Losses available to be carried forward to later years

£ · 0 0

11 Losses used against an earlier year's gain (special circumstances apply - *read the notes on page CGN 12)*

£ · 0 0

12 Losses used against income - amount claimed against 2013–14 income - *read the notes on page CGN 13*

£ · 0 0

13 Losses used against income - amount claimed against 2012–13 income - *read the notes on page CGN 13*

£ · 0 0

14 Income losses of 2013–14 set against gains

£ · 0 0

15 Deferred gains from before 23 June 2010 qualifying for Entrepreneurs' Relief

£ · 0 0

Listed shares and securities

16 Number of disposals - *read the notes on page CGN 13*

17 Disposal proceeds

£ · 0 0

18 Allowable costs (including purchase price)

£ · 0 0

19 Gains in the year, before losses

£ · 0 0

20 If you are making any claim or election, put 'X' in the box

21 If your computations include any estimates or valuations, put 'X' in the box

SA108 2013   Page CG 1   HMRC 12/12

Example

From the following information complete page CG1 for Mrs Smith. Capital transactions carried out during 2013/14 were:

1.11.13 ABC plc shares sold for £20,000. Purchased 10.02.02. Chargeable gain £15,000.

12.05.13 Holiday cottage sold for £150,000. Purchased 21.04.09. Chargeable gain £40,000

23.02.14 XYZ Ltd shares sold for £5,000. Purchased 16.01.10. Allowable loss £8,000.

Mrs Smith had capital losses brought forward from 2012/13 of £3,000.

Solution

Note that shares in a 'plc' are likely to be quoted shares. Shares in a 'Ltd' are always unquoted.

HM Revenue & Customs

Capital gains summary
Tax year 6 April 2013 to 5 April 2014

1 Your name

M R S   S M I T H

2 Your Unique Taxpayer Reference (UTR)

Summary of your enclosed computations

Please read the *Capital gains summary notes* on pages CGN 10 to CGN 13 before filling in this section. **You must enclose your computations, including details of each gain or loss, as well as filling in the boxes.**

3 Total gains *(Boxes 19 + 25 + 31 + 32)*

£ 5 5 0 0 0 . 0 0

4 Gains qualifying for Entrepreneurs' Relief (but excluding gains deferred from before 23 June 2010)
- *read the notes on page CGN 11*

£ . 0 0

5 Gains invested under Seed Enterprise Investment Scheme and qualifying for exemption - *read the notes on page CGN 11 and 12*

£ . 0 0

6 Total losses of the year - *enter '0' if there are none*

£ 8 0 0 0 . 0 0

7 Losses brought forward and used in the year

£ 3 0 0 0 . 0 0

8 Adjustment to Capital Gains Tax - *read the notes*

£ . 0 0

9 Additional liability for non-resident or dual resident trusts

£ . 0 0

10 Losses available to be carried forward to later years

£ . 0 0

11 Losses used against an earlier year's gain (special circumstances apply - *read the notes on page CGN 12*)

£ . 0 0

12 Losses used against income - amount claimed against 2013–14 income - *read the notes on page CGN 13*

£ . 0 0

13 Losses used against income - amount claimed against 2012–13 income - *read the notes on page CGN 13*

£ . 0 0

14 Income losses of 2013–14 set against gains

£ . 0 0

15 Deferred gains from before 23 June 2010 qualifying for Entrepreneurs' Relief

£ . 0 0

Listed shares and securities

16 Number of disposals - *read the notes on page CGN 13*

1

17 Disposal proceeds

£ 2 0 0 0 0 . 0 0

18 Allowable costs (including purchase price)

£ 5 0 0 0 . 0 0

19 Gains in the year, before losses

£ 1 5 0 0 0 . 0 0

20 If you are making any claim or election, put 'X' in the box

21 If your computations include any estimates or valuations, put 'X' in the box

SA108 2013   Page CG 1   HMRC 12/12

Activity 1

Mr Bracknell

Mr Bracknell made the following disposals in 2013/14.

(1)   A house which he bought on 11 April 1988 (an investment property) was sold on 10 September 2013 for £275,000. The chargeable gain was £20,000.

(2)   A painting which he bought on 19 May 2008 was sold on 26 June 2013 for £18,500. The chargeable gain was £3,500.

(3)   Shares in LMN plc which he bought on 3 August 2007 were sold on 30 September 2013 for £10,000 at a loss of £8,000.

Capital losses brought forward were £14,000.

Required:

You are required to complete page CG1 of his tax return.

HM Revenue & Customs

Capital gains summary
Tax year 6 April 2013 to 5 April 2014

1 Your name

2 Your Unique Taxpayer Reference (UTR)

Summary of your enclosed computations

Please read the *Capital gains summary notes* on pages CGN 10 to CGN 13 before filling in this section. **You must enclose your computations, including details of each gain or loss, as well as filling in the boxes.**

3 Total gains *(Boxes 19 + 25 + 31 + 32)*

£ · 0 0

4 Gains qualifying for Entrepreneurs' Relief (but excluding gains deferred from before 23 June 2010)
- *read the notes on page CGN 11*

£ · 0 0

5 Gains invested under Seed Enterprise Investment Scheme and qualifying for exemption - *read the notes on page CGN 11 and 12*

£ · 0 0

6 Total losses of the year - *enter '0' if there are none*

£ · 0 0

7 Losses brought forward and used in the year

£ · 0 0

8 Adjustment to Capital Gains Tax - *read the notes*

£ · 0 0

9 Additional liability for non-resident or dual resident trusts

£ · 0 0

10 Losses available to be carried forward to later years

£ · 0 0

11 Losses used against an earlier year's gain (special circumstances apply - *read the notes on page CGN 12*)

£ · 0 0

12 Losses used against income – amount claimed against 2013–14 income – *read the notes on page CGN 13*

£ · 0 0

13 Losses used against income – amount claimed against 2012–13 income – *read the notes on page CGN 13*

£ · 0 0

14 Income losses of 2013–14 set against gains

£ · 0 0

15 Deferred gains from before 23 June 2010 qualifying for Entrepreneurs' Relief

£ · 0 0

Listed shares and securities

16 Number of disposals - *read the notes on page CGN 13*

17 Disposal proceeds

£ · 0 0

18 Allowable costs (including purchase price)

£ · 0 0

19 Gains in the year, before losses

£ · 0 0

20 If you are making any claim or election, put 'X' in the box

21 If your computations include any estimates or valuations, put 'X' in the box

SA108 2013 Page CG 1 HMRC 12/12

2 Summary

The capital gains summary pages summarise the chargeable gains and allowable losses, and calculate the taxable amount or any losses carried forward.

They can be used to help calculate the capital gains tax liability.

3 Test your knowledge

 Workbook Activity 2

Using the following information, complete the tax return below.

Charlotte French made the following disposals of quoted shares in 2013/14.

Shares	Sale proceeds	Cost
	£	£
June disposal	35,000	18,000
December disposal	21,000	15,000
March disposal	13,500	16,500

HM Revenue & Customs

Capital gains summary
Tax year 6 April 2013 to 5 April 2014

1 Your name

2 Your Unique Taxpayer Reference (UTR)

Summary of your enclosed computations

Please read the *Capital gains summary notes* on pages CGN 10 to CGN 13 before filling in this section. **You must enclose your computations, including details of each gain or loss, as well as filling in the boxes.**

3 Total gains *(Boxes 19 + 25 + 31 + 32)*
£ • 0 0

4 Gains qualifying for Entrepreneurs' Relief (but excluding gains deferred from before 23 June 2010)
- read the notes on page CGN 11
£ • 0 0

5 Gains invested under Seed Enterprise Investment Scheme and qualifying for exemption - *read the notes on page CGN 11 and 12*
£ • 0 0

6 Total losses of the year - *enter '0' if there are none*
£ • 0 0

7 Losses brought forward and used in the year
£ • 0 0

8 Adjustment to Capital Gains Tax - *read the notes*
£ • 0 0

9 Additional liability for non-resident or dual resident trusts
£ • 0 0

10 Losses available to be carried forward to later years
£ • 0 0

11 Losses used against an earlier year's gain (special circumstances apply - *read the notes on page CGN 12*)
£ • 0 0

12 Losses used against income - amount claimed against 2013–14 income - *read the notes on page CGN 13*
£ • 0 0

13 Losses used against income - amount claimed against 2012–13 income - *read the notes on page CGN 13*
£ • 0 0

14 Income losses of 2013–14 set against gains
£ • 0 0

15 Deferred gains from before 23 June 2010 qualifying for Entrepreneurs' Relief
£ • 0 0

Listed shares and securities

16 Number of disposals - *read the notes on page CGN 13*

17 Disposal proceeds
£ • 0 0

18 Allowable costs (including purchase price)
£ • 0 0

19 Gains in the year, before losses
£ • 0 0

20 If you are making any claim or election, put 'X' in the box

21 If your computations include any estimates or valuations, put 'X' in the box

SA108 2013　　　　Page CG 1　　　　HMRC 12/12

Workbook Activity 3

Mrs England

Mrs England made the following disposals in 2013/14.

1   Shares in J&C Plc which she bought on 31 January 2008 were sold on 23 April 2013 for £35,500. The chargeable gain was £15,500.

2   An antique necklace which she bought on 12 July 1990 was sold on 5 June 2013 for £67,000. The chargeable gain was £23,000.

3   Shares in Organigro Ltd which she bought on 20 September 2006 were sold on 30 January 2014 for £12,000 at a loss of £9,000.

Capital losses brought forward were £11,000.

Required:

You are required to complete page CG1 of her tax return.

HM Revenue & Customs

Capital gains summary
Tax year 6 April 2013 to 5 April 2014

1 Your name

2 Your Unique Taxpayer Reference (UTR)

Summary of your enclosed computations

Please read the *Capital gains summary notes* on pages CGN 10 to CGN 13 before filling in this section. **You must enclose your computations, including details of each gain or loss, as well as filling in the boxes.**

3 Total gains *(Boxes 19 + 25 + 31 + 32)*

£   · 0 0

4 Gains qualifying for Entrepreneurs' Relief (but excluding gains deferred from before 23 June 2010)
- *read the notes on page CGN 11*

£   · 0 0

5 Gains invested under Seed Enterprise Investment Scheme and qualifying for exemption - *read the notes on page CGN 11 and 12*

£   · 0 0

6 Total losses of the year - *enter '0' if there are none*

£   · 0 0

7 Losses brought forward and used in the year

£   · 0 0

8 Adjustment to Capital Gains Tax - *read the notes*

£   · 0 0

9 Additional liability for non-resident or dual resident trusts

£   · 0 0

10 Losses available to be carried forward to later years

£   · 0 0

11 Losses used against an earlier year's gain (special circumstances apply - *read the notes on page CGN 12*)

£   · 0 0

12 Losses used against income – amount claimed against 2013–14 income - *read the notes on page CGN 13*

£   · 0 0

13 Losses used against income – amount claimed against 2012–13 income - *read the notes on page CGN 13*

£   · 0 0

14 Income losses of 2013–14 set against gains

£   · 0 0

15 Deferred gains from before 23 June 2010 qualifying for Entrepreneurs' Relief

£   · 0 0

Listed shares and securities

16 Number of disposals - *read the notes on page CGN 13*

17 Disposal proceeds

£   · 0 0

18 Allowable costs (including purchase price)

£   · 0 0

19 Gains in the year, before losses

£   · 0 0

20 If you are making any claim or election, put 'X' in the box

21 If your computations include any estimates or valuations, put 'X' in the box

SA108 2013   Page CG 1   HMRC 12/12

Duties and responsibilities of a tax adviser

Introduction

A tax adviser must ensure that he has the best interests of his clients in mind at all times, whilst ensuring that he complies with his legal duties.

KNOWLEDGE	CONTENTS
Describe the duties and responsibilities of a tax practitioner (1.5 K)	1 Duties and responsibilities 2 Confidentiality 3 Ethical issues 4 Money laundering 5 Tax advice and records

1 Duties and responsibilities

1.1 AAT expectations

The AAT expects its members to:

- master skills and techniques through learning and maintain them through continuing professional development.

- adopt an ethical approach to their employers and to clients.

- acknowledge their professional duty to society as a whole.

- maintain an objective outlook.

- provide professional, high standards of service, conduct and performance at all times.

These expectations are discussed in greater depth in the 'Code of Professional Ethics' that can be found on the website (www.aat.co.uk).

A person advising either a company or an individual on taxation issues has duties and responsibilities towards both:

- his client; and

- HM Revenue and Customs.

An adviser owes the greatest duty to his or her client.

2 Confidentiality

2.1 Dealings with third parties

A tax adviser has an overriding duty of confidentiality towards his client. Under normal circumstances a client's tax affairs should not be discussed with third parties. This duty remains even after the adviser no longer works for the client.

The exceptions to this rule mentioned in the Guidelines are where:

- authority has been given by the client; or

- there is a legal, regulatory or professional duty to disclose e.g. in the case of suspected money laundering.

2.2 Dealings with HM Revenue and Customs

The duty of confidentiality also relates to dealings with HMRC.

However, the tax adviser must ensure that, whilst acting in the client's best interests, he must consult with HMRC staff in an open and constructive manner (see below).

3 Ethical issues

3.1 Dealing with problems

In spite of guidelines being available, there can be situations where the method of resolving an ethical issue is not straightforward.

In those situations additional advice should be sought from:

- a supervisor,
- a professional body, or
- a legal adviser.

3.2 Tax avoidance and tax evasion

Tax avoidance is the use of legitimate means in order to reduce a tax liability. It is acceptable to advise a client on ways in which their tax liabilities may be reduced.

Tax evasion is unlawful. A taxpayer who dishonestly withholds or falsifies information in order to evade tax may be subject to criminal proceedings or suffer civil penalties.

3.3 Dealing with errors in clients' tax returns

Where a tax adviser realises that an error has been made in a client's or employer's tax return he must recommend that the client informs HMRC.

If the client/employer refuses to do so, the member must not act for them in connection with that return or related matters.

Activity 1

Which of the following statements is not correct?

A   Accountants need to follow the rules of confidentiality even in a social environment.

B   If money laundering is suspected, accountants are allowed to break the rules of confidentiality.

C   Rules of confidentiality towards a client must be followed even after the business relationship has ended.

D   Accountants must follow the rules of confidentiality irrespective of the situation.

 Activity 2

When an accountant is advising a client, to whom does he owe the greatest duty of care?

A   HMRC

B   The professional body to which the accountant belongs

C   The client

D   The public

4 Money laundering

4.1   What is money laundering?

Money laundering is the exchange of funds acquired through crime for funds that do not appear to be linked to crime.

The AAT and its members are required to comply with the money laundering laws and regulations.

4.2   Requirements under the laws and regulations

A tax adviser should check the identity of prospective clients via a review of appropriate documentation, for example, a passport.

A firm of accountants must appoint a money laundering officer.

Suspicion that a person is involved in money laundering should be reported to the money laundering officer who will determine whether it needs to be reported to the appropriate authorities.

5 Tax advice and records

5.1 Providing tax advice

When providing tax advice and preparing tax returns, a person should act in the best interests of his client.

However, he must ensure that his services are consistent with the law and are carried out competently.

At all times an adviser 'must not in any way impair integrity or objectivity'.

5.2 Providing information to HM Revenue and Customs / other authorities

The 'Guidelines on Professional Ethics' state that:

'A member should not be associated with any return or communication where there is reason to believe that it:

- contains a false or misleading statement;

- contains statements or information furnished recklessly; or

- omits or obscures information required to be included and such omission or obscurity would mislead the tax authorities.'

5.3 Tax records

The client and the tax adviser must keep records to assist in dealings with and support evidence given to HMRC. This should include invoices, bank statements and working papers.

The records should be kept for one year after the normal filing date, i.e. for 2013/14 the filing date is 31 January 2015, hence records must be kept until 31 January 2016.

However, if the taxpayer receives property income, this time limit is extended to 5 years after the normal filing date (31 January 2020 for 2013/14).

A penalty of up to £3,000 may be charged for failing to keep adequate records.

Activity 3

1   All individuals must submit a tax return – TRUE or FALSE?

2   All tax records should be kept for at least 6 years by an individual – TRUE or FALSE?

6   Summary

Client confidentiality is an adviser's main duty towards the client.

However, his responsibilities include openness in dealing with HMRC and reporting suspicion of money laundering.

Records must be kept by taxpayers and you must know the retention periods.

ANSWERS TO CHAPTER AND WORKBOOK ACTIVITIES

Answers to Chapter and Workbook Activities

2 Principles of income tax

Activity 1

1 **False** – Interest from a building society account is taxable.

2 **False** – Income from an ISA is exempt.

3 **False** – £150 (£120 × 100/80) should be included in Ben's income tax computation.

4 **False** – The basic rate of income tax is 20%; 40% is the higher rate.

Workbook Activity 2

The correct answer is **£9,254**

£		£
32,010 × 20%		6,402
7,130 × 40%		2,852
———		———
39,140		9,254
———		———

Workbook Activity 3

1 **False** – Lottery winnings are exempt

2 **False** – £600 × 100/80 = £750, not £720

3 **True** – Statutory redundancy pay is exempt from income tax

4 **False** – There are three rates of income tax; 20%, 40% and 45%

3 Introduction to employment income

 Activity 1

Contract of service is employment.

Contract for services is self employment.

A high level of control would indicate employment.

 Activity 2

Underwood

Underwood's taxable earnings assessable for 2013/14 are as follows:

	£	£
Basic salary (£950 × 12)		11,400
Bonus paid in May 2013		1,260
		————
		12,660
Less: Allowable expenses		
Subscription	100	
Pension scheme	342	
Payroll giving scheme	200	
	———	(642)
		————
Taxable employment income		12,018
		————

 Activity 3

1   **False** – The bonus will be taxed in 2013/14.

2   **False** – A mileage allowance of 50p per mile would result in an excess taxable on Chen Li.

3   **False** – It is not wholly, exclusively and necessarily incurred.

Workbook Activity 4

The correct answer is **B**.

Egbert

Allowable expenses – 2013/14

	£	£
Entertainment (£46 + £62)		108
General expenses allowance	500	
Less: Used in entertaining customers (35%)	(175)	
Business travelling (65% × £500)		325
Travelling and subsistence		938
Allowable expenses		1,371

The amounts paid to or on behalf of Egbert will all be taxable and included in his employment income (unless covered by a dispensation). However, all the amounts will also be allowable expenses apart from the 35% of the general expenses allowance spent on entertaining.

 Workbook Activity 5

Only **B** is deductible.

Workbook Activity 6

1   The answer is £16,500 (9/12 × £16,000 + 3/12 × £18,000)

2   The answer is £600 which is the bonus received in 2013/14

3   The answer is £400 taxable
     (8,000 × (50p received – 45p allowed)

Workbook Activity 7

Bartholomew

Assessable employment income – 2013/14

	£
Salary	52,000
Bonus (received) – May 2013	7,644
	59,644
Pension contributions (5% paid by employee) (employer's contribution is not taxable)	(2,600)
Assessable employment income	57,044

Workbook Activity 8

The correct answer is **A**.

	£
Salary	45,000
Bonus (received) – June 2013	8,000
	53,000
Less: Travelling expenses	(2,000)
Assessable employment income	51,000

4 Employment income – benefits

Activity 1

The correct answer is **B**.

	£
Basic charge – annual value (no rent paid by employer)	2,400
Expensive property charge	
(£105,000 – £75,000) = £30,000 × 4%	1,200
Use of furniture (20% × £6,500)	1,300
	——
	4,900
Less: Contribution by employee (£100 × 12)	(1,200)
	——
Taxable benefit	3,700
	——

Activity 2

1   **True**

2   **False** – Although often the MV when first made available is the same as the cost to the employer.

3   **False**

4   **True**

Activity 3

1   10% (Emissions between 76 and 94 g/km)

2   5% (Emissions 75 g/km or less)

3   20% (11% + (140 – 95) × $\frac{1}{5}$)
    Round down emissions to 140 g/km

4   35% (11% + (230 – 95 g/km) × $\frac{1}{5}$ = 38%), but maximum is 35%.
    Round down emissions to 230 g/km.

Activity 4

Sue and Paul

1   The correct answer is £2,480.

The amount of the benefit arising is as follows:

	£
£16,000 (the list price) × 28%	4,480
Less: Contribution	(2,000)
Benefit	2,480

The benefit is calculated at the rate of 28% being

$11\% + ((185 - 95) \times {}^1/_5.)$

2   The correct answer is £12,600.

The amount of the benefit arising is as follows:

$(£39,000 - £3,000) \times 35\% = £12,600$

The benefit is calculated at the maximum rate of 35%
$(11\% + (210 - 95) \times {}^1/_5 + 3\% \text{ (diesel)} = 37\%).$

Note that the business mileage driven is of no relevance to the calculations.

 Activity 5

The correct answer is **C**.

	£
Private medical insurance	1,270
Canteen	Exempt
Round sum expense allowance	1,870
Less: Business travel	(550)
Assessable benefits	2,590

Activity 6

1   The correct answer is **D**.

     This is a pool car.

2   The correct answer is **A**.

     The amount of the benefit arising is as follows: £

     Car benefit (35% × £17,000)   5,950
     Fuel benefit (35% × £21,100)   7,385
                                                                   ─────────
                                                                      13,335
     Less Mileage allowance claim for own car   (5,000)
                                                                   ─────────
                                                                       8,335
                                                                   ─────────

     The benefit is calculated at the maximum rate of 35%
     (11% + (240 – 95) × $^1/_5$ = 40% so use maximum).

     The business mileage claim is £5,000
     ((10,000 × 45p) + (2,000 × 25p))

     Raider can claim relief for the business miles he does in his own
     car using the AMAP rates.

 Activity 7

1   **True** – The benefit is (20% × £1,000).

2   **False** – The benefit would be £1,000, the market value of the
     asset.

3   **True**.

4   **False** – There is no benefit if the private use of the van is merely
     incidental.

Workbook Activity 8

Ethelred

		£
1	Season ticket	292
2	Motor car = 23% (W) × (£13,800 – £800)	2,990
	Petrol = 23% (W) × £21,100	4,853
		7,843
3	Private medical insurance (£1,628 – £1,000)	628

Working:

Appropriate percentage: 11% + (155 – 95) × ⅕ = 23%

Workbook Activity 9

William Makepeace

		£	£
1	The correct answer is £825.		
	Car 20% × £8,000 × $\frac{325}{365}$	1,425	
	Less: Contribution	(600)	
			825
2	The correct answer is £3,758.		
	Fuel charge		
	£21,100 × 20% × $\frac{325}{365}$		3,758
3	The correct answer is £1,500.		
	Cheap loan £50,000 × (4% – 1%)		1,500

KAPLAN PUBLISHING

The car benefit percentage: 11% + (140 – 95) × $^1/_5$ = 20%.

The car and petrol benefits are pro rated as the car was unavailable for use for more than 30 consecutive days during November and December 2013. No reduction is made for the 12 day period in July 2013.

No deduction is made for the contribution towards private use petrol as it did not cover the full cost.

Workbook Activity 10

Gordon

1   **False** – School fees are taxable on the cost to the employer

		£	£
2	The correct answer is **A**.		
	Basic car benefit		
	((£25,000 – £1,300) × 35%) (W1)	8,295	
	Contribution towards private use	(1,800)	
		────	6,495
3	The correct answer is **B** – Parking place is exempt		
4	The correct answer is **B**.		
	Provision of asset (computer)		
	(£750 × 20% × 7/12) (W2)		87
			────

Workings:

(W1) Appropriate percentage:

11% + (240 – 95) × $^1/_5$ = 40% restricted to 35%

(W2) The computer was only available from 6 September 2012 and therefore the benefit is prorated for 7 months.

Workbook Activity 11

Gina

Benefits taxable as employment income – 2013/14

	£	£
Mobile telephone – one phone per employee = exempt		Nil
Medical insurance cover		
Premium paid by employer	1,420	
Less: Contribution by Gina	(750)	
	———	670
Beneficial loan		
£10,000 × $\frac{11}{12}$ × 4% (Note)		367
		———
Total taxable benefits		1,037
		———

Note: The loan was only outstanding for 11 months during 2013/14. The average loan is £10,000 throughout the eleven month period. However the interest rate given in the question is an annual percentage and therefore needs to be time apportioned for the eleven month period of the loan.

Workbook Activity 12

Marianne

Employment income – 2013/14

(a) Job-related accommodation

	£	£
Salary		52,000
Other benefits		3,600
		55,600
Living accommodation		Exempt
Other benefits in respect of accommodation		
Heating and lighting	3,000	
Furniture (£20,000 × 20%)	4,000	
	7,000	
Restricted to (10% × £55,600)		5,560
Employment income		61,160

(b) Not job-related accommodation

	£	£
Salary		52,000
Other benefits		3,600
		55,600
Living accommodation:		
Basic charge	1,500	
Expensive charge		
(£150,000 – £75,000) × 4%	3,000	
		4,500
Heating and lighting		3,000
Furniture (£20,000 × 20%)		4,000
Employment income		67,100

Workbook Activity 13

The correct answer is £52,825.

	£
Salary	50,000
Relocation (W1)	2,000
Beneficial loan (W2)	825
Employment income	52,825

Workings:

(1) The first £8,000 of relocation expenses are tax-free provided they are reimbursed expenditure or paid direct to a third party (i.e. you cannot give an £8,000 round sum tax free to the employee).

(£10,000 − £8,000) = £2,000

(2) Beneficial loan:

£30,000 × (4% ORI less 1.25% paid) = £825

Workbook Activity 14

The correct answer is **C**.

	£
Accommodation	8,500
(rent paid by employer higher than annual value)	
Utility services, decorating and repairs	7,000
Use of furniture (£40,000 × 20%)	8,000
Taxable benefits	23,500

Workbook Activity 15

1   The correct answer is £807.
     £32,300 × (4% − 1.5%)   £807

2   The answer is £350
     The bicycle and cycle safety equipment is an exempt
     benefit provided available to employees generally.
     Gym membership is taxable on the cost to the
     employer.   £350

 Workbook Activity 16

Mr Darcy

Employment income – 2013/14

	£
Salary	36,000
Bonus (note)	8,000
	44,000
Less: Pension contributions (7% × £36,000)	(2,520)
Employment income	41,480

Explanation of treatment

The bonus paid in May 2013 is taxable in 2013/14.

 Workbook Activity 17

The correct answer is **D**.

£25,000 × (4% − 1.4%) × 9/12   £487

Workbook Activity 18

The correct answer is **C**.

Workbook Activity 19

1 **YES**
2 **YES**
3 **YES**

Workbook Activity 20

1 **C**
2 **A**
3 **B**
4 **C**
5 **B**

Workbook Activity 21

The answer is **D**.

Child care vouchers provided to a higher rate taxpayer of up to £28 per week are exempt provided they are spent with an approved child carer. The fact that the sales director chose an approved child carer rather than the on-site facilities is irrelevant for tax purposes.
The other items are all taxable.

Workbook Activity 22

The correct answer is **C** = (£4,300 × 20% × 6/12) = £430
The computer was not made available until 1 October 2013 so the benefit must be time apportioned.

Workbook Activity 23

The correct answer is **C** = (£32,000 − £12,000) = £20,000.
The basic charge is the higher of the annual value or rent paid by the employer, which is £32,000, less the rent of £12,000 paid by Leo.

5 Employment income – supplementary pages

Activity 1

HM Revenue & Customs

Employment
Tax year 6 April 2013 to 5 April 2014

Your name
L A   R A I D E R

Your Unique Taxpayer Reference (UTR)

Complete an *Employment* page for each employment or directorship

1 Pay from this employment – the total from your P45 or P60 - *before tax was taken off*
£ 6 2 7 0 0 · 0 0

2 UK tax taken off pay in box 1
£ · 0 0

3 Tips and other payments not on your P60
- *read the Employment notes*
£ · 0 0

4 PAYE tax reference of your employer (on your P45/P60)
/

5 Your employer's name
C O L I S E U M   L T D

6 If you were a company director, put 'X' in the box

7 And, if the company was a close company, put 'X' in the box

8 If you are a part-time teacher in England or Wales and are on the Repayment of Teachers' Loans Scheme for this employment, put 'X' in the box

Benefits from your employment - use your form P11D (or equivalent information)

9 Company cars and vans
- *the total 'cash equivalent' amount*
£ 5 9 5 0 · 0 0

10 Fuel for company cars and vans
- *the total 'cash equivalent' amount*
£ 5 9 1 5 · 0 0

11 Private medical and dental insurance
- *the total 'cash equivalent' amount*
£ 1 2 7 0 · 0 0

12 Vouchers, credit cards and excess mileage allowance
£ · 0 0

13 Goods and other assets provided by your employer
- *the total value or amount*
£ 6 0 0 · 0 0

14 Accommodation provided by your employer
- *the total value or amount*
£ · 0 0

15 Other benefits (including interest-free and low interest loans) - *the total 'cash equivalent' amount*
£ · 0 0

16 Expenses payments received and balancing charges
£ 1 8 5 0 · 0 0

Employment expenses

17 Business travel and subsistence expenses
£ 5 0 5 0 · 0 0

18 Fixed deductions for expenses
£ · 0 0

19 Professional fees and subscriptions
£ · 0 0

20 Other expenses and capital allowances
£ · 0 0

ⓘ Shares schemes, employment lump sums, compensation, deductions and Seafarers' Earnings Deduction are on the *Additional information* pages enclosed in the tax return pack.

SA102 2013   Page E 1   HMRC 12/12

Workbook Activity 2

Maurice Knight

HM Revenue & Customs

Employment
Tax year 6 April 2013 to 5 April 2014

Your name
M A U R I C E   K N I G H T

Your Unique Taxpayer Reference (UTR)

Complete an *Employment* page for each employment or directorship

1 Pay from this employment – the total from your P45 or P60 - *before tax was taken off*
£ 18 1 0 0 . 0 0

2 UK tax taken off pay in box 1
£ 4 3 0 1 . 0 0

3 Tips and other payments not on your P60
- read the Employment notes
£ . 0 0

4 PAYE tax reference of your employer (on your P45/P60)
/

5 Your employer's name

6 If you were a company director, put 'X' in the box

7 And, if the company was a close company, put 'X' in the box

8 If you are a part-time teacher in England or Wales and are on the Repayment of Teachers' Loans Scheme for this employment, put 'X' in the box

Benefits from your employment – use your form P11D (or equivalent information)

9 Company cars and vans
- the total 'cash equivalent' amount
£ 3 2 0 0 . 0 0

10 Fuel for company cars and vans
- the total 'cash equivalent' amount
£ 3 6 0 0 . 0 0

11 Private medical and dental insurance
- the total 'cash equivalent' amount
£ 8 4 0 . 0 0

12 Vouchers, credit cards and excess mileage allowance
£ . 0 0

13 Goods and other assets provided by your employer
- the total value or amount
£ . 0 0

14 Accommodation provided by your employer
- the total value or amount
£ . 0 0

15 Other benefits (including interest-free and low interest loans) - *the total 'cash equivalent' amount*
£ 4 5 0 . 0 0

16 Expenses payments received and balancing charges
£ 5 2 1 0 . 0 0

Employment expenses

17 Business travel and subsistence expenses
£ 3 7 5 0 . 0 0

18 Fixed deductions for expenses
£ . 0 0

19 Professional fees and subscriptions
£ 5 1 0 . 0 0

20 Other expenses and capital allowances
£ 9 5 0 . 0 0

ℹ️ Shares schemes, employment lump sums, compensation, deductions and Seafarers' Earnings Deduction are on the *Additional information* pages enclosed in the tax return pack.

SA102 2013   Page E 1   HMRC 12/12

6 Property income

Activity 1

The correct answer is £2,100

	£
Rental income (£5,000 × 2)	10,000
Less: Expenses	
Agents fees (£1,200 + £700)	(1,900)
Repairs and redecoration	(6,000)
Taxable property income	2,100

Activity 2

1 **False** – The accruals basis is used.

2 **True** – Rental income is first reduced by irrecoverable rents, then the council tax and water rates paid by the landlord are deducted.

3 **False** – The loss must be carried forward and set off against the next available profit from property letting in future years.

Activity 3

Bernard Marks

Taxable property income – 2013/14

Property number	1	2	3	Total
	£	£	£	£
Rental income	3,000	3,500	2,500	9,000
Less: Allowable expenses				
Agent's commission	(300)	(350)	(250)	(900)
Building insurance	(120)	(120)	(120)	(360)
Repairs and maintenance	(560)	(660)	(1,060)*	(2,280)
Council tax	(400)	(450)	(380)	(1,230)
Accountancy fees	(50)	(50)	(50)	(150)
Mortgage interest	(100)	(130)	(90)	(320)
Wear and tear allowance (W)	(260)	(305)	(212)	(777)
Taxable property income	1,210	1,435	338	2,983

*The new kitchen is capital and so is disallowed.

(W) **Wear and tear allowance** = 10% (rental income – council tax)

	1	2	3
Rental income	3,000	3,500	2,500
Council tax	(400)	(450)	(380)
	2,600	3,050	2,120
@ 10%	260	305	212

Activity 4

1 **False** – It simply has to be within the UK or EEA

2 **True** – The property is available for at least 210 days per year

3 **False** – The 105 days can be averaged over several properties

4 **False** – The property can be let to the same person for more than 31 days but the total of all such periods of longer term occupation cannot exceed 155 days

Activity 5

The correct answer is £430.

	£
Rental income (£90 × 52)	4,680
Less: Rent a room relief	(4,250)
Taxable property income	430

If no rent a room relief is claimed

	£
Rental income	4,680
Less: Expenses	(2,100)
Wear and tear allowance (10% × £4,680)	(468)
Taxable property income	2,112

Workbook Activity 6

The correct answer is £3,800.

Computation of taxable property income – 2013/14

	£	£
Rents (£500 × 10 months)		5,000
Less: Repainting windows	700	
Wear and tear allowance (10% × £5,000)	500	
		(1,200)
Taxable property income		3,800

Workbook Activity 7

The correct answer is £2,985.

Computation of taxable property income – 2013/14

	£	£
Rents (£650 × 12)		7,800
Less: Expenses (£300 + £850 + £500)	1,650	
Interest	2,500	
Wear and tear allowance		
(10% × £7,800 – £300 – £850)	665	
		(4,815)
Taxable property income		2,985

Note: The cooker is capital expenditure and is therefore disallowed.

Workbook Activity 8

Rachman

Computation of taxable property income – 2013/14

	£	£
Rents due for 2013/14		26,850
Less: Garden maintenance	500	
Lift maintenance	180	
Normal decorations	800	
Caretaker's wages	5,800	
Insurance etc	269	
Mortgage interest	15,400	
		(22,949)
Taxable property income		3,901

Note: Normal maintenance and repairs are allowable. However, the cost of asphalting the drive (which was in a dangerous state at the time of purchase) would not be deductible being capital in nature.

Workbook Activity 9

James

Computation of rental loss – 2012/13

	£	£
Rents		
(4 × £700) + (6 × £750) – £700 (Note 1)		6,600
Less: Agent's commission	1,163	
Normal redecorations	1,745	
Central heating (Note 2)	–	
Insurance etc	547	
Professional charges	880	
Mortgage interest	3,400	
		(7,735)
Loss (Note 3)		(1,135)

Notes:

(1) Relief is available for irrecoverable rent.

(2) The cost of installing the central heating is not allowable as it represents an improvement rather than ongoing maintenance and is therefore capital in nature.

(3) The loss will be carried forward and offset against future property income.

Workbook Activity 10

The correct answer is **B**.

Workbook Activity 11

1   **FALSE** – This is permitted.

2   **TRUE** – The lodger can occupy more than one room.

3   **FALSE** – It must be furnished.

4   **FALSE** – Such charges must be included.

5   **TRUE** – Wear and tear allowance can be given for furniture but not the actual cost of the furniture

---

 Workbook Activity 12

Arthur

Property income – 2013/14

	Shop 1 £	Shop 2 £
Rents accrued		
(³⁄₁₂ × £3,000 + ⁶⁄₁₂ × £4,000)	2,750	
(£6,000 × ⁶⁄₁₂)		3,000
	2,750	3,000
Less: Insurance	190	300
Ground rent	10	40
Repairs and decorating	3,900	2,000
Accountancy	50	50
Advertising for tenant	100	100
	4,250	2,490
Profit/(loss)	(1,500)	510

Note: Repairs relating to conditions present when the building is purchased are not generally allowable (dry rot in Shop 2).

7 Property income – supplementary pages

Activity 1

Property income

Do not include furnished holiday lettings, Real Estate Investment Trust or Property Authorised Investment Funds dividends/distributions here.

20 Total rents and other income from property

£ 9 0 0 0 . 0 0

21 Tax taken off any income in box 20

£ . 0 0

22 Premiums for the grant of a lease – from box E on the Working Sheet – *read the notes*

£ . 0 0

23 Reverse premiums and inducements

£ . 0 0

Property expenses

24 Rent, rates, insurance, ground rents etc. (1230 + 360)

£ 1 5 9 0 . 0 0

25 Property repairs, maintenance and renewals

£ 2 2 8 0 . 0 0

26 Loan interest and other financial costs

£ 3 2 0 . 0 0

27 Legal, management and other professional fees (900 + 150)

£ 1 0 5 0 . 0 0

28 Costs of services provided, including wages

£ . 0 0

29 Other allowable property expenses

£ . 0 0

Calculating your taxable profit or loss

30 Private use adjustment – *read the notes*

£ . 0 0

31 Balancing charges – *read the notes*

£ . 0 0

32 Annual Investment Allowance

£ . 0 0

33 Business Premises Renovation Allowance (Assisted Areas only) – *read the notes*

£ . 0 0

34 All other capital allowances

£ . 0 0

35 Landlord's Energy Saving Allowance

£ . 0 0

36 10% wear and tear allowance – *for furnished residential accommodation only*

£ 7 7 7 . 0 0

37 Rent a Room exempt amount

£ . 0 0

38 Adjusted profit for the year – from box O on the Working Sheet – *read the notes*

£ 2 9 8 3 . 0 0

39 Loss brought forward used against this year's profits

£ . 0 0

40 Taxable profit for the year (box 38 minus box 39)

£ 2 9 8 3 . 0 0

41 Adjusted loss for the year – from box O on the Working Sheet – *read the notes*

£ . 0 0

42 Loss set off against 2013–14 total income – *this will be unusual – read the notes*

£ . 0 0

43 Loss to carry forward to following year, including unused losses brought forward

£ . 0 0

SA105 2013   Page UKP 2

Workbook Activity 2

Brian Finlay (1)

Property income – 2013/14

	House £	Flat £	Total £
House (4 × £1,000 + 7 × £1,200)	12,400		12,400
Flat (8 × £600)		4,800	4,800
	12,400	4,800	17,200
Expenses:			
Insurance	305		305
Repairs and maintenance	2,010		2,010
Mortgage interest (£500 × 11)	3,700	5,500	9,200
Legal fees	75		75
Services: Service charge (£25 × 11)		275	275
Gardening	520		520
Other expenses (running expenses)	150		150
Wear and tear allowance (10% × £12,400)	1,240		1,240
	8,000	5,775	13,775
Profit/loss	4,400	(975)	3,425
Taxable property income – 2013/14.			3,425

Note: The new washing machine is capital and therefore not an allowable expense.

KAPLAN PUBLISHING

Workbook Activity 3

Property income

Do not include furnished holiday lettings, Real Estate Investment Trust or Property Authorised Investment Funds dividends/distributions here.

20 Total rents and other income from property
£ 1 7 2 0 0 . 0 0

21 Tax taken off any income in box 20
£ . 0 0

22 Premiums for the grant of a lease – from box E on the Working Sheet - *read the notes*
£ . 0 0

23 Reverse premiums and inducements
£ . 0 0

Property expenses

24 Rent, rates, insurance, ground rents etc.
£ 3 0 5 . 0 0

25 Property repairs, maintenance and renewals
£ 2 0 1 0 . 0 0

26 Loan interest and other financial costs
£ 9 2 0 0 . 0 0

27 Legal, management and other professional fees
£ 7 5 . 0 0

28 Costs of services provided, including wages
£ 7 9 5 . 0 0 (275 + 520)

29 Other allowable property expenses
£ 1 5 0 . 0 0

Calculating your taxable profit or loss

30 Private use adjustment – *read the notes*
£ . 0 0

31 Balancing charges – *read the notes*
£ . 0 0

32 Annual Investment Allowance
£ . 0 0

33 Business Premises Renovation Allowance (Assisted Areas only) – *read the notes*
£ . 0 0

34 All other capital allowances
£ . 0 0

35 Landlord's Energy Saving Allowance
£ . 0 0

36 10% wear and tear allowance - *for furnished residential accommodation only*
£ 1 2 4 0 . 0 0

37 Rent a Room exempt amount
£ . 0 0

38 Adjusted profit for the year – from box O on the Working Sheet - *read the notes*
£ 3 4 2 5 . 0 0

39 Loss brought forward used against this year's profits
£ . 0 0

40 Taxable profit for the year (box 38 minus box 39)
£ 3 4 2 5 . 0 0

41 Adjusted loss for the year – from box O on the Working Sheet - *read the notes*
£ . 0 0

42 Loss set off against 2013–14 total income – *this will be unusual - read the notes*
£ . 0 0

43 Loss to carry forward to following year, including unused losses brought forward
£ . 0 0

SA105 2013 — Page UKP 2

8 Investment income

Activity 1

The correct answer is **C**.

			£
			£
First	2,790	taxed at 10%	279.00
Next	2,210	taxed at 20%	442.00
	———		
	5,000		
	———		———
			721.00
			———

Activity 2

Emily

Step 1 – Analyse income

First separate the taxable income into non-savings income, savings income and dividend income. The easiest way to do this is to identify the dividend income then the savings income. The balance (if any) of the taxable income must then be non-savings.

In this case:

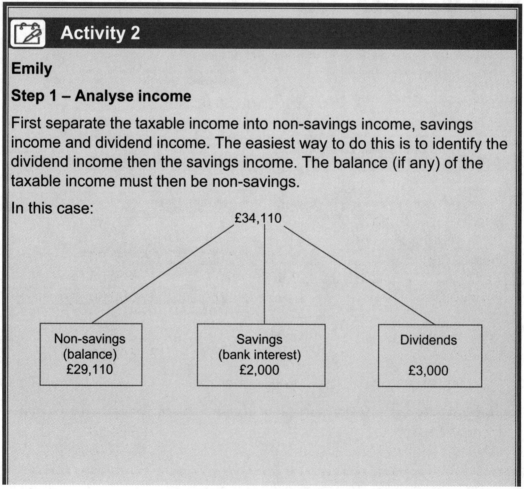

£34,110

| Non-savings (balance) £29,110 | Savings (bank interest) £2,000 | Dividends £3,000 |

Step 2 – Calculation of tax on non-savings income.

The tax liability can then be calculated, first on the non-savings income as follows:

£29,110 × 20%   £5,822.00
                        ————————

Step 3 – Calculation of tax on savings income.

There is still £2,900 of the basic rate band left (£32,010 – £29,110).

This means that all £2,000 of savings income falls into the basic rate band, and will be taxed at 20%.

The tax on savings income is as follows:

£2,000 × 20%   £400.00
                       ————————

Step 4 – Calculation of tax on dividend income.

There is still £900 of the basic rate band left (£32,010 – £29,110 – £2,000).

This means that the first £900 of dividend income will be taxed at 10% with the balance (£2,100) at 32½%.

Tax on dividend income is as follows:

	£
£900 × 10%	90.00
£2,100 × 32½%	682.50
	————
	772.50
	————

Step 5 – In summary:

	£		£
Non-savings	29,110	× 20%	5,822.00
Savings	2,000	× 20%	400.00
Dividends	900	× 10%	90.00
	————		
	32,010		
Dividends	2,100	× 32½%	682.50
	————		
	34,110		
	————		————
Income tax liability			6,994.50
			————

Activity 3

Simon

Step 1 – Analyse income

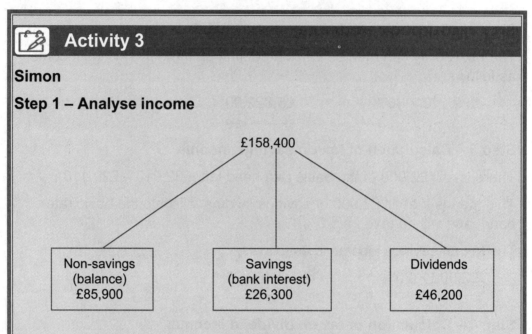

£158,400

| Non-savings (balance) £85,900 | Savings (bank interest) £26,300 | Dividends £46,200 |

Step 2 – Calculation of tax on non-savings income.

The first £32,010 of non-savings income will be taxed at the basic rate.

£32,010 × 20%   £6,402.00

The remainder of the income (£53,890) falls within the higher rate band.

£53,890 × 40%   £21,556.00

Step 3 – Calculation of tax on savings income.

There is still £64,100 of the higher rate band left (£150,000 – £85,900).

This means that all £26,300 of savings income falls into the higher rate band, and will be taxed at 40%.

The tax on savings income is as follows:

£26,300 × 40%   £10,520.00

Step 4 – Calculation of tax on dividend income.

There is still £37,800 of the higher rate band left (£150,000 – £85,900 – £26,300).

This means that the first £37,800 of dividend income will be taxed at 32½% with the balance (£8,400) at 37½%.

KAPLAN PUBLISHING

Tax on dividend income is as follows:

		£
£37,800 × 32½%		12,285.00
£8,400 × 37½%		3,150.00
		15,435.00

Step 5 – In summary:

	£		£
Non-savings	32,010	× 20%	6,402.00
Non-savings	53,890	× 40%	21,556.00
Savings	26,300	× 40%	10,520.00
Dividends	37,800	× 32½%	12,285.00
	150,000		
Dividends	8,400	× 37½%	3,150.00
	158,400		
Income tax liability			53,913.00

Workbook Activity 4

Mr Bundy

Investment income – 2013/14

	Net	Gross	Tax deducted
	£	£	£
Dividends	600	667	67
Bank interest (received net of 20% tax)	51	64	13
Loan note interest (received net of 20% tax) £10,000 × 4% (4% is gross rate)	320	400	80

Workbook Activity 5

Mrs Gubbins
Investment income – 2013/14

	Net	Gross	Tax deducted /tax credit
	£	£	£
Bank interest (received net of 20% tax)	76	95	19
Building society interest (received net of 20% tax)	124	155	31
Dividends (£64 + £121 + £157) (10% tax credit)	342	380	38

Workbook Activity 6

	Net	Gross
Bank interest		
Building society interest		
Interest from NS&I investment accounts		
Interest from gilts		
Loan stock interest f om unquoted companies		

9 Calculating income tax payable

 Activity 1

	Vera £	Agatha £	Henry £	Leon £
Personal age allowance	10,500	10,660	10,660	10,500
Less: Restriction re £26,100				
50% × (£105,000 – £26,100)				
= £39,450 restricted	(1,060)			
50% × (£27,100 – £26,100)		(500)		
50% × (£28,100 – £26,100)			(1,000)	
50% × (£32,100 – £26,100)				
= £3,000 restricted				(1,060)
Personal age allowance	9,440	10,160	9,660	9,440
Less: Restriction re £100,000				
50% × (£105,000 – £100,000)	(2,500)			
	6,940	10,160	9,660	9,440

 Activity 2

The correct answer is **B**.

After deduction of the personal allowance of £9,440, the actual taxable income will be £28,560.

As this is less than £32,010, the whole of the interest will fall into the basic rate band and will be taxed at 20% with a tax credit of 20%.

Activity 3

The correct answer is **C**.

	£
Dividend (£9,360 × 100/90)	10,400
Less Personal allowance	(9,440)
Taxable income	960
Tax at 10%	96.00

Note that the question asked for income tax liability not payable.

The income tax payable would be £Nil after deduction of the 10% tax credit. The excess tax credit cannot be repaid.

Activity 4

Stanley

Income tax computation – 2013/14

	Total £	Other £	Savings £	Dividends £
Employment income				
– Salary	102,485			
– Bonus	38,480			
– Mileage (W)	530			
	141,495	141,495		
Bank interest				
(£2,000 × 100/80)	2,500		2,500	
Building society interest	1,000		1,000	
(£800 × 100/80)				
Dividends	29,000			29,000
(£26,100 × 100/90)				
Total income	173,995	141,495	3,500	29,000
Less: PA (restricted)	(0)	(0)	(0)	(0)
Taxable income	173,995	141,495	3,500	29,000

Income tax

£			£
32,010	× 20%	(other)	6,402.00
109,485	× 40%	(other)	43,794.00
———			
141,495			
3,500	× 40%	(savings)	1,400.00
5,005	× 32.5%	(dividends)	1,626.62
———			
150,000			
23,995	× 37.5%	(dividends)	8,998.12
———			
173,995			
———			———

	£
Income tax liability	62,220.74
Less: Tax deducted at source	
Dividends (£29,000 × 10%)	(2,900.00)
Savings (£3,500 × 20%)	(700.00)
PAYE	(57,800.00)
	———
Income tax payable	820.74
	———

(W) Taxable mileage allowance

	£	£
Income (11,500 × 47p)		5,405
Less: Allowable expense		
10,000 × 45p	4,500	
1,500 × 25p	375	
	———	(4,875)
		———
Taxable amount		530
		———

Activity 5

Hossam

	Total	Other	Savings	Divis
	£	£	£	£
Income	50,000	50,000		
Bank interest (1800 × 100/80)	2,250		2,250	
Dividends (4,500 × 100/90)	5,000			5,000
Total = Net income	57,250	50,000	2,250	5,000
Less Personal allowance	(9,440)	(9,440)		
Taxable income	47,810	40,560	2,250	5,000
£32,010 × 20%	6,402.00			
£8,550 × 40%	3,420.00			
£2,250 × 40%	900.00			
£5,000 × 32.5%	1,625.00			
Income tax liability	12,347.00			

 Workbook Activity 6

Mary – income tax computation 2013/14

		Total
		£
Salary and benefits (£37,900+ £5,200)		43,100
Less 6% pension contribution (£37,900 × 6%)		(2,274)
Dividends (£1,350 × 100/90)		1,500
Total = Net income		42,326
Less Personal allowance		(9,440)
Taxable income		32,886
Other (32,886 -1,500)	£31,386 × 20%	6,277.20
Divis (32,010 – 31,386)	£624 × 10%	62.40
Divis (32,886 – 32,010)	£876 × 32.5%	284.70
Income tax liability		6,624.30

KAPLAN PUBLISHING

Workings:

Mary

Income tax computation – 2013/14

	Total £	Other £	Dividends £
Employment income (W)	40,826	40,826	
Dividends (£1,350 × 100/90)	1,500		1,500
Net income	42,326	40,826	1,500
Less: PA	(9,440)	(9,440)	
Taxable income	32,886	31,386	1,500

Income tax

£			£
31,386	× 20%	(other)	6,277.20
624	× 10%	(dividends)	62.40
32,010			
876	× 32.5%	(dividends)	284.70
32,886			

	£
Income tax liability	6,624.30

	£
Working: Employment income	
Salary	37,900
Car benefit	5,200
	43,100
Less: Pension contributions (6% × £37,900)	(2,274)
Employment income	40,826

Workbook Activity 7

The correct answer is £4,065.

Artemis is entitled to the personal age allowance but it will be reduced to the level of the standard personal allowance because of the level of his income.

The allowance will then be further reduced by 50% × (£110,750 − £100,000) = £5,375 reduction.

Hence the allowance is £4,065 (£9,440 − £5,375).

 Workbook Activity 8

Briony

Income tax computation – 2013/14

	Total £	Other £	Dividends £
Employment income	39,295	39,295	
Trading income	15,415	15,415	
Property income	6,500	6,500	
Dividends (£1,710 × 100/90)	1,900		1,900
Net income	63,110	61,210	1,900
Less: PA	(9,440)	(9,440)	
Taxable income	53,670	51,770	1,900

Income tax

£			£
32,010	× 20%	(other)	6,402.00
19,760	× 40%	(other)	7,904.00
51,770			
1,900	× 32.5%	(dividends)	617.50
53,670			

	£
Income tax liability	14,923.50
Less: Tax deducted at source	
Dividends (£1,900 × 10%)	(190.00)
PAYE	(6,700.00)
Income tax payable	8,033.50

Workbook Activity 9

Sally

The correct answer is **B**.

Income tax computation – 2013/14

	£
Net income	47,965
Less PA	(9,440)
Taxable income	38,525

Income tax

£		£
32,010 at 20%		6,402.00
6,515 at 40%		2,606.00
Income tax liability		9,008.00

Note: The question asks for liability not tax payable so there is no need to deduct the PAYE.

Workbook Activity 10

Jon

Income tax computation – 2013/14

	Total £	Other £	Savings £	Dividends £
Employment income – Salary	39,830	39,830		
NS&I Savings certificates	Exempt			
Gambling winnings	Exempt			
Building society interest				
(£320 × 100/80)	400		400	
Bank interest (£400 × 100/80)	500		500	
Dividends (£1,890 × 100/90)	2,100			2,100
Net income	42,830	39,830	900	2,100
Less: PA	(9,440)	(9,440)		
Taxable income	33,390	30,390	900	2,100

Income tax

£			£
30,390 × 20%	(other)		6,078.00
900 × 20%	(savings)		180.00
720 × 10%	(dividends)		72.00
32,010			
1,380 × 32.5%	(dividends)		448.50
33,390			

Income tax liability	6,778.50
Less: Tax deducted at source	
Dividends (£2,100 × 10%)	(210.00)
Savings (£900 × 20%)	(180.00)
PAYE	(5,850.00)
Income tax payable	538.50

Workbook Activity 11

Marcel

Income tax computation – 2013/14

	Total £	Other £	Savings £	Dividends £
Pension income	9,660	9,660		
Interest on NS Certificates	Exempt			
Government stocks (received gross)	9,400		9,400	
Bank interest (£3,000 × 100/80)	3,750		3,750	
Dividends (£3,600 × 100/90)	4,000			4,000
Net income	26,810	9,660	13,150	4,000
Less: PA				
(£10,500 – ½ (£26,810 – £26,100)	(10,145)	(9,660)	(485)	
Taxable income	16,665	Nil	12,665	4,000

Income tax

£		£
2,790	× 10% (savings)	279.00
9,875	× 20% (savings)	1,975.00
4,000	× 10% (dividends)	400.00
16,665		

	£
Income tax liability	2,654.00
Less: Tax deducted at source	
Dividends (£4,000 × 10%)	(400.00)
Savings (£3,750 × 20%)	(750.00)
PAYE	(280.00)
Income tax payable	1,224.00

Workbook Activity 12

Mr Black

The correct answer is **C**.

Income tax computation – 2013/14

	Total £	Other £	Savings £	Dividends £
Employment income	43,000	43,000		
Bank interest (£28 × 100/80)	35		35	
Dividends (£297 × 100/90)	330			330
Net income	43,365	43,000	35	330
PA	(9,440)	(9,440)		
Taxable income	33,925	33,560	35	330

Income tax

£			£
32,010	× 20%	(other)	6,402.00
1,550	× 40%	(other)	620.00
33,560			
35	× 40%	(savings)	14.00
330	× 32.5%	(dividends)	107.25
33,925			

Income tax liability		7,143.25
Less: Tax deducted at source		
Dividends (£330 × 10%)		(33.00)
Savings (£35 × 20%)		(7.00)
PAYE		(6,420.00)
Income tax payable		683.25

Workbook Activity 13

1 **False** – if the taxpayer's income exceeds £100,000 his personal allowance will be reduced by half of the excess

2 **False** – 10% rate only applies if the savings income falls in the first £2,790 of taxable income

3 **True**

4 **False**

Workbook Activity 14

Louis

Income tax computation – 2013/14

	Total £	Other £	Savings £	Dividends £
Employment income	146,400	146,400		
Bank interest (£5,600 × 100/80)	7,000		7,000	
Dividends (£3,060 × 100/90)	3,400			3,400
Net income	156,800	146,400	7,000	3,400
PA (restricted)	(0)	(0)	(0)	(0)
Taxable income	156,800	146,400	7,000	3,400

Income tax

£			£
32,010	× 20%	(other)	6,402.00
114,390	× 40%	(other)	45,756.00
——————			
146,400			
3,600	× 40%	(savings)	1,440.00
——————			
150,000			
3,400	× 45%		1,530.00
3,400	× 37.5%	(dividends)	1,275.00
——————			
156,800			
——————			——————

		£
Income tax liability		56,403.00
Less: Tax deducted at source		
Dividends (£3,400 × 10%)		(340.00)
Savings (£7,000 × 20%)		(1,400.00)
PAYE		(44,250.00)
		——————
Income tax payable		10,413.00
		——————

 Workbook Activity 15

D is the correct answer.

Mr Ephraim is entitled to an age allowance based on his date of birth. As he was born prior to 6 April 1938, he is entitled to an allowance of £10,660.

However, this is reduced by 50% × (£28,100 − £26,100) = £1,000 reduction. Hence the allowance is £9,660

10 Pension payments and Gift Aid

Activity 1

The correct answer is £8,622.

	£
Salary	50,000
Less Pension contribution (£50,000 × 6%)	(3,000)
	———
	47,000
Less Personal allowance	(9,440)
	———
Taxable income	37,560
	———

Income tax

£	
32,010 × 20%	6,402.00
5,550 × 40%	2,220.00
———	
37,560	
———	
Income tax liability	**8,622.00**
	———

Activity 2

Imogen

Income tax computations – 2013/14

	Total £	Other £	Savings £	Dividends £
Employment income	166,040			
Less: Payroll giving	(2,500)			
	163,540	163,540		
Dividends (£2,790 ×100/90)	3,100			3,100
Net income	166,640	163,540	–	3,100
Less: PA (restricted)	(0)	(0)	(0)	(0)
Taxable income	166,640	163,540	–	3,100

Income tax

£			£
39,910	× 20% (W)	(other)	7,982.00
117,990	× 40%	(other)	47,196.00
157,900	(W)		
5,640	× 45%	(other)	2,538.00
163,540			
3,100	× 37.5%	(dividends)	1,162.50
166,640			

	£
Income tax liability	58,878.50
Less: Tax deducted at source	
Dividends (£3,100 × 10%)	(310.00)
PAYE	(57,180.00)
Income tax repayable	(1,388.50)

(W) Extend tax bands by £7,900 (£6,320 × $^{100}/_{80}$):
– Basic rate band £39,910 (£32,010 + £7,900).
– Additional rate band £157,900 (£150,000 + £7,900).

Activity 3

The correct answer is **B**.

	£
Pension	29,200
Less: Personal allowance (W1)	(9,610)
	────────
Taxable income	19,590
	────────

Income tax
£
| 19,590 × 20% | 3,918.00 |
| | ──────── |

(W1)	**Age allowance**	
	Born before 6 April 1938	10,660
	Less restriction ½ (£28,200 (W2) – £26,100)	(1,050)
		────────
		9,610
		────────

(W2)	**Income limit for age allowance**	
	Total income	29,200
	Less (£800 × 100/80)	(1,000)
		────────
		28,200
		────────

Activity 4

The correct answer is C

Net income for calculating the personal allowance restriction

	£
Salary	106,000
Less: gross Gift Aid	
(£1,600 × 100/80)	(2,000)
Adjusted net income	104,000

Personal allowance

Standard allowance	9,440
Less: ½ (£104,000 – £100,000)	(2,000)
Reduced personal allowance	7,440

Workbook Activity 5

Mr Mars

Income tax computation – 2013/14

	Total £	Other £	Savings £
Trading income	43,765	43,765	
Building society (£480 × 100/80)	600		600
Bank interest (£1,400 × 100/80)	1,750		1,750
Net income	46,115	43,765	2,350
PA	(9,440)	(9,440)	
Taxable income	36,675	34,325	2,350

Income tax		£
34,325 × 20%	(other)	6,865.00
1,185 × 20%	(savings)	237.00
35,510		
1,165 × 40%	(savings)	466.00
36,675		
Income tax liability		7,568.00

Note: Basic rate limit is extended by £3,500 (£2,800 × 100/80) from £32,010 to £35,510.

Workbook Activity 6

Proctor

Income tax computation – 2013/14

	Total £	Other £	Savings £
Employment income (£37,625 + £1,800)	39,425	39,425	
Building society (£576 × 100/80)	720		720
Property income	5,410	5,410	
Net income	45,555	44,835	720
Less: PA	(9,440)	(9,440)	
Taxable income	36,115	35,395	720

Income tax

£			£
35,395 × 20%	(other)		7,079.00
615 × 20%	(savings)		123.00
———			
36,010			
105 × 40%	(savings)		42.00
———			
36,115			
———			———
Income tax liability			7,244.00
			———

Note: The full personal pension premium is allowable as it is less than the maximum amount allowed of £39,425 (100% of earned income).

The basic rate band is therefore extended by £4,000 (£3,200 × 100/80) to £36,010 (£32,010 + £4,000).

The contributions by Proctor's employer are an exempt benefit.

 Workbook Activity 7

Ming Lee

(a) **Maximum pension contribution**

The maximum personal pension contribution that Ming will obtain tax relief for is £47,600 being the higher of £3,600 and 100% of her earnings (£47,600).

Ming would pay the contribution net of basic rate tax:

i.e. £47,600 × 80% = £38,080.

(b)   Income tax computation – 2013/14

	Total	Other	Savings
	£	£	£
Employment income	47,600	47,600	
Building society			
(£6,300 × 100/80)	7,875		7,875
	———	———	———
Net income	55,475	47,600	7,875
Less: PA	(9,440)	(9,440)	
	———	———	———
Taxable income	46,035	38,160	7,875
	———	———	———

Income tax

£				£
38,160	× 20%	(other)		7,632.00
7,875	× 20%	(savings)		1,575.00
———				
46,035				
———				

	———
Income tax liability	9,207.00
Less: Tax deducted at source	
Building society (£7,875 × 20%)	(1,575.00)
PAYE	(9,900.00)
	———
Income tax repayable	(2,268.00)
	———

Note: The basic rate band is extended by £47,600 to £79,610 (£32,010 + £47,600).

Workbook Activity 8

Marjorie

Income tax computation – 2013/14

	Total £	Other £	Savings £	Dividends £
Employment income (£17,000 + £2,330)	19,330			
Less: Pension contributions	(936)			
Trading income	18,394	18,394		
Building society (£200 × 100/80)	250		250	
Dividends (£1,350 × 100/90)	1,500			1,500
Net income	20,144	18,394	250	1,500
Less: PA	(9,440)	(9,440)		
Taxable income	10,704	8,954	250	1,500

Income tax

£			£
8,954	× 20%	(other)	1,790.80
250	× 20%	(savings)	50.00
1,500	× 10%	(dividends)	150.00
10,704			

	£
Income tax liability	1,990.80
Less: Tax deducted at source	
Dividends (£1,500 × 10%)	(150.00)
Savings (£250 × 20%)	(50.00)
PAYE	(1,700.00)
Income tax payable	90.80

Note: Contributions into an occupational pension scheme are an allowable expense against employment income.

Workbook Activity 9

Peter

Income tax computation – 2013/14

	Total £	Other £	Savings £
Employment income	157,350	157,350	
Interest (£2,000 × 100/80)	2,500		2,500
Net income	159,850	157,350	2,500
Less: PA (W)	(6,890)	(6,890)	
Taxable income	152,960	150,460	2,500

Income tax

£			£
86,760	× 20%	(other)	17,352.00
63,700	× 40%	(other)	25,480.00
150,460			
2,500	× 40%	(savings)	1,000.00
152,960			
Income tax liability			43,832.00

Note: The basic rate band is extended by £54,750 ((£38,400 + £5,400) × 100/80) to £86,760 (£32,010 + £54,750).

The higher rate band will also be extended by £54,750. This extends the band to £204,750 (£150,000 + £54,750).

Working: The personal allowance is restricted because adjusted net income exceeds £100,000. The adjusted net income is calculated as follows.

	£
Net income	159,850
Less: Pension contributions (£38,400 × 100/80)	(48,000)
Gift Aid (£5,400 × 100/80)	(6,750)
Adjusted net income	105,100
	(100,000)
	5,100

The personal allowance is £6,890 (£9,440 – (£5,100 × ½)).

Workbook Activity 10

Long Life

The correct answer is **C**.

	£
Net income	31,100
Less PA (£10,500 – ½ (£27,600 (W) – £26,100)	(9,750)
Taxable income	21,350
Income tax at 20%	4,270.00

Working:

	£
Income for age allowance limit calculation £31,100 – (£2,800 × 100/80)	28,600

Workbook Activity 11

1   **False** – Payment to her employer's occupational pension scheme will be deducted from her salary. Her basic rate band is unaffected.

2   **False** – It could affect the PA and hence tax liability of a taxpayer born prior to 6 April 1948.

3   **False** – They are paid gross.

4   **True**

11 Payment and administration

Activity 1

Self assessment

(a) (i) 31 January following the tax year to which the return relates (i.e. 31 January 2015 for 2013/14)

   (ii) 31 October following the tax year to which the return relates (i.e. 31 October 2014 for 2013/14).

(b) (i) There will be an immediate penalty of £100.

   A further penalty of £10 per day for up to 90 days will be charged once the return is more than three months late.

   (ii) In addition to the penalties in part (i), there will be a penalty of 5% of the tax due (minimum £300) once the return is more than six months late.

   Once the return is more than 12 months late there will be a further penalty equal to a percentage of the tax due (minimum £300). The percentage is determined by the reason for the delay.

No deliberate withholding	5%
Deliberate withholding	70%
Deliberate withholding with concealment	100%

Activity 2

1 **False** – Normal date for filing paper returns is 31 October.

2 **False** – Where a return is submitted within three months of the due date the late filing penalty is £100.

3 **True**

4 **False** – The penalty will be 5% because the payment is more than 30 days late and a further 5% because the payment is more than six months late; a total of £125 (10% × £1,250).

Workbook Activity 3

Due dates	£
31 January 2014 and 31 July 2014	2,097.00
31 January 2015 (W)	2,293.12
31 January 2015 and 31 July 2015	3,243.56

Working:

	£
2013/14 Income tax	6,487.12
Less: POA (£2,097 × 2)	(4,194.00)
Final payment	2,293.12

2014/15 payments on account = (£6,487.12 ÷ 2) = £3,243.56.

 Workbook Activity 4

Lewis

1   **True** – The filing date for the 2013/14 return was 31 January 2015. There is a £100 penalty where a return is filed within three months of the due date.

2   **False** – The payment is less than six months late so the penalty will be 5%, not 10%.

3   **False** – If tax is paid late, then interest will be due whether or not a late payment penalty has been imposed.

Workbook Activity 5

Enquiries

(a) • HM Revenue and Customs (HMRC) must normally give written notice within 12 months of the date by which the return was submitted to HMRC.

(b) An enquiry is normally commenced due to:

    • a suspicion that it is incomplete or inaccurate.

    • selection for a random review.

(c) The taxpayer can either:

    • accept HMRC's amendment to his return; or

    • appeal to the Tribunal within 30 days.

 Workbook Activity 6

Income tax self assessment

(a) • Paper income tax returns for 2013/14 should normally be submitted by 31 October 2014.

(b) • On-line income tax returns for 2013/14 should be submitted by 31 January 2015.

(c) • If a tax return is submitted after 31 January following the tax year, a £100 fixed penalty is charged.

    • If it is still outstanding after 3 months, a further penalty of £10 per day may be charged.

    • If it is still outstanding after 6 months, a further penalty of 5% of the tax outstanding is charged.

    • If the return is still outstanding after 12 months, a further penalty of up to 100% of the tax outstanding is charged depending on the reason for the delay.

    • The penalties based on the tax due are each subject to a minimum of £300.

Workbook Activity 7

Ruby Chan (1)

Payments on account for 2013/14

	£
Income tax payable for 2012/13	
£10,320 – £520	9,800
	─────
Payments on account for 2013/14 (£9,800 × 0.5)	4,900
	─────

The payments are due on 31 January 2014 and 31 July 2014.

Balancing payment for 2013/14

Income tax payable for 2013/14	
£17,042 – £800	16,242
Less payments on account as above	(9,800)
	─────
	6,442
	─────

The payment is due on 31 January 2015

Payments on account for 2014/15

	£
Income tax payable for 2013/14 as above	16,242
	─────
Payments on account for 2014/15 (£16,242 × 0.5)	8,121
	─────

The payments are due on 31 January 2015 and 31 July 2015.

Workbook Activity 8

Ruby Chan (2)

(i) If you fail to file your 2013/14 return until 31 May 2015, you will be charged an initial fixed penalty of £100.

In addition, you may be charged £10 per day for up to 90 days once the return is more than three months overdue.

(ii) If you do not pay the 2013/14 balancing payment until 31 May 2015, then the payment (£6,442) will attract an interest charge from 31 January 2015 to 30 May 2015 inclusive. In addition a 5% late payment penalty will be imposed as the payment is more than 30 days late.

 Workbook Activity 9

Self assessment

(i) (1) 31 January in the tax year (i.e. 31 January 2014).

(2) 31 July following the tax year (i.e. 31 July 2014).

(3) 31 January following the tax year (i.e. 31 January 2015).

(ii) • Each of payments 1 and 2 is half the income tax liability (net of any tax deducted at source) in respect of 2012/13 (the preceding income tax year).

• Payment 3 is the balancing payment, i.e. it is the amount of the final tax liability for the year, less payments 1 and 2 and any tax deducted at source in 2013/14.

12 Introduction to capital gains tax

Activity 1

1	**NO**	A greyhound is a wasting chattel (tangible moveable property with a life of less than 50 years) and is therefore exempt.
2	**YES**	Gifts are still chargeable disposals and shares are a chargeable asset.
3	**NO**	Disposals on death are not chargeable disposals.
4	**NO**	Cars are exempt assets regardless of whether they are sold for a profit or a loss.
5	**NO**	Gifts to charity are not chargeable disposals.
6	**YES**	Principal Private Residence relief only applies to an individual's main home, therefore the sale of a holiday home is not exempt (see Chapter 13).

Activity 2

The correct answer is **A**.

Explanation

Taxable gains are defined as net chargeable gains after the deduction of the annual exempt amount, as follows:

	£
Total chargeable gains (£60,000 + £12,000)	72,000
Less Capital loss	(4,000)
	————
Net chargeable gains	68,000
Less: Annual exempt amount	(10,900)
	————
Taxable gain	57,100
	————

Activity 3

1   The correct answer is **B**.

2   The correct answer is **C**.

Explanation

	2012/13 £	2013/14 £
Current gains	15,000	16,300
Current losses	(17,000)	(4,000)
		12,300
Brought forward losses*		(1,400)
	Nil	10,900
Annual exempt amount	Wasted	(10,900)
		Nil
Loss carried forward		
(£17,000 – £15,000)	2,000	
(£2,000 – £1,400)		600

*Utilised to reduce gains to annual exempt amount.

Workbook Activity 4

1   **YES**   Shares are a chargeable asset.

2   **NO**   Motor cars are exempt assets.

3   **YES**   A gift is a chargeable disposal and Principal Private Residence relief only applies to an individual's main home, therefore the gift of a holiday home is not exempt.

4   **NO**   Chattels sold at a gain where the consideration is £6,000 or less are exempt assets.

5   **YES**   A gift is a chargeable disposal. The antique is treated as having been sold for its market value of £15,000.

Workbook Activity 5

1   **True.**

2   **False** – Capital losses cannot be set against anything except gains.

3   **False** – Current year losses must be relieved in full but brought forward losses are only utilised to the extent that they reduce net gains to the level of the annual exempt amount.

4   **False** – Gains are taxed at 28% for higher rate taxpayers.

 Workbook Activity 6

Mary

1   The correct answer is **B**.

2   The correct answer is **C**.

Explanation

1   Net chargeable gains for 2013/14 are £9,500 (£12,500 – £3,000). As this is less than the annual exempt amount, the loss brought forward of £4,000 is carried forward to 2014/15.

2   If Mary had only made the chargeable gain of £12,500 in 2013/14, losses brought forward of £1,600 would have been offset to reduce the gain to the level of the annual exempt amount. The balance of the capital losses of £2,400 (£4,000 – £1,600) would have been carried forward.

Workbook Activity 7

Carl

The correct answer is **A**.

	£
Chargeable gains for the year (£9,900 + £11,400)	21,300
Less: Current year capital losses	(2,500)
Net chargeable gains for the year	18,800
Less: Capital losses brought forward	(3,400)
Net chargeable gains	15,400
Less: Annual exempt amount	(10,900)
Taxable gains	4,500

Workbook Activity 8

Misha

The correct answer is **B**.

	£
Chargeable gains (£16,800 + £11,400)	28,200
Less: Annual exempt amount	(10,900)
Taxable gains	17,300
£8,110 (£32,010 – £23,900) × 18%	1,459.80
£9,190 (£17,300 – £8,110) × 28%	2,573.20
Capital gains tax liability	4,033.00

13 Calculation of individual gains and losses

Activity 1

Paul

The correct answer is B.

	£
Sales proceeds	145,000
Less: Allowable cost	(108,000)
Chargeable gain	37,000

Note: The fees of £2,000 in June 2005 were incurred by the seller, not Paul; therefore they are not an allowable deduction.

The **chargeable** gain is **before** deducting the annual exempt amount.

Activity 2

Mr Windsor

	£	£
(1) **Painting (non-wasting chattel)**		
Sales proceeds	6,600	
Less: Allowable cost	(3,500)	
	3,100	
Chargeable gain cannot exceed:		
⅝ × (sale proceeds – £6,000)		
= ⅝ × (£6,600 – £6,000)		1,000
C/f		1,000

B/f		1,000

(2) House

Sale proceeds	75,000	
Less: Allowable cost		
Original (April 1988)	(5,000)	
Enhancement (June 1993)	(10,000)	
Chargeable gain		60,000

(3) Car – exempt asset   Nil

(4) Plot of land (part disposal)

Sale proceeds	20,000	
Less: Allowable cost		

$$\frac{A}{A+B} \times £8,000$$

$$\frac{20,000}{20,000 + 60,000} \times £8,000 \quad (2,000)$$

Chargeable gain	18,000
Total chargeable gains	79,000

Activity 3

1 Market value used as disposal is between connected persons.

2 No gain or loss basis as transfer between spouses. Actual proceeds are irrelevant.

3 Actual proceeds used as transfer not between connected persons and not a deliberate sale at undervalue.

Activity 4

Mr Rialto

			£
Gain before relief			144,000
PPR exemption			

		Months
1 July 2001 – 31 October 2004	Occupied	40
1 November 2004 – 31 December 2005	Employed in UK	14
1 January 2006 – 30 June 2008	Occupied	30
1 July 2008 – 31 August 2013	Absent (note 1)	36
		120

	£
120/146 (note 2) × £144,000	(118,356)
Chargeable gain	25,644

Notes:

1 The last 36 months of ownership are always treated as a period of occupation. Accordingly, the period of absence from 1 September 2010 to 31 August 2013 is deemed occupation.

The beginning of the period of absence, from 1 July 2008 to 31 August 2010, cannot be treated as a period of occupation as Mr Rialto did not live in the property both before and after the period of absence.

2 Mr Rialto owned the property for a period of 146 months from 1 July 2001 to 31 August 2013.

Workbook Activity 5

Alfie

The correct answer is £25,000.

	£
Disposal proceeds	170,000
Less: Cost	(120,000)
Enhancement cost	(25,000)
Chargeable gain	25,000

 Workbook Activity 6

Lisa

The correct answer is £19,725.

	£
Disposal proceeds	56,250
Less: Selling costs	(3,375)
	52,875
Less: Cost	(32,500)
Incidental purchase costs	(650)
Chargeable gain	19,725

 Workbook Activity 7

1 **False** – The A / (A + B) formula should be used to calculate the allowable cost.

2 **False** – Advertising costs are an allowable selling cost.

3 **True**

4 **True** – Proceeds will be deemed to be £6,000 as a picture is a chattel and it has been sold for less than £6,000 but bought for more. The loss will therefore be (£6,000 – £8,000) = £2,000.

Workbook Activity 8

Asset	Sale proceeds	Cost	Statement
1	£8,000	£4,000	Gain restricted to 5/3 rule
2	£14,000	£20,000	Calculate loss as normal
3	£16,000	£7,000	Calculate gain as normal
4	£4,000	£9,000	Sale proceeds to be £6,000
5	£3,000	£2,000	Exempt asset

Workbook Activity 9

Whahid

The correct answer is **C**.

Explanation

	£
Proceeds	45,000
Less: Cost	
£28,000 × £45,000 / (£45,000 + £15,000)	(21,000)
Chargeable gain	24,000

Workbook Activity 10

1   £Nil – PPR exemption applies throughout.

2   £200,000, the house was never used as his PPR.

3   £10,000 (£200,000 × 1/20):

       First 3 years – exempt – actual occupation

       Next 4 years – exempt – working elsewhere in the UK

       Next 3 years – exempt – absent for any reason

       Next 1 year – chargeable under PPR rules

       Next 9 years – exempt – actual occupation

Workbook Activity 11

Mitch

Occupation	Non-occupation
1.7.03 – 30.6.09	1.7.09 – 30.9.10
1.10.10 – 30.9.13 (last three years)	

14 Shares and securities

 Activity 1

Petra

The correct answer is **A**.

Explanation

A is the correct answer because the share identification rules match shares in the following priority

1   Shares acquired on the same day as the disposal – not applicable here.

2   Shares acquired in the following 30 days – 50 shares acquired on 5 January 2014.

3   Shares in the share pool (all acquisitions up to date of disposal).

Activity 2

Ken

October 2013 disposal of 2,000 shares identified with:

		£
(a)	Shares acquired on the same day	400
(b)	Shares from share pool	1,600
		2,000

Sale proceeds are £33,000 for 2,000 shares

(a) 10 October 2013 acquisition

	£
Sale proceeds ($\frac{400}{2,000} \times$ £33,000)	6,600
Cost	(6,000)
Chargeable gain	600

(b) Share pool

	£
Sale proceeds ($\frac{1,600}{2,000} \times$ £33,000)	26,400
Cost (W)	(4,000)
Chargeable gain	22,400
Total chargeable gains	23,000

Workings: **Share pool**	**Number**	**Cost**
		£
February 1997 purchase	1,800	3,100
September 2006 purchase	1,200	4,400
	3,000	7,500
October 2013 disposal	(1,600)	(4,000)
Pool balance c/f	1,400	3,500

Activity 3

Mr Jones

	£
Sale proceeds	36,000
Less: Cost (W)	(10,414)
Chargeable gain	25,586

Workings: **share pool**	*Number*	*Cost*
		£
June 1990 purchase	4,200	11,600
August 2004 rights issue ($\frac{1}{3} \times 4{,}200$) = 1,400 × £5.60	1,400	7,840
	5,600	19,440
October 2013 disposal $\frac{3{,}000}{5{,}600} \times £19{,}440$	(3,000)	(10,414)
Pool balance c/f	2,600	9,026

 Workbook Activity 4

Ben

The correct answer is **C**.

Explanation

The share identification rules match shares in the following priority

1   Shares acquired on the same day as the disposal – not applicable here.

2   Shares acquired in the following 30 days – 500 shares acquired on 5 September 2013.

3   Shares in the share pool.

Workbook Activity 5

Tony

	£
Sale proceeds (9,000 × £14)	126,000
Less: Cost (W)	(50,625)
Chargeable gain	75,375

Workings: **Share pool**	*Number*	*Cost* £
August 2002 purchase (15,000 × £6)	15,000	90,000
January 2005 bonus issue	1,000	
	16,000	90,000
November 2012 disposal $\frac{9,000}{16,000} \times £90,000$	(9,000)	(50,625)
Pool balance c/f	7,000	39,375

Workbook Activity 6

Canrad

The correct answer is **B**.

Explanation

	£
Proceeds	8,580
Less: Cost (W)	(3,928)
Chargeable gain	4,652

Working: Share pool	Shares number	Cost £
July 2009 purchase	1,750	2,625
May 2010 purchase	200	640
	1,950	3,265
June 2011 rights issue (1 for 10) @ £3.40	195	663
	2,145	3,928
November 2013 sale	(2,145)	(3,928)
	Nil	Nil

Workbook Activity 7

David

The correct answer is **D**.

Explanation

Working: Share pool	Shares number	Cost £
October 2000 purchase	2,000	4,000
March 2006 purchase	1,000	3,000
	3,000	7,000
February 2008 rights issue (1 for 5) @ £4.00	600	2,400
	3,600	9,400
September 2013 sale	(400)	(1,044)
	3,200	8,356

15 Capital gains tax summary pages

Activity 1

HM Revenue & Customs

Capital gains summary
Tax year 6 April 2013 to 5 April 2014

1 Your name

M R B R A C K N E L L

2 Your Unique Taxpayer Reference (UTR)

Summary of your enclosed computations

Please read the *Capital gains summary notes* on pages CGN 10 to CGN 13 before filling in this section. **You must enclose your computations, including details of each gain or loss, as well as filling in the boxes.**

3 Total gains *(Boxes 19 + 25 + 31 + 32)*

£ 2 3 5 0 0 · 0 0

4 Gains qualifying for Entrepreneurs' Relief (but excluding gains deferred from before 23 June 2010) *- read the notes on page CGN 11*

£ · 0 0

5 Gains invested under Seed Enterprise Investment Scheme and qualifying for exemption *- read the notes on page CGN 11 and 12*

£ · 0 0

6 Total losses of the year *- enter '0' if there are none*

£ 8 0 0 0 · 0 0

7 Losses brought forward and used in the year

£ 4 6 0 0 · 0 0

8 Adjustment to Capital Gains Tax *- read the notes*

£ · 0 0

9 Additional liability for non-resident or dual resident trusts

£ · 0 0

10 Losses available to be carried forward to later years

£ 9 4 0 0 · 0 0

11 Losses used against an earlier year's gain (special circumstances apply *- read the notes on page CGN 12*)

£ · 0 0

12 Losses used against income – amount claimed against 2013–14 income *- read the notes on page CGN 13*

£ · 0 0

13 Losses used against income – amount claimed against 2012–13 income *- read the notes on page CGN 13*

£ · 0 0

14 Income losses of 2013–14 set against gains

£ · 0 0

15 Deferred gains from before 23 June 2010 qualifying for Entrepreneurs' Relief

£ · 0 0

Listed shares and securities

16 Number of disposals *- read the notes on page CGN 13*

1

17 Disposal proceeds

£ 1 0 0 0 0 · 0 0

18 Allowable costs (including purchase price)

£ 1 8 0 0 0 · 0 0

19 Gains in the year, before losses

£ · 0 0

20 If you are making any claim or election, put 'X' in the box

21 If your computations include any estimates or valuations, put 'X' in the box

SA108 2013 | Page CG 1 | HMRC 12/12

Workbook Activity 2

Charlotte French

HM Revenue & Customs

Capital gains summary
Tax year 6 April 2013 to 5 April 2014

1 Your name

C H A R L O T T E

F R E N C H

2 Your Unique Taxpayer Reference (UTR)

Summary of your enclosed computations

Please read the *Capital gains summary notes* on pages CGN 10 to CGN 13 before filling in this section. **You must enclose your computations, including details of each gain or loss, as well as filling in the boxes.**

3 Total gains *(Boxes 19 + 25 + 31 + 32)*

£ 23 000 . 00

4 Gains qualifying for Entrepreneurs' Relief (but excluding gains deferred from before 23 June 2010) - *read the notes on page CGN 11*

£ . 00

5 Gains invested under Seed Enterprise Investment Scheme and qualifying for exemption - *read the notes on page CGN 11 and 12*

£ . 00

6 Total losses of the year - *enter '0' if there are none*

£ 3 000 . 00

7 Losses brought forward and used in the year

£ . 00

8 Adjustment to Capital Gains Tax - *read the notes*

£ . 00

9 Additional liability for non-resident or dual resident trusts

£ . 00

10 Losses available to be carried forward to later years

£ . 00

11 Losses used against an earlier year's gain (special circumstances apply - *read the notes on page CGN 12*)

£ . 00

12 Losses used against income - amount claimed against 2013–14 income - *read the notes on page CGN 13*

£ . 00

13 Losses used against income - amount claimed against 2012–13 income - *read the notes on page CGN 13*

£ . 00

14 Income losses of 2013–14 set against gains

£ . 00

15 Deferred gains from before 23 June 2010 qualifying for Entrepreneurs' Relief

£ . 00

Listed shares and securities

16 Number of disposals - *read the notes on page CGN 13*

3

17 Disposal proceeds

£ 69 500 . 00

18 Allowable costs (including purchase price)

£ 49 500 . 00

19 Gains in the year, before losses

£ 23 000 . 00

20 If you are making any claim or election, put 'X' in the box

21 If your computations include any estimates or valuations, put 'X' in the box

SA108 2013   Page CG 1   HMRC 12/12

Workbook Activity 3

Mrs England

HM Revenue & Customs

Capital gains summary
Tax year 6 April 2013 to 5 April 2014

1 Your name

M R S   E N G L A N D

2 Your Unique Taxpayer Reference (UTR)

Summary of your enclosed computations

Please read the *Capital gains summary notes* on pages CGN 10 to CGN 13 before filling in this section. **You must enclose your computations, including details of each gain or loss, as well as filling in the boxes.**

3 Total gains *(Boxes 19 + 25 + 31 + 32)*

£ 3 8 5 0 0 . 0 0

4 Gains qualifying for Entrepreneurs' Relief (but excluding gains deferred from before 23 June 2010)
– *read the notes on page CGN 11*

£ . 0 0

5 Gains invested under Seed Enterprise Investment Scheme and qualifying for exemption – *read the notes on page CGN 11 and 12*

£ . 0 0

6 Total losses of the year – *enter '0' if there are none*

£ 9 0 0 0 . 0 0

7 Losses brought forward and used in the year

£ 1 1 0 0 0 . 0 0

8 Adjustment to Capital Gains Tax – *read the notes*

£ . 0 0

9 Additional liability for non-resident or dual resident trusts

£ . 0 0

10 Losses available to be carried forward to later years

£ . 0 0

11 Losses used against an earlier year's gain (special circumstances apply – *read the notes on page CGN 12*)

£ . 0 0

12 Losses used against income – amount claimed against 2013–14 income – *read the notes on page CGN 13*

£ . 0 0

13 Losses used against income – amount claimed against 2012–13 income – *read the notes on page CGN 13*

£ . 0 0

14 Income losses of 2013–14 set against gains

£ . 0 0

15 Deferred gains from before 23 June 2010 qualifying for Entrepreneurs' Relief

£ . 0 0

Listed shares and securities

16 Number of disposals – *read the notes on page CGN 13*

1

17 Disposal proceeds

£ 3 5 5 0 0 . 0 0

18 Allowable costs (including purchase price)

£ 2 0 0 0 0 . 0 0

19 Gains in the year, before losses

£ 1 5 5 0 0 . 0 0

20 If you are making any claim or election, put 'X' in the box

21 If your computations include any estimates or valuations, put 'X' in the box

SA108 2013   Page CG 1   HMRC 12/12

16 Duties and responsibilities of a tax adviser

 Activity 1

The answer is **D**.

The duty of confidentiality can be overridden if the client gives authority or if there is a legal, regulatory or professional duty to disclose.

 Activity 2

The correct answer is **C**.

 Activity 3

1   **False** – Individuals only have to submit a tax return if they are required to do so by HMRC.

2   **False** – Personal records must be kept for one year from the filing date of 31 January and business records, such as for property income, for 5 years from the filing date

MOCK ASSESSMENT
AQ2013

1 Mock Assessment Questions AQ2013

You should attempt and aim to complete EVERY task.

Each task is independent. You will not need to refer to your answers to previous tasks.

Read every task carefully to make sure you understand what is required.

Where the date is relevant, it is given in the task data.

Both minus signs and brackets can be used to indicate negative numbers UNLESS task instructions say otherwise.

You must use a full stop to indicate a decimal point.

Task 1 (9 marks)

(1) What percentage would be used to calculate the benefit for the following diesel cars provided to employees for a mixture of business and private use during 2013/14?

    (a)   127 g/km (Choices: 0%, 15%, 19%, 20%)

    (b)   210 g/km (Choices: 15%, 34%, 35%, 37%)

    (c)   91 g/km (Choices: 10%, 13%, 15%, 18%)

    (d)   72 g/km (Choices: 5%, 8%, 10%, 13%)

(2) A petrol van with CO_2 emissions of 147 g/km is provided to Emmanuel for business and private use between 6 April 2013 and 5 October 2013. The list price of the van is £18,200.

    What is the taxable benefit?

    A   £1,500

    B   £1,911

    C   £3,822

    D   £3,000

(3) Jake is provided with the use of a Toyota IQ car on 6 November 2013 by his employer. The list price of the car is £16,000 and Jake made a capital contribution of £1,800 towards the cost of the car. The CO_2 emissions are 139 g/km and it has a petrol engine. The company pays for all the running costs of the car including fuel.

(a)   **What is the taxable benefit for 2013/14 for the use of the car?**

£

(b)   **What is the fuel benefit for 2013/14?**

£

Task 2   **(10 marks)**

(1)   On 6 June 2013, Sue was provided with a flat to live in, purchased by her employer in 2012 for £126,000. The flat had an annual value of £2,500 and is not job related accommodation. It has furniture supplied by her employer and valued at £15,000 when Sue moved in. Her employer also paid her gas bill of £125. The official rate of interest is 4%.

(a)   **What is the accommodation benefit (only) for 2013/14?**

(b)   **What are the total ancillary benefits for 2013/14?**

(2)   On 10 December 2011, Rona was provided with a loan of £18,000 from her employer. The interest rate charged is 1.5%. Rona repaid £1,500 of the loan during 2013/14. The official rate of interest is 4%.

Using the average method, how much is the taxable benefit for the loan for 2013/14?

(3)   Engelbert is loaned the use of a television by his employer. The television cost £650 when first provided on 1 May 2013. Engelbert does not have any business use of the television but he does pay £5 per month to his employer for the use of the television from 1 May 2013.

What is Engelbert's taxable benefit for the use of the television during 2013/14?

(4) **Mark the following statements as true or false**

	True	False
There is no assessable benefit for the provision of a company bicycle when bicycles are available to all staff.		
An employer pays a private medical insurance premium of £800 for an employee. The employee does not reimburse the employer. If the employee joined the scheme privately the cost would be £1,100. The assessable benefit for the employee is £1,100.		

(5) **Mark the following benefits as taxable or exempt**

	Taxable	Exempt
Childcare vouchers provided to an employee of £45 per week. The employee, who is a basic rate taxpayer, spent the vouchers with an approved childminder.		
A second mobile phone provided to an employee.		
A car parking space in a multi-storey car park near the place of work.		
An employer contribution to an employee's pension scheme.		

Task 3   (10 marks)

(a) Joan Miller has two properties that she rents out;

   (1) Two bedroom unfurnished flat. This was occupied throughout 2013/14. The monthly rent was £620 until 31 December 2013 and then it increased to £680. Joan paid an agents fee of 5% of the total rental income, gardening fees of £200 for 2013/14 and bought a new kitchen for the house costing £5,000.

(2) Three bedroom furnished house. This was occupied until 5 November 2013 at a monthly rent of £750 and was not re-occupied for the rest of 2013/14. Joan paid mortgage interest of £50 per month on this property.

Joan has a property loss brought forward of £1,500 from 2012/13.

Calculate the property income to be entered into the income tax computation for 2013/14 for both properties using the following table.

	Flat £	House £
Income		
Expenses		

(b) Mark the following statements as true or false.

	True	False
Income from property is taxed on a receipts basis.		
In order to receive the special treatment as furnished holiday accommodation, properties must be available for short term letting all year round.		
Joseph receives rent of £4,000 per year from letting a room in his own house. For 2013/14 he must claim rent-a-room relief by 31 January 2016.		
Bad debts, (i.e. rents not received), are ignored when calculating 10% wear and tear allowance for a furnished letting.		

Task 4 (6 marks)

(1) Complete the following table to show the amount of income to be included in the personal income tax computation.

	Amount received £	Included in income tax computation £
Building society interest	52	
Dividend received	153	
ISA interest	80	
NS&I Bank Interest	110	
Premium Bond prize received by a person aged 65	50	

(2) **Which one of the following statements about dividends received is incorrect?**

A   Dividends are taxed as if received net of a 10% tax credit.

B   Shares held in ISAs produce exempt dividends.

C   Taxpayers under 16 are exempt from paying any tax on dividends received.

D   Dividends falling into the additional rate band are taxed at 37.5%

Task 5   **(12 marks)**

Novak who is 27 provides you with the following information:

(1)   His gross annual salary up to 31 December 2013 was £21,000.He received a pay rise to an annual salary of £23,500 on 1 January 2014.

(2)   He received a bonus of £550 on 15 April 2013 which related to the financial year ended 31 December 2012.

He received a bonus of £610 on 15 April 2014 which related to the financial year ended 31 December 2013

(3)   Novak pays £10 per month to charity through the payroll giving scheme.

(4)   He has had the use of a company car from 1 July 2013. The annual assessable benefit for this car is £5,600.

(5)   Novak paid 6% of his salary to his employer's occupational pension scheme. Novak's employers contribute 5% of his salary to the pension scheme.

(6)   During 2013/14 Novak received interest from an ISA of £250, interest from government stocks of £400 and dividends of £450.

Complete the following table showing the figure that may be included in Novak's taxable income for 2013/14. Use whole pounds only. If your answer is zero then please put '0'. Do not use brackets or minus signs.

	£
Salary	
Bonus	
Employee pension contribution	
Employer's pension contribution	
Car benefit	
Payroll giving	
ISA interest	
Interest on government stocks	
Dividends	
Personal allowance	
Taxable income	

Task 6 (10 marks)

During 2013/14 Lauren, who is 75 years old had a gross salary of £26,100 from which £3,100 of PAYE has been deducted. She also received dividends of £900. Lauren pays £640 to Oxfam each year through the Gift Aid scheme.

Calculate her total <u>income tax payable or repayable</u> for 2013/14 using the table set out below.

Task 7 (10 marks)

(a) Neil has never previously completed a self assessment tax return.

He is worried that he should be completing a tax return for 2013/14 as he has recently started receiving rent and has requested information from you concerning the completion of tax returns and the due dates of payment of tax.

In particular he wishes to know:

- when he should tell HMRC about his new rental income and the consequences of not informing them

- when his 2013/14 tax return will need to be submitted

- the penalties arising for the late submission of a return

- when the balance of his income tax for 2013/14 will be payable (he does not need to make payments on account)

- the consequences of late payment of the tax due

Write brief notes answering Neil's questions.

(b) Which one of the following statements is not correct?

A   A member should adopt an ethical approach to their work for employers and clients

B   You can disclose details about a client's tax affairs provided they have given you permission.

C   An AAT member has a duty of confidentiality to a client even after the member has retired from practice.

D   If an AAT member cannot resolve an ethical issue they should seek advice from their supervisor, a professional body or the police.

(c) How many years from the filing date (31 January 2015) should documents relating to property income for 2013/14 be kept?

Task 8 (7 marks)

Using the following information, complete the tax return below:

John is employed by Becks Ltd. His form P60 for 2013/14 shows:

	£
Gross pay	45,000
Tax deducted	7,905

His form P11D for 2013/14 shows the following:

Car benefit	4,890
Fuel benefit	4,320
Use of company home cinema equipment	350
Camera given to John after use by another employee	125
Interest free loan	240
Expenses allowances received	6,000
Private medical insurance – premium paid by employer	865
Expenses paid by John:	
Subscription to the Institute of Surveyors	475
Hotel bills whilst working away	5,220

Employment

Tax year 6 April 2013 to 5 April 2014

Your name

Your Unique Taxpayer Reference (UTR)

Complete an *Employment* page for each employment or directorship

1 Pay from this employment – the total from your P45 or P60 - *before tax was taken off*

£ · 0 0

2 UK tax taken off pay in box 1

£ · 0 0

3 Tips and other payments not on your P60 - *read the Employment notes*

£ · 0 0

4 PAYE tax reference of your employer (on your P45/P60)

/

5 Your employer's name

6 If you were a company director, put 'X' in the box

7 And, if the company was a close company, put 'X' in the box

8 If you are a part-time teacher in England or Wales and are on the Repayment of Teachers' Loans Scheme for this employment, put 'X' in the box

Benefits from your employment - use your form P11D (or equivalent information)

9 Company cars and vans - *the total 'cash equivalent' amount*

£ · 0 0

10 Fuel for company cars and vans - *the total 'cash equivalent' amount*

£ · 0 0

11 Private medical and dental insurance - *the total 'cash equivalent' amount*

£ · 0 0

12 Vouchers, credit cards and excess mileage allowance

£ · 0 0

13 Goods and other assets provided by your employer - *the total value or amount*

£ · 0 0

14 Accommodation provided by your employer - *the total value or amount*

£ · 0 0

15 Other benefits (including interest-free and low interest loans) - *the total 'cash equivalent' amount*

£ · 0 0

16 Expenses payments received and balancing charges

£ · 0 0

Employment expenses

17 Business travel and subsistence expenses

£ · 0 0

18 Fixed deductions for expenses

£ · 0 0

19 Professional fees and subscriptions

£ · 0 0

20 Other expenses and capital allowances

£ · 0 0

ⓘ **Shares schemes, employment lump sums, compensation, deductions and Seafarers' Earnings Deduction** are on the *Additional information* pages enclosed in the tax return pack.

SA102 2013   Page E 1   HMRC 12/12

Task 9   **(12 marks)**

(1) Romana sold a painting for £11,500 in October 2013. She had originally purchased the painting in August 1999 for £4,800. She had the painting professionally cleaned at a cost of £150 in August 2013 to prepare it for sale.

What is the gain or loss on the sale of this asset?

```



```

(2) Stefan sold an antique pocket watch for £2,800 in September 2013, which had originally been purchased for £1,900 in June 1993.

What is the gain or loss on the sale of this asset?

```



```

(3) Paula sold a painting to her brother for £15,000. The painting cost Paula £11,520 in June 2005. The market value of the painting at the date of the sale was £17,200.

What is the gain or loss on the sale of this asset?

```



```

(4) Alex attends a party with the following people.

His girlfriend, his brother, his sister and her husband, his cousin and finally Alex's grandfather also attends.

How many of these people are connected with Alex for capital gains purposes?

A   6

B   5

C   4

D   3

(5) Sally sold a diamond ring for £5,200 in August 2013. She had purchased the ring for £7,150 in November 2012.

Which of the following applies to calculating the gain/loss on disposal?

    A   The loss is calculated as normal

    B   The sales proceeds are deemed to be £6,000

    C   There is a restriction on the gain of:
           5/3 × (gross sales proceeds − £6,000)

    D   The gain is calculated as normal

    E   Rings are exempt from tax

(6) Sheena sold 3 acres of land for £28,000. She bought 10 acres in July 1992 for £32,000. The value of the remaining 7 acres at the date of sale was £90,000.

What is the gain/loss on this disposal?

Task 10 (8 marks)

Mai sold 4,200 shares in Toby Ltd for £8.50 per share in May 2013. She purchased 3,500 shares in Toby Ltd for £16,800 in April 2009, she purchased a rights issue of 1 for 4 at £3.60 per share in November 2011 and she received a bonus issue of 1 for 3 in January 2013.

Clearly showing the balance of shares and their value to carry forward, calculate the gain made on these shares. All workings must be shown in your calculations.

Task 11 (6 marks)

(a) John bought a house for £52,000 on 1 February 1998. He lived in the house until 31 March 1999 when he went travelling. He returned to the house on 1 June 2007 and lived in it until 30 November 2012 when he moved into his girlfriend's flat. The house was sold for £180,000 on 1 June 2013.

(i) Total period of ownership ....months

(ii) Total period of actual and deemed residence ....months

(iii) Chargeable gain on sale £................................

(b) **Mark the following statements as true or false?**

	True	*False*
Capital losses can be offset against taxable income if the taxpayer has no capital gains in the year.		
Current year capital losses must be deducted from current year capital gains even where the gains are less than the annual exempt amount.		

(c) Jenna had gains of £35,800 for 2013/14 in respect of quoted shares sold on the stock market. She also had capital losses brought forward of £4,000 from 2012/13 which arose when she sold a painting to her brother. She is a higher rate taxpayer.

What is her capital gains tax liability for 2013/14?

2 Mock Assessment Answers AQ2013

Task 1

(1) (a) 20% (11% + 1/5 (125 − 95) + 3%)

(b) 35% (11% + 1/5 (210 − 95) + 3%)= 37% so restricted to 35%

(c) 13% (10% + 3%)

(d) 8% (5% + 3%)

(2) The answer is A.

Van benefit for 6 months is £1,500 (£3,000 × 6/12)

(3) (a) £1,124

(£16,000 − £1,800) = £14,200 × 19% (W) × 5/12

Working for % = 11% + 1/5(135 − 95) = 19%

(b) £1,670

(£21,100 × 19% × 5/12)

Task 2

(1) (a) The answer is £3,783

(£2,500 + 4% (£126,000 − £75,000)) × 10/12 = £3,783

(b) The answer is £2,625.

(£15,000 × 20% × 10/12) + £125 = £2,625

(2) The answer is £431.

(£18,000 + £16,500)/2 × (4% − 1.5%) = £431

(3) The answer is £64.

(£650 × 20%) × 11/12 − (£5 × 11) = £64

(4)

	True	False
There is no assessable benefit for the provision of a company bicycle when bicycles are available to all staff.	✓	
An employer pays a private medical insurance premium of £800 for an employee. The employee does not reimburse the employer. If the employee joined the scheme privately the cost would be £1,100. The assessable benefit for the employee is £1,100.		✓

Notes:

(1) Company bicycles must be available to staff generally.

(2) The assessable benefit for the private medical insurance is based on the cost to the employer.

(5)

	Taxable	Exempt
Childcare vouchers provided to an employee of £45 per week. The employee, who is a basic rate taxpayer, spent the vouchers with an approved childminder.		✓
A second mobile phone provided to an employee.	✓	
A car parking space in a multi-storey car park near the place of work.		✓
An employer contribution to an employee's pension scheme.		✓

Task 3

(a)

	Flat £	House £
Income		
£620 × 9 + £680 × 3	7,620	
£750 × 7		5,250
Expenses		
Agents fees (5% × £7,620)	(381)	
Gardening fees	(200)	
New kitchen is capital	Nil	
Mortgage interest (£50 × 12)		(600)
Wear and tear allowance		
£5,250 × 10%		(525)
Property income	7,039	4,125
Total property income		11,164
Less Loss b/f		(1,500)
Taxable property income		9,664

(b)

	True	False
Income from property is taxed on a receipts basis.		✓
In order to receive the special treatment as furnished holiday accommodation, properties must be available for short term letting all year round.		✓
Joseph receives rent of £4,000 per year from letting a room in his own house. For 2013/14 he must claim rent-a-room relief by 31 January 2015.		✓
Bad debts, (i.e. rents not received), are ignored when calculating 10% wear and tear allowance for a furnished letting.		✓

Notes:

(1) Property income is taxed on an accruals basis not receipts

(2) Properties need to be available for short term letting for seven months in the year, not all year,

(3) Rent a room applies automatically if rents are ≤ £4,250.

(4) Wear and tear allowance is calculated on rents less bad debts less amounts paid by the landlord which are the tenant's responsibility.

Task 4

(1)

	Amount received	Included in income tax computation
	£	£
Building society interest *(× 100/80)*	52	65
Dividend received *(× 100/90)*	153	170
ISA interest	80	Exempt
NS&I Bank Interest *(received gross)*	110	110
Premium Bond prize received by a person aged 65	50	Exempt

(2) The answer is C.

Taxpayers under 16 are not automatically exempt from income tax on dividends. However, they do not usually have to pay tax because their income is usually less than the personal allowance.

Task 5

	£
Salary	21,625
Bonus	550
Employee's pension contribution (a)	1298
Employer's pension contribution	0
Car benefit (b)	4,200
Payroll giving	120
ISA interest (c)	0
Interest on government stocks (c)	400
Dividends	500
Personal allowance	9,440
Taxable income	16,417

Workings:

(a)   Employee's pension contribution £1,298 (£21,625 × 6%). Note that in an assessment it would not matter if you rounded this up or down.

(b)   Car benefit £4,200 (£5,600 × 9/12)

(c)   ISA interest is exempt. Interest from government stocks is received gross.

Task 6

	Total	Other income	Divis
	£	£	£
Salary	26,100	26,100	
Dividends (£900 × 100/90)	1,000		1,000
Net income	27,100		
Less Age PA £10,660			
less ½ (£27,100 – £800 £26,100)	(10,560)	(10,560)	
Taxable income	16,540	15,540	1,000
£15,540 × 20%	3,108.00		
£1,000 × 10%	100.00		
Income tax liability	3,208.00		
Less Dividend tax credits	(100.00)		
PAYE	(3,000.00)		
Tax payable	108.00		

The Gift Aid payment is grossed up to £800 (£640 × 100/80) and reduces the net income for the purpose of calculating the personal allowance

Task 7

Notification of new income

(a) Neil must notify HMRC of his new untaxed income by 5 October 2014.

Failure to notify HMRC can result in a penalty which is calculated as a percentage of any tax unpaid at 31 January 2015.

Submission of the tax return

The taxpayer has the choice of filing a paper return or filing electronically on line.

The date by which a return must be filed depends on the method used.

For 2013/14

- All completed and signed paper returns must normally be filed by 31 October 2014

- All on line (electronic) returns must be filed by 31 January 2015

If a 2013/14 return is not issued in good time by HMRC then it must be filed within three months of the date of issue if this is later than the normal due date.

Penalties for late submission

Immediate penalty	£100
Delay of more than three months	£10 per day
Delay of more than six months	5% of tax due
Delay of more than 12 months	Tax related penalty

The due date for the balance of income tax outstanding

The balance of income tax is due on 31 January 2015.

The consequences of late payment

(i) Interest is charged, calculated on a daily basis, running from due date of payment to the date the tax is actually paid.

(ii) Penalties are due, calculated as follows:

5% of tax outstanding if more than 30 days late

A further 5% due if more than 6 months late.

A further 5% due if more than 12 months late.

(b) The answer is D.

Statements A to C are correct.

If an AAT member cannot resolve an ethical issue they should seek advice from their supervisor or their professional body. They do not seek advice from the police.

(c) 5 years

Task 8

HM Revenue & Customs

Employment
Tax year 6 April 2013 to 5 April 2014

Your name
J O H N

Your Unique Taxpayer Reference (UTR)

Complete an *Employment* page for each employment or directorship

1 Pay from this employment – the total from your P45 or P60 – *before tax was taken off*
£ 4 5 0 0 0 . 0 0

2 UK tax taken off pay in box 1
£ 7 9 0 5 . 0 0

3 Tips and other payments not on your P60
– *read the Employment notes*
£ . 0 0

4 PAYE tax reference of your employer (on your P45/P60)

5 Your employer's name
B E C K S   L T D

6 If you were a company director, put 'X' in the box

7 And, if the company was a close company, put 'X' in the box

8 If you are a part-time teacher in England or Wales and are on the Repayment of Teachers' Loans Scheme for this employment, put 'X' in the box

Benefits from your employment – use your form P11D (or equivalent information)

9 Company cars and vans
– *the total 'cash equivalent' amount*
£ 4 8 9 0 . 0 0

10 Fuel for company cars and vans
– *the total 'cash equivalent' amount*
£ 4 3 2 0 . 0 0

11 Private medical and dental insurance
– *the total 'cash equivalent' amount*
£ 8 6 5 . 0 0

12 Vouchers, credit cards and excess mileage allowance
£ . 0 0

13 Goods and other assets provided by your employer
– *the total value or amount* (350 + 125)
£ 4 7 5 . 0 0

14 Accommodation provided by your employer
– *the total value or amount*
£ . 0 0

15 Other benefits (including interest-free and low interest loans) – *the total 'cash equivalent' amount*
£ 2 4 0 . 0 0

16 Expenses payments received and balancing charges
£ 6 0 0 0 . 0 0

Employment expenses

17 Business travel and subsistence expenses
£ 5 2 2 0 . 0 0

18 Fixed deductions for expenses
£ . 0 0

19 Professional fees and subscriptions
£ 4 7 5 . 0 0

20 Other expenses and capital allowances
£ . 0 0

ℹ Shares schemes, employment lump sums, compensation, deductions and Seafarers' Earnings Deduction are on the *Additional information* pages enclosed in the tax return pack.

SA102 2013   Page E 1   HMRC 12/12

Task 9

(1)   Romana

	£
Proceeds	11,500
Less: Selling costs	(150)
Net sales proceeds	11,350
Less: Cost	(4,800)
Gain	6,550

5/3 (£11,500 – £6,000) = £9,167

Chargeable gain	£6,550

(2)   Stefan

This is an exempt disposal as the watch is a chattel bought and sold for less than £6,000

(3)   Paula

	£
Proceeds = Market value	17,200
Less: Cost	(11,520)
Chargeable gain	5,680

Market value has been used because Paula
and her brother are connected persons.

(4)   The answer is C.

Alex is connected with everyone except his girlfriend and his cousin.

(5) The answer is B.

When a chattel is sold for less than £6,000 but was purchased for more than £6,000, the taxpayer can deem the gross proceeds of sale to be £6,000 in order to receive at least some capital loss.

(6) The answer is £20,407.

	£
Proceeds	28,000
Less: Cost (£28,000÷(£28,000 + £90,000)) × £32,000	(7,593)
Chargeable gain	20,407

The cost of the land sold must be found using the A/A+B formula
A = £28,000 B = £90,000

Task 10

Shares

		£	
Sales proceeds	(£8.50 × 4,200)	35,700	
Less: Cost (Pool)		(14,365)	
Chargeable gain		21,335	
Pool		Number	Cost (£)
4/09 Purchase		3,500	16,800
11/11 Rights	1 for 4 at £3.60	875	3,150
		4,375	19,950
1/13 Bonus	1 for 3	1,458	Nil
		5,833	19,950
5/13 Sale		(4,200)	(W)(14,365)
Balance c/f		1,633	5,585
Working	4,200/5,833		
	× £19,950	= £14,365	

Task 11

(a) (i)   184 months

   (ii)   122 months

   (iii) Gain

	£
Sales proceeds	180,000
Less: Cost	(52,000)
	———
Gain before relief	128,000
Less: PPR exemption (W) (122/184 × £128,000)	(84,870)
	———
Chargeable gain	43,130
	———

Date	Total months	Exempt months	Comments
1.2.98 – 31.3.99	14	14	Occupation
1.4.99 – 31.3.02	36	36	3 years any reason
1.4.02 – 31.5.07	62		
1.6.07 – 30.11.12	66	66	Occupation
1.12.12 – 31.5.13	6	6	Last 3 years
	———	———	
Total	184	122	
	———	———	

(b)

	True	False
Capital losses can be offset against taxable income if the taxpayer has no capital gains in the year.		✓
Current year capital losses must be deducted from current year capital gains even where the gains are less than the annual exempt amount.	✓	

(c)   The answer is £6,972

	£
Gains	35,800
Less: Annual exempt amount	(10,900)
Taxable gains	24,900
Tax at 28%	£6,972

Jenna cannot use the loss on disposal to her brother against gains generally, only on future gains on assets sold to her brother

MOCK ASSESSMENT
AQ2010

1 Mock Assessment Questions AQ2010

This assessment is in TWO sections.

You must show competence in each section.

You should therefore attempt and aim to complete EVERY task in EACH section.

Each task is independent. You will not need to refer to your answers to previous tasks.

Read every task carefully to make sure you understand what is required.

Where the date is relevant, it is given in the task data.

Both minus signs and brackets can be used to indicate negative numbers UNLESS task instructions say otherwise.

You must use a full stop to indicate a decimal point.

SECTION 1

Task 1.1

(1) **Which of the following statements are true?**

   (i)   If a self assessment tax return is filed 2 months late, the penalty cannot exceed £200

   (ii)   For 2013/14, the 31 January 2015 is known as the filing date

   A   (i) and (ii)

   B   (i) only

   C   (ii) only

   D   Neither

(2) **If a taxpayer has to make payments on account for 2013/14, when are they due?**

   A   31.7.2013 and 31.1.2014

   B   31.7.2014 and 31.1.2015

   C   31.1.2014 and 31.7.2014

   D   31.1.2014 and 31.1.2015

Task 1.2

Which one of the following statements is not correct?

A   A member should adopt an ethical approach to their work for employers and clients

B   You can disclose details about a client's tax affairs provided they have given you permission.

C   An AAT member has a duty of confidentiality to a client even after the member has retired from practice.

D   If an AAT member cannot resolve an ethical issue they should seek advice from their supervisor, a professional body or the police.

Task 1.3

For each statement, tick either self employment or employment

	Employment	Self employment
Provision of own equipment		
Paid holidays		
Having to correct mistakes at your own expense		

Task 1.4

(1)   Stuart provides you with the following information about his employment income.

- His gross annual salary up to 31 December 2013 was £21,000

- His gross annual salary up to 31 December 2014 was £23,500

- He received a bonus of £550 on 15 April 2013 which related to the financial year ended 31 December 2012.

- He received a bonus of £610 on 15 April 2014 which related to the financial year ended 31 December 2013

- He received a bonus of £720 on 15 April 2015 which related to the financial year ended 31 December 2014.

(a) **What is his taxable salary for 2013/14?**

    A   £23,500

    B   £21,625

    C   £21,000

    D   £21,417

(b) **What is his taxable bonus for 2013/14?**

    A   £550

    B   £458

    C   £610

    D   £638

(2) Puccini pays £1,200 to a personal pension scheme.

Mark the following statements as true or false.

	True	*False*
The £1,200 is net of 20% tax relief.		
Puccini's pension provider can recover tax of £240 from HMRC to invest in Puccini's pension scheme.		
Provided his relevant earnings are no more than the annual allowance, Puccini can invest a figure equal to his relevant earnings into the pension scheme and obtain tax relief		
Income from furnished holiday lettings is not included in the figure of relevant earnings for pension purposes.		

Task 1.5

(1) What percentage would be used to calculate the benefit for the following diesel cars provided to employees for a mixture of business and private use during 2013/14?

    (a)   127 g/km (Choices: 0%, 15%, 19%, 20%)

    (b)   210 g/km (Choices: 15%, 34%, 35%, 37%)

    (c)   91 g/km (Choices: 10%, 13%, 15%, 18%)

    (d)   72 g/km (Choices: 5%, 8%, 10%, 13%)

(2) A petrol van with CO_2 emissions of 147 g/km is provided to Emmanuel for business and private use between 6 April 2013 and 5 October 2013. The list price of the van is £18,200.

What is the taxable benefit?

A   £1,500

B   £1,911

C   £3,822

D   £3,000

(3) Jake is provided with the use of a Toyota IQ car on 6 November 2013 by his employer. The list price of the car is £16,000 and Jake made a capital contribution of £1,800 towards the cost of the car. The CO_2 emissions are 139 g/km and it has a petrol engine. The company pays for all the running costs of the car including fuel.

(a) What is the taxable benefit for 2013/14 for the use of the car?

£ [   ]

(b) What is the fuel benefit for 2013/14?

£ [   ]

Task 1.6

(1) On 6 June 2013, Sue was provided with a flat to live in, purchased by her employer in 2012 for £126,000. The flat had an annual value of £2,500 and is not job related accommodation. It has furniture supplied by her employer and valued at £15,000 when Sue moved in. Her employer also paid her gas bill of £125. The official rate of interest is 4%.

(a) What is the accommodation benefit (only) for 2013/14?

A   £2,083

B   £4,540

C   £3,783

D   £1,700

(b) What are the total ancillary benefits for 2013/14?

A   £2,625

B   £15,125

C   £3,125

D   £12,625

(2) On 10 December 2011, Rona was provided with a loan of £18,000 from her employer. The interest rate charged is 1.5%. Rona repaid £1,500 of the loan during 2013/14. The official rate of interest is 4%.

Using the average method, how much is the taxable benefit for the loan for 2013/14?

A   £690

B   £431

C   £450

D   £412

(3) Engelbert is loaned the use of a television by his employer. The television cost £650 when first provided on 1 May 2013. Engelbert does not have any business use of the television but he does pay £5 per month to his employer for the use of the television from 1 May 2013.

What is Engelbert's taxable benefit for the use of the television during 2013/14?

A   £130

B   £119

C   £70

D   £64

(4) **Mark the following statements as true or false**

	True	*False*
There is no assessable benefit for the provision of a company bicycle when bicycles are available to all staff.		
An employer pays a private medical insurance premium of £800 for an employee. The employee does not reimburse the employer. If the employee joined the scheme privately the cost would be £1,100. The assessable benefit for the employee is £1,100.		

Task 1.7

Mark the following benefits as taxable or exempt

	Taxable	Exempt
Childcare vouchers provided to an employee of £45 per week. The employee, who is a basic rate taxpayer, spent the vouchers with an approved childminder.		
A second mobile phone provided to an employee.		
A car parking space in a multi-storey car park near the place of work.		
An employer contribution to an employee's pension scheme.		

Task 1.8

(1) Toby uses his own car for business travel. During 2013/14 he travelled 21,000 business miles and 3,000 personal miles. His employer pays him 34p per business mile.

What will be his tax position?

    A   He can claim an allowable expense of £860.

    B   He will have a taxable amount of £1,890.

    C   He will claim an allowable expense of £110.

    D   He will claim an allowable expense of £2,310.

(2) Olivia pays £30 per month to a Cat Protection charity through the payroll giving scheme.

What is the impact of this?

    A   £30 per month is deducted from her employment income, reducing her taxable amount of income.

    B   This has no impact.

    C   If she is a higher rate taxpayer, then her basic rate band is extended by £30 per month.

    D   If she is a higher rate taxpayer, then her basic rate band is extended by £38 per month.

(3) Jerry is self employed. He has taxable profits of £28,000 for 2013/14 and no other income. He pays £50 per month to a private pension scheme.

What effect will the payments to the private pension scheme have on his income tax liability?

A   It will increase

B   It will decrease

C   It will have no impact

(4) Cruz is the finance director of a large company and incurred the following costs personally during 2013/14.

Which one is deductible from his employment income?

A   Subscription to the local golf club where he often meets clients

B   Travel between the two offices of his employer

C   The cost of a course on public speaking to make him feel more confident when speaking to clients

D   Cost of two new suits bought to impress clients

(5) During 2013/14, Joe donated £50 per month to a national charity through the Gift Aid scheme. His only income was a salary of £50,000.

How much of his taxable income will be taxed at the basic rate in 2013/14?

A   £30,010

B   £32,610

C   £32,760

D   £32,677

Task 1.9

(1)   Complete the following table to show the amount of income to be included in the personal income tax computation.

	Amount received £	Included in income tax computation £
Building society interest	52	
Dividend received	153	
ISA interest	80	
NS&I Bank Interest	110	
Premium Bond prize received by a person aged 65	50	

(2)   Which of the following is the correct treatment for interest from Government Stocks (also known as Gilts)?

A   It is exempt from income tax.

B   It is grossed up by multiplying by 100/80 and then entered into the personal income tax computation.

C   It is entered into the income tax computation at the amount received.

Task 1.10

Which of the following statements about dividends received is incorrect?

A   Dividends are taxed as if received net of a 10% tax credit.

B   Shares held in ISAs produce exempt dividends.

C   Taxpayers under 16 are exempt from paying any tax on dividends received.

D   Dividends falling into the additional rate band are taxed at 37.5%

Task 1.11

Read the following statements about ISAs and mark each one as true or false

	True	False
Only taxpayers resident in the UK can have an ISA.		
You have to be at least 18 to open a cash ISA.		
The maximum amount that can be invested in an ISA is £11,520 per tax year.		
When a taxpayer invests the maximum amount into an ISA they can invest the whole amount in a cash ISA.		
A taxpayer can open a new ISA every year.		
ISAs are government regulated investments.		

Task 1.12

During 2013/14 Lauren, who is 75 years old had a gross salary of £26,100 from which £3,100 of PAYE has been deducted. She also received dividends of £900.

Calculate her total <u>income tax payable or repayable</u> for 2013/14 using the table set out below.

Task 1.13

Neil has never previously completed a self assessment tax return.

He is worried that he should be completing a tax return for 2013/14 as he has recently started receiving rent and has requested information from you concerning the completion of tax returns and the due dates of payment of tax.

In particular he wishes to know:

- when he should tell HMRC about his new rental income and the consequences of not informing them

- when his 2013/14 tax return will need to be submitted

- the penalties arising for the late submission of a return

- when the balance of his income tax for 2013/14 will be payable (he does not need to make payments on account)

- the consequences of late payment of the tax due

Write brief notes answering Neil's questions.

Task 1.14

Using the following information, complete the tax return below:

John is employed by Becks Ltd. His form P60 for 2013/14 shows:

	£
Gross pay	45,000
Tax deducted	7,905

His form P11D for 2013/14 shows the following:

Car benefit	4,890
Fuel benefit	4,320
Use of company home cinema equipment	350
Camera given to John after use by another employee	125
Interest free loan	240
Expenses allowances received	6,000
Private medical insurance – premium paid by employer	865

Expenses paid by John:

Subscription to the Institute of Surveyors	475
Hotel bills whilst working away	5,220

Employment
Tax year 6 April 2013 to 5 April 2014

Your name

Your Unique Taxpayer Reference (UTR)

Complete an *Employment* page for each employment or directorship

1 Pay from this employment – the total from your P45 or P60 – *before tax was taken off*

£   · 0 0

2 UK tax taken off pay in box 1

£   · 0 0

3 Tips and other payments not on your P60 – *read the Employment notes*

£   · 0 0

4 PAYE tax reference of your employer (on your P45/P60)

   /

5 Your employer's name

6 If you were a company director, put 'X' in the box

7 And, if the company was a close company, put 'X' in the box

8 If you are a part-time teacher in England or Wales and are on the Repayment of Teachers' Loans Scheme for this employment, put 'X' in the box

Benefits from your employment – use your form P11D (or equivalent information)

9 Company cars and vans – *the total 'cash equivalent' amount*

£   · 0 0

10 Fuel for company cars and vans – *the total 'cash equivalent' amount*

£   · 0 0

11 Private medical and dental insurance – *the total 'cash equivalent' amount*

£   · 0 0

12 Vouchers, credit cards and excess mileage allowance

£   · 0 0

13 Goods and other assets provided by your employer – *the total value or amount*

£   · 0 0

14 Accommodation provided by your employer – *the total value or amount*

£   · 0 0

15 Other benefits (including interest-free and low interest loans) – *the total 'cash equivalent' amount*

£   · 0 0

16 Expenses payments received and balancing charges

£   · 0 0

Employment expenses

17 Business travel and subsistence expenses

£   · 0 0

18 Fixed deductions for expenses

£   · 0 0

19 Professional fees and subscriptions

£   · 0 0

20 Other expenses and capital allowances

£   · 0 0

ℹ Shares schemes, employment lump sums, compensation, deductions and Seafarers' Earnings Deduction are on the *Additional information* pages enclosed in the tax return pack.

SA102 2013   Page E 1   HMRC 12/12

SECTION 2

Task 2.1

Which one of the following statements is correct?

A The first £4,250 of furnished holiday letting income is tax free.

B If two people own a property together then each one is entitled to claim rent -a-room relief of £4,250.

C Rent received from letting property to a member of your family is an exempt activity.

D Wear and tear allowance can be claimed for furnished holiday accommodation.

Task 2.2

Joan Miller has two properties that she rents out;

(1) Two bedroom unfurnished flat. This was occupied throughout 2013/14. The monthly rent was £620 until 31 December 2013 and then it increased to £680. Joan paid an agents fee of 5% of the total rental income, gardening fees of £200 for 2013/14 and bought a new kitchen for the house costing £5,000.

(2) Three bedroom furnished house. This was occupied until 5 November 2013 at a monthly rent of £750 and was not re-occupied for the rest of 2013/14. Joan paid mortgage interest of £50 per month on this property.

Joan has a property loss brought forward of £1,500 from 2012/13.

Calculate the property income to be entered into the income tax computation for 2013/14 for both properties using the following table.

	Flat £	House £
Income		
Expenses		

Task 2.3

(1) Abraham rents out a furnished room in his own home to a lodger. The weekly rent is £100 per week and weekly expenses for heating, lighting and repairs are £81 per week.

What is the minimum amount of rental income on which Abraham will be assessed for a full tax year?

A   £950

B   £988

C   £520

D   £468

(2) **Mark the following statements as true or false**

	True	*False*
Income from property is taxed on a receipts basis.		
In order to receive the special treatment as furnished holiday accommodation, properties must be available for short term letting all year round.		
Joseph receives rent of £4,000 per year from letting a room in his own house. For 2013/14 he must claim rent-a-room relief by 31 January 2016.		
Bad debts, (i.e. rents not received), are ignored when calculating 10% wear and tear allowance for a furnished letting.		

(3) **How many years from the filing date (31 January 2015) should documents relating to property income for 2013/14 be kept?**

Task 2.4

(1) Romana sold a painting for £11,500 in October 2013. She had originally purchased the painting in August 1999 for £4,800. She had the painting professionally cleaned at a cost of £150 in August 2013 to prepare it for sale.

What is the gain or loss on the sale of this asset?

(2) Stefan sold an antique pocket watch for £2,800 in September 2013, which had originally been purchased for £1,900 in June 1993.

What is the gain or loss on the sale of this asset?

(3) Paula sold a painting to her brother for £15,000. The painting cost Paula £11,520 in June 2005. The market value of the painting at the date of the sale was £17,200.

What is the gain or loss on the sale of this asset?

(4) Alex attends a party with the following people.

His girlfriend, his brother, his sister and her husband, his cousin and finally Alex's grandfather also attends.

How many of these people are connected with Alex for capital gains purposes?

A   6

B   5

C   4

D   3

Task 2.5

Jenna had gains of £35,800 for 2013/14 in respect of quoted shares sold on the stock market. She also had capital losses brought forward of £4,000 from 2012/13 which arose when she sold a painting to her brother. She is a higher rate taxpayer.

What is her capital gains tax liability for 2013/14?

A   £5,852

B   £9,960

C   £3,762

D   £6,972

Task 2.6

Mai sold 4,200 shares in Toby Ltd for £8.50 per share in May 2013. She purchased 3,500 shares in Toby Ltd for £16,800 in April 2009, she purchased a rights issue of 1 for 4 at £3.60 per share in November 2011 and she received a bonus issue of 1 for 3 in January 2013.

Clearly showing the balance of shares and their value to carry forward, calculate the gain made on these shares. All workings must be shown in your calculations.

Task 2.7

(1) Sally sold a diamond ring for £5,200 in August 2013. She had purchased the ring for £7,150 in November 2012.

Which of the following applies to calculating the gain/loss on disposal?

A   The loss is calculated as normal

B   The sales proceeds are deemed to be £6,000

C   There is a restriction on the gain of:
    5/3 × (gross sales proceeds – £6,000)

D   The gain is calculated as normal

E   Rings are exempt from tax

(2) Sheena sold 3 acres of land for £28,000. She bought 10 acres in July 1992 for £32,000. The value of the remaining 7 acres at the date of sale was £90,000.

What is the gain/loss on this disposal?

A   £18,400

B   £20,407

C   (£4,000)

D   £9,507

Task 2.8

John bought a house for £52,000 on 1 February 1998. He lived in the house until 31 March 1999 when he went travelling. He returned to the house on 1 June 2007 and lived in it until 30 November 2012 when he moved into his girlfriend's flat. The house was sold for £180,000 on 1 June 2013.

(i)   Total period of ownership ....months

(ii) Total period of actual and deemed residence
      ....months

(iii) Chargeable gain on sale £.................................

Task 2.9

Mark the following statements as true or false?

	True	False
Capital losses can be offset against taxable income if the taxpayer has no capital gains in the year.		
Current year capital losses must be deducted from current year capital gains even where the gains are less than the annual exempt amount.		
Capital losses brought forward are deducted from current year capital gains before the deduction of current year capital losses.		

2 Mock Assessment Answers AQ2010

Task 1.1

(1) The answer is C.

The penalty for a tax return filed 2 months late would be £100 so the first statement is false.

(2) The answer is C.

Task 1.2

The answer is D.

Statements A to C are correct.

If an AAT member cannot resolve an ethical issue they should seek advice from their supervisor or their professional body. They do not seek advice from the police.

Task 1.3

	Employment	Self employment
Provision of own equipment		✓
Paid holidays	✓	
Having to correct mistakes at your own expense		✓

Task 1.4

(1) (a) The answer is B.

(9/12 × £21,000) + (3/12 × £23,500) = £21,625

(b) The answer is A.

The bonus received during 2013/14 is taxable during 2013/14.

(2)

	True	*False*
The £1,200 is net of 20% tax relief.	✓	
Puccini's pension provider can recover tax of £240 from HMRC to invest in Puccini's pension scheme.		✓
Provided his relevant earnings are no more than the annual allowance, Puccini can invest a figure equal to his relevant earnings into the pension scheme and obtain tax relief.	✓	
Income from furnished holiday lettings is not included in the figure of relevant earnings for pension purposes.		✓

Note: The pension provider can recover 20/80 of the amount paid by Puccini to invest on the scheme. This is £300 not £240.

Task 1.5

(1) (a) 20% (11% + 1/5 (125 – 95) + 3%)

   (b) 35% (11% + 1/5 (210 – 95) + 3%) = 37% so restricted to 35%

   (c) 13% (10% + 3%)

   (d) 8% (5% + 3%)

(2) The answer is A.

   Van benefit for 6 months is £1,500 (£3,000 × 6/12)

(3) (a) £1,124

   (£16,000 – £1,800) = £14,200 × 19% (W) × 5/12

   Working for % = 11% + 1/5(135 – 95) = 19%

   (b) £1,670

   (£21,100 × 19% × 5/12)

Task 1.6

(1) (a) The answer is C.

($2,500 + 4\% ($126,000 − $75,000)) × 10/12 = $3,783

(b) The answer is A.

($15,000 × 20% × 10/12) + £125 = £2,625

(2) The answer is B.

(£18,000 + £16,500)/2 × (4% − 1.5%) = £431

(3) The answer is D.

(£650 × 20%) × 11/12 − (£5 × 11) = £64

(4)

	True	False
There is no assessable benefit for the provision of a company bicycle when bicycles are available to all staff.	✓	
An employer pays a private medical insurance premium of £800 for an employee. The employee does not reimburse the employer. If the employee joined the scheme privately the cost would be £1,100. The assessable benefit for the employee is £1,100.		✓

Notes:

(1) Company bicycles must be available to staff generally.

(2) The assessable benefit for the private medical insurance is based on the cost to the employer.

Task 1.7

	Taxable	Exempt
Childcare vouchers provided to an employee of £45 per week. The employee, who is a basic rate taxpayer, spent the vouchers with an approved childminder.		✓
A second mobile phone provided to an employee.	✓	
A car parking space in a multi-storey car park near the place of work.		✓
An employer contribution to an employee's pension scheme.		✓

Task 1.8

(1)   The answer is C.

	£
Mileage allowance received (34p × 21,000)	7,140
Mileage allowance permitted:	
First 10,000 miles × 45p	(4,500)
Next 11,000 miles × 25p	(2,750)
Shortfall of allowance received	(110)

(2)   The answer is A.

(3)   The answer is C.

Jerry will receive basic rate tax relief at source. He is not a higher rate taxpayer so there is no further relief available. Accordingly, the pension contributions will not affect his income tax liability.

(4)   The answer is B.

Employees can only deduct the costs of expenses incurred wholly, exclusively and necessarily in connection with their employment. Answers A, C and D do not meet this test.

(5)   The answer is C.

£32,010 + (£50 × 12 × 100/80)

Task 1.9

(1)

	Amount received £	Included in income tax computation £
Building society interest *(× 100/80)*	52	65
Dividend received *(× 100/90)*	153	170
ISA interest	80	Exempt
NS&I Bank Interest *(received gross)*	110	110
Premium Bond prize received by a person aged 65	50	Exempt

(2)   The answer is C.

Interest on government stocks is taxable and is received gross.

Task 1.10

The answer is C.

Taxpayers under 16 are not automatically exempt from income tax on dividends. However, they do not usually have to pay tax because their income is usually less than the personal allowance.

Task 1.11

	True	False
Only taxpayers resident in the UK can have an ISA.	✓	
You have to be at least 18 to open a cash ISA.		✓
The maximum amount that can be invested in an ISA is £11,520 per tax year.	✓	
When a taxpayer invests the maximum amount into an ISA they can invest the whole amount in a cash ISA.		✓
A taxpayer can open a new ISA every year.	✓	
ISAs are government regulated investments.	✓	

Task 1.12

	Total	Other income	Divis
	£	£	£
Salary	26,100	26,100	
Dividends (£900 × 100/90)	1,000		1,000
Net income	27,100		
Less Age PA £10,660			
less ½ (£27,100 – £26,100)	(10,160)	(10,160)	
Taxable income	16,940	15,940	1,000
£15,940 × 20%	3,188.00		
£1,000 × 10%	100.00		
Income tax liability	3,288.00		
Less Dividend tax credits	(100.00)		
PAYE	(3,000.00)		
Tax payable	188.00		

Task 1.13

Notification of new income

Neil must notify HMRC of his new untaxed income by 5 October 2014.

Failure to notify HMRC can result in a penalty which is calculated as a percentage of any tax unpaid at 31 January 2015.

Submission of the tax return

The taxpayer has the choice of filing a paper return or filing electronically on line.

The date by which a return must be filed depends on the method used.

For 2013/14

–   All completed and signed paper returns must normally be filed by 31 October 2014

–   All on line (electronic) returns must be filed by 31 January 2015

If a 2013/14 return is not issued in good time by HMRC then it must be filed within three months of the date of issue if this is later than the normal due date.

Penalties for late submission

Immediate penalty	£100
Delay of more than three months	£10 per day
Delay of more than six months	5% of tax due
Delay of more than 12 months	Tax related penalty

The due date for the balance of income tax outstanding

The balance of income tax is due on 31 January 2015.

The consequences of late payment

(i)   Interest is charged, calculated on a daily basis, running from due date of payment to the date the tax is actually paid.

(ii)   Penalties are due, calculated as follows:

5% of tax outstanding if more than 30 days late

A further 5% due if more than 6 months late.

A further 5% due if more than 12 months late.

Task 1.14

HM Revenue & Customs

Employment
Tax year 6 April 2013 to 5 April 2014

Your name

`J O H N`

Your Unique Taxpayer Reference (UTR)

Complete an *Employment* page for each employment or directorship

1 Pay from this employment – the total from your P45 or P60 – *before tax was taken off*

£ `4 5 0 0 0 . 0 0`

2 UK tax taken off pay in box 1

£ `7 9 0 5 . 0 0`

3 Tips and other payments not on your P60 – *read the Employment notes*

£ `. 0 0`

4 PAYE tax reference of your employer (on your P45/P60)

` / `

5 Your employer's name

`B E C K S   L T D`

6 If you were a company director, put 'X' in the box

7 And, if the company was a close company, put 'X' in the box

8 If you are a part-time teacher in England or Wales and are on the Repayment of Teachers' Loans Scheme for this employment, put 'X' in the box

Benefits from your employment – use your form P11D (or equivalent information)

9 Company cars and vans – *the total 'cash equivalent' amount*

£ `4 8 9 0 . 0 0`

10 Fuel for company cars and vans – *the total 'cash equivalent' amount*

£ `4 3 2 0 . 0 0`

11 Private medical and dental insurance – *the total 'cash equivalent' amount*

£ `8 6 5 . 0 0`

12 Vouchers, credit cards and excess mileage allowance

£ `. 0 0`

13 Goods and other assets provided by your employer – *the total value or amount* (350 + 125)

£ `4 7 5 . 0 0`

14 Accommodation provided by your employer – *the total value or amount*

£ `. 0 0`

15 Other benefits (including interest-free and low interest loans) – *the total 'cash equivalent' amount*

£ `2 4 0 . 0 0`

16 Expenses payments received and balancing charges

£ `6 0 0 0 . 0 0`

Employment expenses

17 Business travel and subsistence expenses

£ `5 2 2 0 . 0 0`

18 Fixed deductions for expenses

£ `. 0 0`

19 Professional fees and subscriptions

£ `4 7 5 . 0 0`

20 Other expenses and capital allowances

£ `. 0 0`

ℹ Shares schemes, employment lump sums, compensation, deductions and Seafarers' Earnings Deduction are on the *Additional information* pages enclosed in the tax return pack.

SA102 2013   Page E 1   HMRC 12/12

SECTION 2

Task 2.1

The answer is D.

The £4,250 exemption applies only to letting a part of your own house, not furnished holiday lettings.

The £4,250 is per property not per person.

Letting property to a family member is a normal taxable activity.

Task 2.2

	Flat £	House £
Income		
£620 × 9 + £680 × 3	7,620	
£750 × 7		5,250
Expenses		
Agents fees (5% × £7,620)	(381)	
Gardening fees	(200)	
New kitchen is capital	Nil	
Mortgage interest (£50 × 12)		(600)
Wear and tear allowance		
£5,250 × 10%		(525)
Property income	7,039	4,125
Total property income		11,164
Less Loss b/f		(1,500)
Taxable property income		9,664

Task 2.3

(1)   The answer is D.

Abraham's annual rent of £5,200 (£100 × 52) is more than £4,250 so he can either be taxed on the normal basis or elect for rent–a–room treatment.

On the normal basis his rental income assessment is:

£5,200 – (£81× 52) expenses – (£5,200 × 10%) wear and tear

= £468

Using rent-a-room his taxable income is £5,200 – £4,250 = £950.

The minimum amount of rental income is therefore £468.

(2)

	True	False
Income from property is taxed on a receipts basis.		✓
In order to receive the special treatment as furnished holiday accommodation, properties must be available for short term letting all year round.		✓
Joseph receives rent of £4,000 per year from letting a room in his own house. For 2013/14 he must claim rent-a-room relief by 31 January 2015.		✓
Bad debts, (i.e. rents not received), are ignored when calculating 10% wear and tear allowance for a furnished letting.		✓

Notes:

- Income from property is taxed on an accruals basis.
- Properties may be let on long term lets for no more than 155 days per year.
- If rents are below £4,250 then rent-a-room treatment is automatic so no claim needed.
- Bad debts must be deducted from rents before calculating wear and tear allowance.

(3)   5 years

Task 2.4

(1) Romana

	£
Proceeds	11,500
Less: Selling costs	(150)
Net sales proceeds	11,350
Less: Cost	(4,800)
Gain	6,550

5/3 (£11,500 – £6,000) = £9,167

Chargeable gain	£6,550

(2) Stefan

This is an exempt disposal as the watch is a chattel bought and sold for less than £6,000

(3) Paula

	£
Proceeds = Market value	17,200
Less: Cost	(11,520)
Chargeable gain	5,680

Market value has been used because Paula and her brother are connected persons.

(4) The answer is C.

Alex is connected with everyone except his girlfriend and his cousin.

Task 2.5

The answer is D.

	£
Gains	35,800
Less: Annual exempt amount	(10,900)
Taxable gains	24,900
Tax at 28%	£6,972

Jenna cannot use the loss on disposal to her brother against gains generally, only on future gains on assets sold to her brother

Task 2.6

Shares

		£	
Sales proceeds	(£8.50 × 4,200)	35,700	
Less: Cost (Pool)		(14,365)	
Chargeable gain		21,335	
Pool		Number	Cost (£)
4/09 Purchase		3,500	16,800
11/11 Rights	1 for 4 at £3.60	875	3,150
		4,375	19,950
1/13 Bonus	1 for 3	1,458	Nil
		5,833	19,950
5/13 Sale		(4,200)	(W)(14,365)
Balance c/f		1,633	5,585
Working	4,200/5,833		
	× £19,950	= £14,365	

Task 2.7

(1) The answer is B.

When a chattel is sold for less than £6,000 but was purchased for more than £6,000, the taxpayer can deem the gross proceeds of sale to be £6,000 in order to receive at least some capital loss.

(2) The answer is B.

	£
Proceeds	28,000
Less: Cost (£28,000÷(£28,000 + £90,000)) × £32,000	(7,593)
Chargeable gain	20,407

The cost of the land sold must be found using the A/A+B formula
A = £28,000 B = £90,000

Task 2.8

(i) 184 months

(ii) 122 months

(iii)

	£
Gain	
Sales proceeds	180,000
Less: Cost	(52,000)
Gain before relief	128,000
Less: PPR exemption (W) (122/184 × £128,000)	(84,870)
Chargeable gain	43,130

Date	Total months	Exempt months	Comments
1.2.98 – 31.3.99	14	14	Occupation
1.4.99 – 31.3.02	36	36	3 years any reason
1.4.02 – 31.5.07	62		
1.6.07 – 30.11.12	66	66	Occupation
1.12.12 – 31.5.13	6	6	Last 3 years
Total	184	122	

Task 2.9

	True	False
Capital losses can be offset against taxable income if the taxpayer has no capital gains in the year.		✓
Current year capital losses must be deducted from current year capital gains even where the gains are less than the annual exempt amount.	✓	
Capital losses brought forward are deducted from current year capital gains before the deduction of current year capital losses.		✓

APPENDIX

Advice on answering
extended writing tasks

Personal tax – advice on extended writing tasks

There's only one task in the Personal tax computer based assessment (CBA) that may need you to provide a written response. Karen Boyd, the Chief Examiner, offers some tips to help you understand the best way to answer this task, which will always be marked by an AAT assessor.

Layout of answer

Before we look at the technical aspects of this task, we should begin by considering the practical issues.

Firstly, it's important you understand that the software in which you are answering the task is **not** Microsoft Word. So there's no:

- spell checker
- grammar checker
- automatic correcting of typos.

You won't see any different coloured lines highlighting any of these issues. It's quite clear from assessments we've marked so far that too many students are not proofreading their answers, and are failing to correct obvious mistakes.

So, when you type:

"i DON'T LIKE ANWSERING WRITEN QUETSIONS."

… this is exactly how it will look to the assessor. While the sentence can be read and understood, it's poor practice and would certainly not be allowed in the workplace.

You **must** proofread what you've written and correct any obvious spelling and grammatical errors. There's often a mark for presentation of the answer, and the assessor is looking for whether the way you've presented your work would be acceptable in the workplace. This mark is independent of the technical answer, and what we look for is whether a client would find the answer acceptable from a visual perspective.

Length of answer

It may not be obvious when you first look at the answer box on the screen, but this is a never-ending answer box. When you get to the last visible line, you can scroll down for extra writing space. So don't start your answer assuming that it needs to be condensed or short.

You should also remember that in many cases, the model answer the assessor is working from is in much more depth than the answer you'd need to give to gain full marks. It's acknowledged that it can be very difficult to write every aspect of all the areas applicable in a written question, and usually it's not necessary to do so.

Before you start to type

You **must** read the question in detail. We've noticed that students often scan read a question, decide what it's about in an instant and then write the answer without giving any thought or consideration to the details. You should:

- read through once to get the general feel of the question
- read through again, slower this time, concentrating on key words or phrases
- plan your answer, ensuring all key areas are covered
- decide the structure of your answer, considering where you'll use things like an email, a memo or bullet points
- type up your answer
- proofread your answer, correcting any errors.

Too many times it would seem that students only follow the fifth of these points. If you do this it **will** affect your marks.

Consider exactly who you're writing to. Most likely it will be a client, so this needs to influence your approach.

Remember, if the client is writing to you for advice, they don't know the answer. We often see students give half answers which the assessor will understand, but which a client would not. As a result, they lose marks.

Similarly, be sure to avoid:
- abbreviations
- technical jargon
- SMS/text message speak.

Technical content

What exactly are you going to write?

Let's take the written task from the AQ2010 sample assessment, updated.

Shania has written to you with the following query:

"I am writing to you for some clarification on my father's tax affairs. He is no longer capable of handling his own money, and I have a letter of authorization allowing me to deal with his tax matters.

I have received notification from HMRC of how much tax he has to pay for 31 January 2014. It says he owes £1,400 from 2012/13, and needs to pay £3,500 for 2013/14. I thought he had paid all the tax due for 2012/13, so I don't understand what the £1,400 is for. Also, I know that he has hardly any income this tax year, so where does the £3,500 come from?

If you could explain this to me, it would be much appreciated."

You need to respond appropriately to her query.

Let's break this task down to see exactly what you need to do.

The first line is an introduction only, and gives you the name of the person you are addressing.

The first paragraph of her query is also background, but lets you know two things.

1. It's fine to discuss the father's affairs with Shania.
2. As this tax bill is not hers, Shania will have no understanding of how it has arisen or why, and so you need to explain this in simple but detailed terms.

The second paragraph is the crux of the query, and you must spend time working out the figures and dates from the information given. Let's take a look at the details.

There's a total tax bill of £4,900 to be paid on 31 January 2014. Shania can't understand this, as she knows her father has little income for 2013/14.

Now, ask yourself this question: before you started studying Personal Tax, did you know how payments on account worked? For the majority of people, the answer is 'No'; so you need to put yourself in Shania's position and consider how you're going to clearly and simply explain the £4,900 her father needs to pay.

The question already tells you that £1,400 is from 2012/13, so that must be the balancing figure from that year. But why would there be a balancing figure? You need to explain the payments on account system, but in very simple terms.

Before you read any further, write your answer to this question and then compare it to the examples below.

Your answer

Now consider the following three typical student answers. Read them carefully and decide how well they answer the question, before reading the feedback from the Chief Examiner.

Answer 1

Half of the tax liability for any year is paid by 31 January in that tax year, and the other half is paid by 31 July following the tax year. This is based on an estimate, using the preceding tax year's liability. Therefore, when your father paid his tax liability on 31 January 2013 and 31 July 2013 for 2012/13, this was based on his liability for 2011/12. When the final figures were sent to HMRC, they have worked out that these two instalments are not enough to cover the full liability; hence the £1,400 is the balance of tax due.

Feedback from the Chief Examiner

Answer 1 is from the model answer and will obviously get full marks.

Answer 2

This is to do with the payments on account system. You need to pay half of your tax bill on 31 January in the year and the other half on 31 July in the year. Anything still to pay needs paying on 31 January after that. So the £1,400 is what is left from 2012/13.

Feedback from the Chief Examiner

Answer 2 has some good points. Firstly, it uses short sentences, which always makes it easier to read and understand. There are no jargon words. It would therefore get the mark for communication.

However, the crux of the answer, explaining the payments on account, is a problem. The assessor will know which year the answer is referring to, but there's no way a client would. When the answer says '31 January in the year', which year is the student referring to? The tax year, the financial year or the calendar year?

A client wouldn't understand this, so dates written in this manner will lose the student marks. This answer would attract a few marks, but certainly not full marks.

Answer 3

This is to do with POA. You need to pay half of your tax bill in January in the year, and other half in July following that. Then anything left over to pay gets paid in January after that. So the £1,400 is what is left from 2012/13.

Feedback from the Chief Examiner

Answer 3 will simply attract no marks at all. How will a client know what POA means? A day in January in some year also means nothing, and the last sentence is lifted from the question.

How did you do?

Now be honest, and compare the three examples above to your answer and see which one you're the closest to. Ask yourself these questions.
- Have I used abbreviations?
- Have I given the day, month and year accurately?
- Have I proofread my answer?

To finish off, let's consider the rest of the model answer to the question and see if you can understand how to judge the quality of your answer. Again, be honest with yourself on this.

Do you, for instance, realise that as Shania knows her father has 'hardly any income' she needs to understand the implications of this? This leads to the last paragraph of the answer where you can explain to her that he may be entitled to a refund; but that if he makes an incorrect claim to reduce his payments, this may have negative implications.

And finally, when you start the written question in Personal Tax, remember this sequence:
- read
- read again
- plan
- structure
- type
- read once again.

Note: below is the full answer to the question to help you.

Half of the tax liability for any year is paid by 31 January in that tax year, and the other half is paid by 31 July following the tax year. This is based on an estimate, using the preceding tax year's liability. Therefore, when your father paid his tax liability on 31 January 2013 and 31 July 2013 for 2012/13, this was based on his liability for 2011/12.

When the final figures were sent to HMRC, they have worked out that these two instalments are not enough to cover the full liability; hence the £1,400 is the balance of tax due.

As explained, the instalment on 31 January 2014 for this current tax year is based on the accurate liability for 2012/13. If he overpays for 2013/14, he will receive a refund from HMRC.

However, he can claim to reduce these instalments if he knows that his income will not be as high as it was last year. Whilst this is fine, your father needs to be careful. If he makes an incorrect claim to reduce these instalments, then HMRC will charge him interest on the difference between what should have been paid and what was actually paid.

INDEX

KAPLAN PUBLISHING